Praise for *The People's Republic of A.*

"Twenty-Five years after the bloodsh[...] emerging. This reconstruction, by [...] National Public Radio, is as important for Western readers as it is for the new Chinese generation that has grown up since 1989 and knows little of what happened." *–The Economist*

"Courageous... Lim moves nimbly between the individuals' narratives and broader reflections, interspersing both with short, poignant vignettes... written with verve." *–The New York Review of Books*

"Louisa Lim peers deep into the conflicted soul of today's China. Twenty-five years after the bloody suppression of pro-democracy demonstrations in Beijing, the government continues to deploy its technologies of forgetting to silence those who dare to remember and deter those who want to inquire. But the truth itself does not change; it only finds new ways to come out. Lim gives eloquent voice to the silenced witnesses, and uncovers the hidden nightmares that trouble China's surface calm." –Andrew J. Nathan, coeditor, *The Tiananmen Papers*

"With her carefully researched and beautifully reported *The People's Republic of Amnesia: Tiananmen Revisited*, Louisa Lim helps not only restore several important missing pieces of Chinese posterity that were part of the demonstrations in 1989, but also reminds us that a country which loses the ability to remember its own past honestly risks becoming rootless and misguided." –Orville Schell, Arthur Ross Director, Center on US-China Relations, Asia Society

"In *The People's Republic of Amnesia* veteran China correspondent Louisa Lim skillfully weaves the voices that 'clamor against the crime of silence' to recover for our collective memory the most pivotal moment in modern China's history." –Paul French, author of *Midnight in Peking*

"This book is essential reading for understanding the impact of mass amnesia on China's quest to become the world's next economic superpower." –Jan Wong, author of *Red China Blues* and *A Comrade Lost and Found*

"A deeply moving book—thoughtful, careful, and courageous. The portraits and stories it contains capture the multi-layered reality of China, as well as reveal the sobering moral compromises the country has made to become an emerging world power, even one hailed as presenting a compelling alternative to Western democracies." –Shen Tong, former student activist and author of *Almost a Revolution*

"Lim's intimate history of the events of 1989 deepens our understanding of what happened, and touches our hearts with its humanity. Lim brings the history to our doorsteps, reminding us that we aren't so different from those who lived and shaped history and tragedy. *The People's Republic of Amnesia* is a wholly original work of history that will alter how China in 1989 is understood, and felt." –Adam Minter, author of *Junkyard Planet*

"[Louisa Lim's] book is haunted by the voices of those who remember and tell her their stories. By breaking the silence, they represent a collective memory that has been officially repressed. Ms Lim opens yet another wound—the crackdown by the army in Chengdu, 'the other Tiananmen', also in June 1989, less publicised but no less brutal." –*The Times*

"The book is an excellent investigation into how nearly everyone in China has managed to internalise government censorship. Even those who go off to study at the top liberal universities in America are, she notes, so steeped in the Party's bogus patriotic education that they cannot even begin to accept there could be any other versions of their country's history than the official one." –*The Literary Review*

THE PEOPLE'S REPUBLIC OF AMNESIA

TIANANMEN REVISITED

LOUISA LIM

OXFORD
UNIVERSITY PRESS

OXFORD

UNIVERSITY PRESS

Oxford University Press is a department of the University of Oxford.
It furthers the University's objective of excellence in research, scholarship,
and education by publishing worldwide. Oxford is a registered trademark of
Oxford University Press in the UK and certain other countries.

Published in the United States of America by
Oxford University Press
198 Madison Avenue, New York, NY 10016, United States of America

Library of Congress Cataloging-in-Publication Data
Lim, Louisa.
The People's Republic of amnesia : Tiananmen revisited / Louisa Lim.
pages cm
1. China—History—Tiananmen Square Incident, 1989.
2. China—History—Tiananmen Square Incident, 1989—Influence.   I. Title.
DS779.32.L55 2014
951.05′8—dc23
2013044312

ISBN 978-0-19-934770-4 (hardback);
978-0-19-022791-3 (paperback)

Printed in Canada
on acid-free paper

To those who dare speak out

CONTENTS

AUTHOR'S NOTE

To write about present-day China requires an almost impossible calculation, weighing the risks and consequences of every sentence. It is like juggling in the dark, given the void of information into which these words fall. The very need for these acts of reckoning is also the reason why this book is necessary. As the boundaries of what is considered politically acceptable in China narrow, the subtle algebra of self-censorship has steadily diminished free expression both within China's borders and beyond. This process has quickened in recent years, as the Chinese government has expelled some foreign journalists and denied visas to others. Because my family has made China its home for the past decade, I could not help but contemplate these issues as I decided whether to write this book. But one question kept nagging: if I—with all the freedoms available to me—chose not to write about June 4th, then would anyone else document these stories for the historical record? Historical fact should not be held hostage, and the line between compliance and collusion is vanishingly thin.

I owe an enormous debt to those who have shared their stories with me, especially as most do not have the option of being able to publish their own accounts or to leave China. All were aware that they were taking a risk in talking about the sensitive topic of June 4th to a Western journalist. As I wrote these chapters, I wrestled with the question of whether to strip out their details to try to protect them, and for a very small number of my interviewees, I did indeed take that step. But most of those who spoke to me are so well known, and their experiences so unique, that their identities cannot be disguised. These people gave me permission to use their real names, and I know these decisions were not taken lightly. I hope that this book will honor the trust they have placed in me to tell their stories.

None of the people with whom I spoke inside China knew that I would write about the brutal crackdown in the city of Chengdu in June 1989. I only began to discover what had happened there during a chance meeting with Tang Deying, whose teenage son was beaten to death in police custody in June 1989. I did not begin further research on Chengdu until after I had left China. In writing this book, I hope to begin a conversation about the "other Tiananmens" that took place beyond the capital, to remember the victims of the crackdown, and to break the code of silence in China that surrounds discussion of 1989.

January 2014

TIMELINE

APRIL–JUNE 1989

April 15	Death of deposed CCP General Secretary Hu Yaobang.
April 16	Students mobilize on some Beijing campuses.
April 17	First student march to Tiananmen.
April 18–19	Student sit-in at Xinhuamen ends in scuffles with police.
April 21	100,000 students gather on Tiananmen Square.
April 22	Hu Yaobang's memorial service is held inside Great Hall of the People; three students kneel on steps outside.
April 24	Beijing Autonomous Federation of Students formed. Class boycott begins.
April 26	*People's Daily* editorial labels the student movement "turmoil."
April 27	Massive demonstations against April 26th editorial.
May 4	CCP General Secretary Zhao Ziyang pledges no "major" turmoil during a speech to the Asian Development Bank.
May 13	Student hunger strike begins in Beijing.

May 14	Elected student representatives meet officials, but talks break down.
May 15	USSR President Mikhail Gorbachev begins state visit to Beijing.
May 17	More than a million people march in Beijing.
May 18	Premier Li Peng meets student leaders at the Great Hall of the People.
May 19	Zhao Ziyang visits students on the square during his last public appearance. Students end their hunger strike. Troops attempt to enter Beijing ahead of martial law, but citizens block their advance.
May 20	Martial law is officially declared at 10 A.M.
May 23	Troops pull back to the outskirts of Beijing.
May 27	Students vote unanimously to retreat at the end of May, but decision is immediately overturned.
May 28	Zhao Ziyang's secretary Bao Tong is arrested.
May 29	Thirty-foot-high Goddess of Democracy statue unveiled.
June 3	Four intellectuals begin hunger strike.
June 3–4	Thousands of troops deployed into central Beijing. Troops open fire on civilians; tanks roll into Tiananmen Square. Preliminary Chinese reports say 241 people died; eyewitnesses believe the figure is higher.
June 4	Protests against the violent suppression break out in dozens of cities across China, including Chengdu.
June 5	Foreign media film a young Chinese man standing in the path of a column of tanks; he becomes known as Tank Man.
June 9	Central Military Commission Chairman Deng Xiaoping makes his first appearance since the crackdown, saying the government has suppressed a counterrevolutionary rebellion.

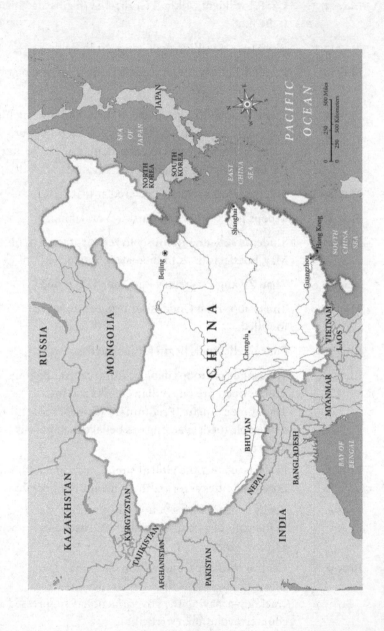

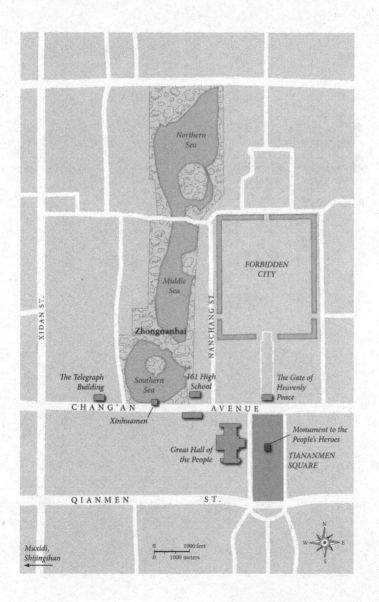

Northern
Sea

FORBIDDEN
CITY

XIDAN ST.

Middle
Sea

NANCHANG ST.

Zhongnanhai

The Telegraph
Building

Southern
Sea

161 High
School

The Gate of
Heavenly
Peace

CHANG'AN   AVENUE

Xinhuamen

Monument to the
People's Heroes

Great Hall of
the People

TIANANMEN
SQUARE

QIANMEN   ST.

Muxidi,
Shijingshan

0   1000 feet

0   1000 meters

N
W   E
S

Introduction

In the dim predawn light, they swarmed into the square, converging from all directions, their flags and banners waving high. There was an air of heightened expectancy, nervousness, and excitement, footsteps quickening to a run as they crossed the grey emptiness so vast that it could contain 60 soccer fields. This was not Tiananmen Square 1989, but Tiananmen Square 2014. These thousands of people had come out at four in the morning not to protest against corruption or censorship; they had come to witness the daily flag-raising ceremony that has become a solemn celebration of China's national identity. For these secular pilgrims, Tiananmen Square invokes neither those who occupied the square in 1989 nor the government's violent repression. For them, the square is the political and symbolic heart of the nation, as much today as it was for the Ming dynasty emperors who built the original square in the 1420s. Over the course of the past quarter-century, in an extraordinary sleight of hand, China's rulers have managed to transform this site of national shame into one of national pride. How has this act of excising the collective memory been achieved, and at what cost?

As I joined the crowds straining toward the flagpole at daybreak that summer morning, I found myself squeezed against a tiny, grizzled out-of-towner with pungent breath and an unfortunate habit of snorting like a piglet. "Don't push!" he shouted between snorts, as he himself pushed forward into the crush of bodies. On my other side was a high school grammar teacher, a cheerful woman in her mid-20s, who was accompanying 1,372 junior high students on a school trip from the city of Chongqing, a southwestern mega-city that has become the world's biggest municipality with 30 million residents. She had maneuvered herself toward the front, showing blithe disregard for the group of 12-year-olds she was supposed to be supervising. They were standing obediently in orderly rows way at the back, where they could see little but a sea of heads. Another teacher was patrolling their lines, barking into a megaphone, "Watch your bags! Everybody watch your bags!" Looking behind me, it was impossible to tell if the crowd was 20-deep or 40-deep, but a sea of tiny heads pixilated the square as far as the eye could see.

A murmur ran through the crowd. Something had happened far off under Tiananmen, the Gate of Heavenly Peace. "Are they coming?" "What's happening?" Only those in the front row could see, and disjointed fragments of their commentary began filtering back. "They're coming! They're coming! They're under the portrait of Chairman Mao! They're marching forward!"

Two columns of 18 guards each were solemnly goose-stepping in the direction of the flagpole, those in the front bearing a folded Chinese flag. It was difficult to see anything at all in the gaps between the mosaic of cell phones and iPads wobbling aloft. The sky was brightening, with tendrils of white cloud standing out against the pale blue-grey. Everyone was jostling, jiggling, grumbling. But when the strains of China's national anthem rang out from the loudspeakers, an immediate, awed silence fell upon the crowd, religious in its intensity. Even my neighbor stopped snorting for a full two minutes.

As the flag glided up the flagpole, the hush was broken by a cantata of clicks from cameras and smart phones. Two soldiers saluted at the crowd while their comrades faced the flagpole, rifles with bayonets across their chests, symbolically poised to defend the flag with their lives. Policemen eyed the masses warily; opposite me, a plainclothes policeman in a Nike shirt standing behind the police ropes incongruously clutched a long black umbrella while his eyes scoped the crowds. As the national anthem came to an end, spontaneous cries of *"Hao! Hao!"*—"Good! Good!"—echoed through the crowd.

By now, an orange glow was creeping across the sky. It was the perfect photo moment, and this single thought was clearly shared by every one of the thousands of people on the square. When the policemen lifted the rope corralling the crowds, hundreds began running flat-out toward the flagpole. They got only as far as another barrier, which had suddenly materialized a few hundred yards away. Immediately, the square was transformed into a mass photo session: A middle-aged matron in a sequined Mickey Mouse T-shirt beamed winsomely; nearby, a young man in red track shoes struck a hip-hop pose with the national flag in the background. The students from Chongqing arranged themselves in neat tiers according to height, shouting *"Qiezi!"* - "Eggplant!" - for the camera, the Chinese equivalent of "Cheese!"

My neighbors were exultant. "I'm so moved!" the school teacher enthused, beaming widely. Patriotism was beating in her heart, she said, for today she had finally achieved what she had been dreaming of for years.

I couldn't help myself. I asked her whether she ever thought about the students and their supporters who camped out on this very spot a quarter-century ago, with their demands for cleaner government and greater democracy; or whether she even knew about the tanks and guns used against the unarmed bystanders in the approach to the square. Her face fell. I had cast a pall over the moment, behaving in the stereotypical way of the doubting Western media.

"This problem is quite sensitive," she replied hesitantly, "Let's not talk about it now. Let's live in today's world and not dwell on the past."

I suddenly wondered whether out of the thousands of people gathered on the square that morning, I might be the only one dwelling on 1989. Actually, our very presence there was partly due to the post-Tiananmen policy of promoting ideological education, bolstered by popular pride at the metamorphosis that China has undergone in the past quarter of a century. The leadership has transformed the lives of their populace, lifting hundreds of millions out of grinding poverty and rebuilding the face of the country with brand-new cities brimming with gleaming skyscrapers, all linked by wide highways and state-of-the-art high-speed railways.

Tiananmen, too, has been remade, but its darker notes cannot help but echo through time. In the Ming and Qing dynasties, it was the site of public trials, even gruesome acts of torture like *lingchi*, or "death by a thousand cuts." Even Tiananmen's name—the Gate of Heavenly Peace—is by no means as peaceful as it sounds; it was named by the Manchus, who were not very proficient in Chinese, in 1651 in the early years of the Qing dynasty. The translation of the original Manchu name is the "Gate of Heaven's Pacification," perhaps a more fitting reflection of the fledgling empire that was busy suppressing resistance and launching deadly campaigns of conquest to expand its territory.

After Chairman Mao came to power, his vision was to create a gigantic political stage for his own veneration, by building what was then the world's biggest public square. After the flag ceremony was finished, as I walked toward Mao's final resting place, his hulking mausoleum, I came across a group of elderly men and women sitting on the ground, looking exhausted.

"Are you alright?" I asked.

"Yes, we're fine," they replied, shading their heads from the rising sun with folded newspapers. "We're just resting."

The sight of them brought to mind my encounter years earlier with one of the architects who had shaped modern Beijing. Zhang Kaiji was 92 when I met him, with the outspokenness born of great age and frustration. He had designed and supervised the construction of the two museums flanking the square to mark the 10th anniversary of Communist rule in 1959—and he had completed this herculean task in just 10 months. Almost half a century later, he was still regretting what he had done, "Tiananmen Square is too big. We wanted to show how great our country was. At that time, there was a feeling that bigger was better, but I think that is wrong. It was just to show off. It wasn't really to serve the people."

What he regretted most was not designing a space on a human scale, where the elderly could sit on benches and watch their grandchildren toddling around. Indeed, what had happened in 1989 was that, for at least seven weeks, the people had reclaimed the square as their own.

Like almost every aspect of Chinese politics, economics, and diplomacy today, the flag-raising ritual itself is intricately intertwined with the fallout from the Tiananmen protests. In the 1980s, just three soldiers were responsible for hoisting the flag every morning. In 1991, facing a crisis in confidence, the government designed a new ceremony to boost patriotism and brought in the 36 goose-stepping flag guards. The success of this strategy was illustrated by the piles of luggage heaped about the square, belonging to out-of-towners who traipsed over from Beijing's main train station a couple of miles from the square, dragging their bags behind them. Two hundred million people have witnessed the upgraded flag-raising, which has become a rite of national communion, since it was introduced in 1991.

Chinese people are practiced at not dwelling on the past. One by one, episodes of political turmoil have been expunged from official history or simply forgotten: from the anti-Rightist movement in 1957 that persecuted hundreds of thousands of people, some of whom were sent to labor camps, tortured, or even driven to suicide; to the Great Famine in the late 1950s and early 1960s, which resulted in the deaths of an estimated 36 million people; to the suffering—impossible to measure—of the Cultural Revolution in the mid-1960s to the mid-1970s; to the Democracy Wall movement of 1979; to the failed student movement in 1986 and 1987. In a world now linked by the Internet and smart phones, when new prosperity has enabled large numbers of Chinese to travel overseas, an act of collective amnesia should be harder to manage. Indeed, in the aftermath of Tiananmen, so plentiful were the eyewitness accounts of the events on the square that publishing houses worldwide were rejecting them, citing the saturation of the market. Writing from his hiding place in the basement of a U.S. embassy building in Beijing, astrophysicist Fang Lizhi, one of China's preeminent dissidents, baldly stated that the multiplicity of Tiananmen literature heralded "the failure of the 'Technique of Forgetting History,' which has been an important device of rule by the Chinese Communists." Facts would no longer be so easy to cover up, he wrote, and history could not possibly be forgotten.

A quarter-century later, that prediction has largely been forgotten inside China, along with the events of 1989 and even Fang Lizhi himself. Those who continue to remember are consigned to a

life on the periphery, since moving on—not dwelling on the past—
has become a key survival tactic, perhaps the most important one.
Young Chinese people have little idea of, or little interest in, what
happened.

The forgetting began almost immediately. Just before the 10th
anniversary of the killings, a film professor named Cui Weiping
wrote, "A massive secret has become a massive vacuum...this
secret is like a poison that has contaminated the air we breathe and
our whole life and spirit." By the 20th anniversary, she concluded
that if the situation remained unchanged, "June 4th will no longer
be a crime committed by a small group of people, but one in which
we all participated."

• • • •

I have spent a decade working as a journalist in China, watching
my Chinese counterparts being muzzled, as the "vacuum" swelled
to encompass ever more "sensitive" topics. Tiananmen has become
one of the most sensitive of them all. Even for the participants themselves, the events of 1989 have become half-stories, only partially
remembered, some chapters blazing in vivid Technicolor, others
faded into grey. Memory—individual as well as national—is fickle,
sculpted by the exigencies of vanity and convenience, as well as the
distortions created by political dictates. The accounts given in this
book cannot be considered infallible; above all, the stories I tell are
human journeys in memory and forgetting.

Tiananmen was not the only site of tragedy in 1989. One episode that is at risk of being entirely lost to history is the crackdown
in the southwestern city of Chengdu, where protesters, enraged by
what happened in Beijing, swarmed into the streets, battled with the
police, and were brutally put down; those deaths went almost unnoticed, even at the time. I have tried to piece together these events
through the eyes of multiple witnesses, many of whom kept notes
and took photos, yet did not share their stories until now.

The passage of a quarter-century may render recollections hazy
and partial, but collectively, the voices in this book clamor against
the crime of silence.

1 :: Soldier

Plumes of smoke from fires frame the Gate of Heavenly Peace, as soldiers pile the students' possessions to burn them. No civilians are present. This world is inhabited only by khaki-clad, helmeted men whose sole task is destroying evidence. The soldiers pore over a flotsam of hastily abandoned tents, sleeping bags, and papers. A swathe of red banners tumbles along the ground, its scarlet a visceral echo of the bloodshed preceding this scene. It is June 4th, 1989, early in the morning; the violence is unseen but ever present.

Swarms of armored personnel carriers, their guns stark against Tiananmen Gate, stand where Chairman Mao stood 40 years earlier in 1949 to declare the founding of the People's Republic of China. Tank after tank is lined up in front of the most politically charged site in China.

These scenes at Tiananmen were witnessed only by the army. The students had finally straggled out of the square after seven weeks, leaving at gunpoint as 150,000 soldiers were mobilized in a massive military operation. The number of dead still remains unknown. The preliminary Chinese account put it at 241, including 23 soldiers. The Chinese Red Cross initially estimated that 2,600 people had died, a figure basically corroborated by the Swiss ambassador who had visited Beijing's hospitals and claimed 2,700 had died, but both quickly withdrew these figures under diplomatic pressure. A U.S. diplomatic cable from June 22, 1989 concluded that such numbers were not unreasonable "given the nature of the conflict and the weapons used by the PLA." In any case, the numbers do not convey the sheer sense of betrayal as the People's Army turned its weapons on its own people.

For one of the soldiers involved, it took time—days, weeks, even years—to make sense of his role in what happened. To this day, the scenes he captured on the square as a 17-year-old military photographer obsess him. Today, Chen Guang is a painter whose artwork reverberates with echoes of that night; he creates whole collections that he knows cannot be publicly shown in mainland China. That night bisects his life. He will never regain the innocence he once had or forget what had taken it from him. It also bisects the life of the nation; China's modern history pivots on that night—though it is unspoken and increasingly unknown among the younger generation.

Perhaps the most sinister of all Chen Guang's pictures are the most innocuous: propped up against the wall, a triptych of almost identical paintings of a wristwatch. It is a silver-colored wristwatch with a metal strap, a cream face, and a cheap jewel set at 12:00. Under that is a red outline of the Gate of Heavenly Peace set above the word "Beijing." Beneath the watch's central pivot is a small sketch of an olive-helmeted soldier, his face resolute and determined. Along the bottom of the watch in small Chinese characters are the words "June 89 to Commemorate the Quelling of the Turmoil." This watch was the souvenir given to all martial law troops who took part in the suppression of the pro-democracy movement.

• • • •

Chen Guang was waiting for me by the side of a potholed road, watching a pack of stray dogs scavenge among grubby plastic bags spinning in the wind. A slight, sprightly figure with shaggy salt-and-pepper hair, he wore a well-cut black coat with a fashionable, detachable collar. In this outer suburb of Beijing, grey factories push up against spartan brick bungalows, all melting into the never-ending horizon of urban sprawl punctuated by pointillist piles of trash. Chen led me to his studio tucked away in the inner depths of a printing factory where no one cared about what he was painting. An air of diffidence distinguished Chen Guang from the brash painter-entrepreneurs making millions from China's art boom. His decision to paint pictures that cannot be shown has shut him out from the easy money and "insta-fame" that have become the badges of success.

As a child, Chen Guang's dream of becoming an artist had seemed impossibly aspirational. He was born to a factory worker father and a housewife mother in a farming town in the poverty-stricken county of Shangqiu in Henan province, a place that has since become notorious as the ground zero of an AIDS epidemic. Desperately poor peasant farmers had sold their only commodity—their blood—to government-sponsored blood collectors, who pooled the blood, skimmed off the plasma, and then re-infused the remaining red blood cells back into the farmers, facilitating the spread of AIDS through the area's farming villages. Though Chen was unaffected by the crisis, his poor grades at school had left him with dim prospects. "People thought you had to either find a job or join the army," he told me. "There was no third path." So in the spring of 1988, at just 16 years of age, he dropped out of high school. The minimum age for enlisting in the People's Liberation Army was 18. He lied about his age, hoping that military service would provide him with a springboard into the prestigious military art academy.

Joining the army was a decision Chen regretted from the very moment he boarded the train for his new barracks in Zhangjiakou in Hebei province. From day one, he was exhausted by the unremittingly grueling routines of army life. Each day started at 5:30 a.m., with an obligatory cross-country run in cold so bitter that it made him retch. By the time he returned to base, a thin layer of ice had formed on his cotton cap. The day's activities consisted mostly of endless drilling and political education sessions, in which the soldiers listened to army officers reading the PLA newspaper out loud and then painstakingly explaining the correct understanding of each article. Worst of all was the lack of sleep; soldiers were forced to get up several times a night to stand watch, participate in nighttime training sessions, and endure emergency inspections, during which they were required to leap out of their beds to pack up their entire kits in five minutes flat. By May 1989, having been in the army for just over a year, Chen Guang was disillusioned. Nothing had prepared him for the rigors of army life, which had taken a toll on his health, leaving him struggling with chronic bronchitis and diarrhea.

One May day as his unit was drilling, a warning siren suddenly began to blare. The order had come down: His unit was being deployed to Beijing to defend the capital from "serious upheaval." Chen and his fellow soldiers did not know what this meant. At the time, they had little idea that there had been massive demonstrations snaking through the capital's streets in an unprecedented display of public protest. They did not know that students had first marched in mid-April to mourn the sudden death of reformist leader Hu Yaobang, and then—emboldened by the government's restrained response—had begun to issue calls for press freedom, democracy, and an end to corruption. They did not know that many thousands of workers, even from government ministries, had joined the marches. They did not know that there were divisions at the highest level of government about how to deal with the protests, with the reformers pitted against the conservatives. And they did not know—yet—that they themselves were to become pawns in a political game with the highest stakes.

For the most part, the soldiers—raw country boys in their teens—didn't expend much energy thinking about what they were heading into. If anything, it seemed like an adventure. Few of them had visited the capital before, and they were finally being offered the chance. "We weren't scared, we thought it would be fun," said Chen Guang, laughing wheezily as he remembered their naïve excitement. "We felt that going to Beijing would be more fun than doing drills at base." Their barracks in Zhangjiakou were about 100 miles from the capital, but the journey took the soldiers two days and two nights, packed tightly into green army trucks bumping over isolated and winding mountain roads.

For soldiers hoping for some fun, the Chinese capital initially seemed even more boring than barracks life. Chen Guang's unit was billeted at a PLA shooting range in Shijingshan, 12 miles due west of Beijing. With no drilling grounds available, they spent every day listening to articles read out loud from the PLA Daily and the People's Daily. They were repeatedly told that an extremely small number of troublemakers with ulterior purposes had taken advantage of the situation. This minority, they were told, was opposed to the leadership of the Communist Party and the Socialist system. Its aim was to sow dissension among the people and plunge the country into chaos. The army must be resolute and comply with the orders of the party. For Chen Guang, the mission was clear-cut. As a soldier trained in the art of obedience, the very thought of questioning an order—even in the privacy of his own head—was impossible.

On May 19th, as China's Premier Li Peng declared martial law would go into effect the following day, the order the soldiers had been waiting for was finally issued: to secure Tiananmen Square. Their convoy set out from the barracks, but had only traveled a few miles before the trucks were swamped by successive waves of people surging forward to enclose them. Each time they nosed forward, a new wave of people crested around them, backed up by trucks and buses blocking the roads. The soldiers were hemmed in by this outpouring of humanity whose aim was to block the troops' advance into the city. For Chen, this was a turning point. "It didn't feel fun anymore," he remembered. "It felt real."

Those surrounding the trucks were both students and ordinary citizens. Trying to employ reason against the use of force, they deployed a continuous stream of talk to counter the political education the soldiers had been receiving inside their barracks, with one speaker taking over from another. This continued day and night. The students and citizens spread newspapers on the ground and slept in front of the wheels of the PLA trucks. They told the soldiers that their duty was to protect the border regions and ensure the safety of Chinese territory, and not to deploy to the capital where their presence was not needed. This combination of earnest students and kindly grandmothers argued and pleaded with the young men in the trucks not to use violence against the Chinese people. The soldiers were under orders not to reply; they were packed so tightly into their trucks, they had to take turns sitting down.

This was not at all the kind of reception that Chen had been expecting. "The atmosphere was not like some kind of turmoil," he remembered. "The students were very friendly, with bright smiles. Their spirit was welcoming." Three days and four nights passed as it became increasingly clear that the PLA chiefs had neither prepared for this eventuality nor formed a strategy for the next step. Each soldier was carrying only one bread roll. At first, the troops refused offers of sustenance from the students, but as the hours stretched into days, they were unable to bear their hunger. "A few people accepted," Chen Guang remembered. "And then the students were so enthusiastic—they really wanted to feed us—that you could only refuse them so many times, then you felt embarrassed and accepted." People gave instant noodles, bread, fruit, and mineral water to the grateful troops, and slowly the barriers between the besiegers and the besieged crumbled.

As the days passed, the citizens began to vary the topics of their lectures, tiring of the one-note pleas against violence. Instead, Chen remembered listening to a riff on the meaning of life, followed by a lecture on the spread of corruption within China. For Chen, this unexpected civic education was beginning to have an effect, "All at once you felt like you hadn't understood this society. Does China really have that many corrupt people? Is there so much injustice? You suddenly started to think about these problems. Before that, you didn't have that kind of consciousness. Though you couldn't talk to the students, their words had an effect on your mind." Once Chen had mentally formulated such questions, they led to other questions that he had never considered, which in turn led to doubts, "You might have said that our army was big and powerful, but at that time, we didn't feel big and powerful. We felt very useless."

Slowly the soldiers began to relax, lowering their guard to chat with the residents about their hometowns and their lives. At one point, the PLA—clearly worried about fraternization—began dropping leaflets from helicopters, warning the soldiers not to believe rumors and to remain resolute. The students scooped these up, hoping to keep them from the soldiers. By then, Chen was already unable to bridge the gaping disconnect between what he was seeing and the army's repeated warnings against troublemakers with ulterior motives. "You began to wonder which of the students were the bad ones. But it was hard to say who the bad ones were. Everyone seemed so normal."

Finally, the order came to return to the barracks in Shijingshan. It did not feel in the least like a humiliating withdrawal. Beijingers set off firecrackers along the route of the soldiers' retreat. The troops' own relief combined with the students' elation to create an atmosphere of triumphant festivity. Banners were even hung from buildings en route with slogans like "The PLA came on orders. We support you" and "There is no disorder in Beijing. You guys go on home."

Chen's unit was not the only one to have had this experience. At least seven PLA divisions had tried to enter the city around the same time to impose martial law. Their orders were to converge on the capital from the west, the southwest, the south, the east, and the north. All were immobilized by the sea of civilians and eventually forced to retreat, with some even finding it difficult to return to base.

The people had stood up to the army—using nothing but their bodies and their wits—and had won. For the students, this was a major triumph, a sign that their movement had become a mass movement. They saw it as tantamount to an admission by the government that it had lost the trust of the people who granted its prerogative to rule, the traditional "mandate of heaven." According to the Confucian philosopher Mencius, while heaven gave the ruler the right to rule, heaven sees with the eyes of its people, and hears with the ears of its people.

The people's victory—which only increased the urgency of the central government's need to regain control—was to be short-lived. Martial law was not rescinded. After returning to the garrison, the troops spent the next 10 days in a fog of intense ideological education. Their only task was to listen to lectures that warned them about the turmoil in Beijing and the importance of their mission to protect the capital. Then the order came for a second time: to secure Tiananmen Square.

• • • •

The first time Chen Guang told me his story, he avoided giving too many details of that long night. He revealed his role on June 4th only gradually. The next time we met, I visited him in his new home in Songzhuang, a modest farming village 16 miles east of Beijing that has tried to reinvent itself as an art hub.

Instead of peasants selling watermelons by the roadside, artists squatted in the dust hawking bad Van Gogh copies or shaky line drawings of Chairman Mao drinking tea. Art supply shops had supplanted all others to the extent that purchasing gold-flecked calligraphy paper had become far easier than buying staples like fruit. The proliferation of art museums was exemplified by their names: the Czech China Contemporary Art Gallery, the National Defense Art Zone, and the African Art Museum. But even the biggest and the flashiest, Songzhuang Art Museum, was empty during my last few visits, its doors chained and windows covered in dust. These deserted exhibition spaces were testaments to the failure of the "build it and they will come" school of central planning. The authorities' investment of $13 million to create a "cultural and creative industry" cluster in Songzhuang had attracted some 4,000 artists, but it did not appear to have resulted in an economically viable artistic destination.

Chen Guang's new home was inside a building site, hidden behind a bright blue corrugated iron fence. The approach was unpromising, consisting of a yellow dirt road frequented only by delivery trucks. But nestled out of view was a row of handsome three-story grey brick buildings. Although he was unable to show his work inside China, he was evidently doing reasonably well selling it overseas, as he had just bought a pair of neighboring industrial studios with 25-feet-high ceilings and chic mezzanine balconies. Sandwiched between two construction sites, his studio was a bright, airy refuge from the hammering and drilling emanating from the dozen 16-story buildings that were sprouting up behind his apartment.

Inside, two decades worth of paintings were propped up against the wall, carefully protected in bubble wrap. They represented and reinforced his memories of that night. As we sipped green tea and he chain-smoked, he told me what had happened.

The first sign that the troops would take a more covert approach to enter Beijing was the arrival on June 3rd at the shooting range of a truck piled high with civilian clothing. The authorities were determined that any second attempt to enter Beijing would not be derailed in the same way. Each soldier was ordered to pick out a civilian outfit to hide his true identity. Chen Guang chose a pair of navy-blue trousers and a grey T-shirt. Instead of entering the capital in trucks, as before, the mufti-clad soldiers were ordered to make their own way into central Beijing by subway, bus, or even on foot. The rendezvous point was the Great Hall of the People at Tiananmen Square before 6:00 on that same evening.

At the time, Chen Guang was taking antibiotics for asthma and diarrhea, leading his superiors to fear that he might not be strong enough to reach the square on his own. He was ordered to travel to Tiananmen Square inside a converted public bus. When he saw it, he noticed that all the seats had been removed to make room for crates of guns and ammunition that were stacked up to the window ledges. Chen Guang, crouching alongside the crates, was the only passenger on the bus. His first emotion was relief that he was getting a ride, thereby avoiding the danger of getting lost in the huge, unfamiliar city.

The bus crawled into Beijing. It was blocked only once by a crowd of students who glanced inside perfunctorily and then let it continue on its way. At that time, Chen had no idea how lucky he had been. In fact, his journey was so smooth that he was one of the first soldiers to arrive at the Great Hall of the People, getting there at 3:30 p.m., more than two hours before the rendezvous time. He was ordered to unpack the bus and carry the guns inside. As he grappled with armfuls of submachine guns—five or six at a time—and hauled them into the Great Hall of the People, Chen's hands and clothes became coated with the black grease in which the guns had been packed for preservation. As he toted the guns into the cavernous atrium, he saw that it was filling up with troops in plainclothes trying to find their own units. Once they had done so, they were given strips of colored cloth, each identifying a different unit, to tie around their arms until they could change into uniform. Chen was used to seeing the Great Hall of the People on the news, peopled by tidy tiers of delegates applauding politely as they attended annual meetings of the National People's Congress. When he saw this hallowed place filling up with armed soldiers, he felt as though he had fallen through the cracks into an alternate, incomprehensible universe.

At around 6:00 p.m., the soldiers of Chen's unit—now wearing their uniforms—were given a new task. They were told that they must rescue arms and ammunition that criminals had stolen from a bus that had been apprehended near the Telegraph building, close to the Xidan intersection of Chang'an Avenue. "Only then did I start feeling very afraid," he remembered, as it dawned on him that a soldier just like himself had been discovered escorting weapons into central Beijing.

The next day he heard that, in the early hours of the morning of June 4th, a 25-year-old soldier named Liu Guogeng was murdered by a mob near to where the guns were taken. The image of his dead body became iconic in the state-run Chinese media since it illustrated the real dangers faced by the martial law troops; Liu's burned corpse had been suspended by the neck from a blackened public bus, naked but for his socks, an army hat incongruously perched on his head. He was instantly elevated to martyr status. His weeping father was shown on television being consoled by the country's leaders.

According to an official account, Liu's unit had been surrounded on Chang'an Avenue, where protesters had disabled some of the vehicles carrying troops and ammunition toward the back of the column. When Liu realized what had happened, he returned on foot to help his unit. The approved version of history, released in a book called *The Truth about the Beijing Turmoil*, describes what then happened, "A group of rioters turned upon them ferociously. Bricks, bottles, and iron sticks rained on their heads and chests. The driver was knocked unconscious there and then. Liu Guogeng was first beaten to death by some thugs, then his body was burned and strung on a bus. Afterwards, his body was disemboweled by a savage rioter." This was part of an aggressive propaganda initiative in the initial aftermath of the killings, during which the government tried to saturate the country with its version of events.

On the streets, a widely circulated alternative version of events was that Liu had shot four people with his AK47 and was lynched after he ran out of ammunition. In fact, the photos of him hanging from a bus had been framed in such a way as to exclude the slogans scrawled in the dirt on the side of the bus: "He killed four people! Murderer! The People Must Win! Pay Back the Blood Debt!" To Chen, the sight of a soldier's corpse suspended from the same kind of public bus in which he had transported weapons signaled something altogether different. "This guy was doing the same thing as me," he told me confidently, shrugging off the discrepancies.

On the evening of June 3rd, following orders to recapture the stolen weapons, Chen Guang's battalion went out the backdoor on the west side of the Great Hall of the People, only to be met by a surging crowd once again using the sea-of-humanity tactic to swamp the soldiers. Chen and his battalion were immobilized. Protesters were still lecturing them, but now they were doing something more, "Bricks came flying at us, from I don't know where, and glass bottles. Some hit us in the head. Some soldiers' faces were covered in blood. We soldiers held onto each other very tightly, as the bricks and bottles bounced off our helmets."

The troops had received no orders, so they simply sat down cross-legged outside the hall. At one point, they even engaged in a sing-off against those surrounding them, a farcical competition that may have lulled the students into a false sense of security. The soldiers belted out military songs, trying to drown out the students' rendition of the Communist anthem, the "Internationale." After about three and a half hours—sometime around 9:30 p.m.— the troops were ordered to retreat back into the Great Hall of the People. Bricks smashed against the windows as they waited inside.

Then a period of high tension began. The troops stood lined up behind the massive doors to the square, waiting for the order. By about midnight, ammunition had been distributed—four clips per person, each carrying around 50 or 60 bullets, one clip to be loaded into the gun and the three others to be slung across their chests. "Of course I was afraid," Chen Guang said, his hands shaking as he poured another cup of delicate green tea. "When you have a gun with no bullets, it's meaningless. It's not even as dangerous as a kitchen knife. But once the bullets have been loaded, it's dangerous."

Nerves were so taut that there were numerous accidental discharges, bullets flying through the ceiling of the hall. "At 9:30 p.m. when we went back inside, they said we were going to head straight out.

Then at 10:00 p.m., 11:00 p.m., then 12:00 a.m, we were supposed to be heading out. Instead we were just waiting and waiting, standing there, holding our guns and waiting."

Chen had lost track of time when suddenly the doors swung open. The order had come to clear the square. As he stood with his detachment on the steps in front of the Great Hall of the People, permission to shoot was passed through the ranks. "At that time, it wasn't as if there was a direct order, but the guys in front would tell the guys behind them that if you run into danger, you can open fire. And that's an order from above. It was just spread down the line from person to person."

Chen was gripping his gun so tightly that his hands were shaking. One of his unit's leaders saw him struggling and decided that he was unfit for the task ahead. A stills camera was pushed into his hands. He was to work with the unit's cameraman, who was grappling with a heavy television camera. Chen went back into the Great Hall and climbed the marble staircases to the roof, from where he snapped pictures and listened to gunfire slowly coming closer, as units farther away fought their way toward Tiananmen Square, the heart of the city. Down below, he saw the soldiers opening fire. But from his vantage point, he couldn't tell whether they were firing warning shots into the air or firing directly at the students, tiny as ants, who were slowly retreating back toward the grey column of the Monument to the People's Heroes, a 10-story-high obelisk near the center of the square. Soldiers advanced toward them and tanks approached from both east and west.

When he climbed back down the marble staircases, he discovered that the ground floor of the Great Hall of the People had been turned into a makeshift field hospital. Hundreds of injured soldiers lay on the floor, many bleeding profusely, as they were tended by nurses.

Chen struggled to process the enormity of what he was seeing through the viewfinder of his camera. Occasionally, he was assailed by the same flashes of doubt he had felt when his truck had been stopped by the masses. "I started to feel conflicted. There were so many injured people lying on the first floor. You would think, 'How could something so big happen?'"

Outside, he watched as the last of the students—a few thousand—left the square from the southeast corner. As Chen later learned, the students had held a vote by voice on whether to stay or go, and though both sides shouted equally loudly, the decision had been made to leave. Chen's initial emotion was enormous relief because, despite the injuries he had witnessed, he believed any major loss of life had been avoided. He continued to watch as an armored car crashed into the Goddess of Democracy, the lumpen sister to the Statue of Liberty, that had been erected by art students just a few days earlier and had become an instant icon for the movement. After the first collision, the statue wobbled, but it did not fall. It took three or four more attempts before it slowly keeled over. And he watched as a line of armored cars careened over the tents in which only hours earlier students had been living. Chen insisted that he did not see any people killed in the square—either civilians or military—nor did he at any time fire a gun himself.

When the sun came up, the extent to which central Beijing had become a war zone was clear. Hulks of burnt-out armored vehicles and tanks dotted the square's expanse. Some of the trees lining Chang'an Avenue had caught fire, leaving smoldering black trunks flanking the boulevard. Even the railings separating the pavement from the road were black with soot. Despite all this, Chen Guang's overriding emotion was utter relief. He had heard gunfire, yet he still believed the square had been cleared without any major loss of life. That morning at around 7:00, he slept deeply—the slumber of exhaustion and relief—for two hours.

The unit's first task was to restore the square to normality by expunging any trace of what had happened. All the possessions left behind by fleeing students were to be heaped into big piles and burned: battered bicycles, bags of belongings, tents, banners, and the crumpled papers of their speeches. By then it was raining, and rivulets of black water from the sooty piles ran across the square, darkening its surface. These were the scenes that Chen Guang captured with his camera. Some of the negatives he kept; others he hid, propelled by some instinct he could not explain.

It was then that Chen spotted something that has obsessed him ever since. Tangled in the spokes of a bicycle's wheel was a braid of woman's hair, secured with a red rubber band. Who was this young woman, and what had she been thinking as she brushed her hair that morning and carefully plaited it? Under what circumstances could that braid have been hacked off? And where was she now? As the rain pelted down, flames from the soldiers' pyres engulfed the braid, which hissed and crackled as it burned.

A quarter of a century later, the echoes of that moment still reverberate throughout Chen Guang's work. His latest series of portraits depicts people having their hair cut, wet tendrils of severed hair lying on their bare shoulders. The detail is photographic, the effect eerily unsettling. These are pictures born of a quarter-century of unresolved guilt, of one man's post-Tiananmen posttraumatic stress disorder.

• • • •

Within months of June 4th, Chen Guang managed to gain a transfer into the Military Art Academy on the strength of his copy of Van Gogh's *Sunflowers*. In 1992, he won entrance to China's best art school, the Central Academy of Fine Arts in Beijing. Then located just a stone's throw from Tiananmen Square, its students had been the ones who created the iconic Goddess of Democracy statue. During the three years he studied at the academy, he kept his military past a secret from all but a few close friends. "It wasn't that I was afraid. I just didn't want to talk about it. I didn't want to bring up that stuff. I didn't even want to think about that stuff."

His denial lasted for almost 15 years, though the events of that day continued to loop through his mind almost endlessly. First, he committed to canvas the same scenes he had captured on film in the aftermath of the killing. Pictures of fire devouring piles of rubbish in Tiananmen Square; flames licking the base of a lamppost standing among a wasteland of devastation; soldiers sorting through debris, guns slung carelessly over their backs. He placed one photo he took that day of the cleanup effort into a wooden chest that he painted white, the color of mourning in China, ringed by shards of a mirror, so that anyone looking in sees his or her own face surrounded by splintered reflections of destruction. This is, he believes, his confession.

Perhaps unsurprisingly, Chen Guang's artwork was incomprehensible to his military comrades, who suspected he was using it to insult the government. Many have now risen to senior positions in the government bureaucracy, in part due to the honor accrued from their actions that day in June. "Because they participated in the 'suppression of counterrevolutionary turmoil,' as the government calls it, some were promoted," Chen Guang told me. Few have questioned whether the repression was the right move. "They didn't think it was a bad thing at all. They felt it was necessary. To this day, they feel it was necessary."

Even his artist friends wish Chen would choose other subject matter. In the go-go capitalism of China's ever-ballooning art bubble, his decision to forgo profit to depict this most charged moment in the country's recent history was viewed as stubborn, retrograde, and simply eccentric. More than that, his choices were overtly confrontational, forcing viewers to admit the existence of events that most would rather not remember. There is a cost to taking such a path, Chen admitted. "You definitely pay a very big price. You find that the world is no longer yours. China's mainstream society is no longer yours." The political nature of his work means that it cannot be exhibited, posted online, or even created in front of those who might report him to the authorities. So Chen has shut himself out from the clubby sociability of the art world. He has not married nor has he had children, finding it difficult to form close attachments. His work—and the isolation required to produce it—is not conducive to relationships.

Could he have behaved otherwise on that June night? This is a question he has struggled to answer. "Of course there is guilt," he admitted. "Over a long period of time, you realize that there were many things you could have chosen not to do." But if there were other choices, the callow 17-year-old soldier did not realize it at the time. He was well trained, and his job was to obey. Desertion never once crossed his mind.

• • • •

Some soldiers did rebel, however. The most famous conscientious objector was Major General Xu Qinxian, the commander of the

38th Group Army, traditionally the most elite division. The major general refused to agree to the deployment of troops in mid-May when the troops' transports became bogged down by citizens. Xu's own account of what happened, which was not made public for two decades, was relayed to me by Yang Jisheng, a retired Xinhua journalist who has been fearless in his pursuit of historical truth. Yang met Xu twice and has provided the fullest account of what happened.

In May of 1989, Xu had been following the protests while laid up in a hospital suffering from kidney stones and had become opposed to the idea of using the PLA to crush the students. On May 17th, he was in a good mood, having just expelled a kidney stone, when the deputy commander of the Beijing military region, Li Laizhu, called a meeting of military commanders. Li announced the verbal order to mobilize troops and asked each commander for an expression of support. All the commanders complied except for Xu Qinxian, who replied that he could not follow a verbal order; he needed a written order. Li replied, "There are no written orders today. We'll get them later. That's what happens in wartime." Xu responded, "Now is not a time of war. I cannot implement a verbal order." Li told Xu he must telephone his political commissar—a political officer assigned by the Communist Party—to tell him of his decision. In a phone call, Xu told his commissar, "I am communicating that I will not take part. This has nothing to do with me." Then he returned to the hospital, a convenient place of shelter in times of political crisis in China.

Xu told friends that he was prepared to be executed for insubordination. "I would rather be beheaded than be seen as a criminal by history!" He was indeed arrested in the hospital shortly afterward. His party membership was stripped from him, and he was sentenced to five years of imprisonment. Xu spent four years in Qincheng Prison near Beijing, where China's most famous political prisoners have traditionally been held, followed by one year in a police hospital. On his release, he was told to retire to Shijiazhuang in Hebei province, where he received treatment commensurate with that of a deputy commander. Since then, he has lived under state surveillance, his freedoms sharply curtailed. In photos taken with Yang Jisheng several years ago, Xu looks less like a major general than a portly, retired government servant, perched on the edge of a cream leather sofa, his eyes shaded by the capacious dark glasses favored by a previous generation of leaders.

Xu has spoken publicly only twice about his role—once to Yang Jisheng and once to a foreign radio station. For these two exceedingly brief interviews, his already limited freedom was rescinded. From then on, he was escorted to the doctor and was temporarily banned from visiting Beijing. "He's very cautious," Yang said. "He spoke very carefully. He didn't speak very openly." Yang is sure of one thing: Xu Qinxian has never regretted the insubordination that cost him his career and his freedom. However, as the most senior army officer who refused to act against his conscience, he remains— even 25 years later—a potent symbol.

Xu was not the only soldier to refuse to follow orders. In a classified speech, it was revealed that 21 officers at division-level command or higher, and 90 other officers of lesser rank, had "breached discipline in a serious manner during the struggle to crush the counterrevolutionary rebellion." Nonetheless, the act of insubordination by the commander of the 38th Group Army was to have a profound effect on the way that ordinary soldiers were treated at the square.

Another ex-soldier from a different division described to me how his company's leadership was suddenly reshuffled and new leaders were put in charge days before they were sent to Tiananmen. The scenes he described from his deployment on the night of June 3rd were like something from a dystopian nightmare: civilians weeping as they watched ammunition being distributed to the troops; young soldiers running into the city on foot in a dazed panic, with those at the front shooting warning shots into the air. After the clearing of the square, every soldier in his company was ordered to hand over his ammunition, leaving their weapons as empty showpieces. But this ex-soldier told me that he had seen a visiting commander being accompanied by machine-gun-toting bodyguards, though the troops he was inspecting had no ammunition. He believed that the PLA, paranoid about the loyalty of its troops, was taking all necessary precautions against a mutiny or, worse still, an outright armed rebellion.

• • • •

Chen Guang's anguished guilt about June 4th does not seem to have been shared by Deng Xiaoping, who as chairman of the Central Military Commission was ultimately in charge of the army. His daughter later told his biographer Ezra Vogel that he never once doubted that he had made the correct decision. Deng had laid his groundwork carefully. By forcing every military commander to *biaotai*, meaning to state his attitude toward the imposition of martial law—the test of loyalty that Xu Qinxian failed—he ensured that everyone was incriminated in the act of violence.

It is significant that Deng Xiaoping's first public appearance after the suppression was to congratulate the martial law troops on June 9th, five days after the killings. He began by offering his condolences on the deaths of soldiers, a courtesy he did not extend to civilians killed by his army. He then labeled the protest movement as "counterrevolutionary turmoil" aimed at overthrowing the Socialist system and establishing a "totally Western-dependent bourgeois republic." Deng's speech set in place the party orthodoxy that both the protests and their suppression were inevitable: "This storm was bound to come sooner or later," he declared. "It was just a matter of time and scale."

Deng's speech to the martial law troops was more than just a thank you from on high. A quarter-century later, this post-suppression justification reads like his living will, setting out the future political direction of the country by emphasizing that, while China's economic reform and opening up should continue at an accelerated pace, this should not be accompanied by similarly fast political liberalization. Deng also laid in place the theoretical basis for strengthening the security apparatus: "From now on, we should pay attention when handling such problems. As soon as a trend emerges, we should not allow it to spread."

Over the years, Beijing has progressively softened its language as it moves to conceal and neuter those heady weeks of the student movement and its ensuing violent repression. Deng's "counterrev-olutionary turmoil" has morphed over time into plain "turmoil" and then a "political storm." Nowadays, if it is referred to at all, it is often called the "June 4th incident," a term notable for its blandness. Just one year after the killings, when American interviewer Barbara Walters asked then-President Jiang Zemin how he looked back on the events of 1989, he told her that it was "much ado about nothing."

Though the language may have changed, the Communist Party has not budged in its official assessment of the events. Speaking on the 2013 anniversary, Foreign Ministry Spokesman Hong Lei emphasized that judgment, saying, "A clear conclusion has al-ready been made concerning the political turmoil that happened in the late 1980s." Identical sentiments are repeated every year, de-spite cyclical hopes that new men at the top might bring about a reassessment.

In that first post-Tiananmen appearance, Deng Xiaoping praised the martial law troops repeatedly, stating, "The People's Army is truly a great wall of iron and steel of the party and state." Chen Guang's memories of that period paint a very different picture. As Deng Xiaoping was congratulating the troops, Chen's unit was still stationed at the Great Hall of the People, sleeping on the floor. The troops spent their days obsessing over their gnawing hunger, since at that point, all their rations were being airlifted in by helicopter, and one day's rations consisted only of a single packet of instant noodles to be split among three men. Chen says the ravenous, ex-hausted troops were shocked and baffled by the lack of supplies.

This detail is repeated in a book published by the People's Liberation Army, *One Day of Martial Law*, which paints a vivid pic-ture of the scene inside the packed Great Hall of the People after three days in which the soldiers had only eaten small quantities of instant noodles, "The warriors were now bearing the torture of hunger. Some were snuggled up close to each other, some were lying on one side, some were squatting, some were lost in thought star-ing at the ceiling." The officer who wrote the piece, a senior colonel, describes how he followed the sound of weeping to discover a young soldier driven to tears by hunger, lying in a fetal position, his knees pulled up against his chest. In a pep talk, the senior colonel tells the troops, "This struggle is complicated and intense. We must fear neither death nor hardship. Hunger is testing us. The senior officers and other comrades are suffering hunger just like you."

That much, at least, may not have been true. According to Chen, the military leadership was still based at the Great Hall of the People and was being fed in grand style, served by waitresses who would wheel them trolleys of food kept warm under glass domes covered with white napkins. As the waitresses' heels clacked across the marble floors, the soldiers' catcalls spread from the ground floor up through the second and third stories to echo across the entire Great Hall of the People. Watching this spectacle made Chen Guang think about the social structure, how China's privileged classes operated in full view of ordinary people with their approbation, and how these pockets of privilege had become entrenched in the army.

Chen Guang described the mood as angry and bitter. The soldiers ripped up the carpets, threatening to use the carpet rods as weapons. "It was like being at the battlefield," he said, grimacing as he remembered the subsistence rations. He spent a total of 10 days billeted in the Great Hall of the People. For the next decade, the smell of instant noodles made him retch.

• • • •

It was drizzling during my final visit to Songzhuang, which looked even more depressed than ever. The artists had disappeared from the roadsides, and the streets seemed eerily empty. Something else was missing, though it took me some time to figure out what it was. It was the absence of noise. The ever-present hum and buzz of construction had stopped. The building sites had fallen silent. Most of the half-finished buildings had been draped in enormous white banners emblazoned with red Chinese characters reading "This building is an illegal construction, and has already been sealed by the government." The banners also included warnings that purchases of "apartments with limited-property rights" did not enjoy any legal protection.

This was something I had never before seen during more than two decades in China. Given the raft of necessary planning permissions, it seemed impossible that such buildings could have been built without the knowledge of the relevant government departments. Nobody I asked believed the official line. It appeared that these apartments were part of a compromise, technically illegal, that allowed urban buyers to purchase cheap apartments constructed on rural land in exchange for giving up some of their property rights. Despite its illegality, this happened all over China, accounting for one fifth of all property under construction, according to one estimate. But in Songzhuang, there had recently been a political reshuffle, resulting in a crackdown on this practice. Most people believed this was basically a government-backed shakedown that would allow local officials to wring more funds from the property developers. The chance of the half-finished buildings actually being torn down, everyone seemed to agree, was precisely nil.

All the construction sites around Chen Guang's new house had also fallen silent, and the big development outside his back window was shrouded in white banners, giving it a funereal air. This, Chen Guang sighed, was one of the hazards of life in China. Policies could be reversed at the drop of a hat, with no warning whatsoever. He had invested the proceeds from all his years of art into his studio and the neighboring one, which he had bought with an eye to expansion. Now they were suddenly surrounded by illegal buildings. Was he worried? I asked him. "The reality in China is like this," he replied. "There's no point worrying." He was, he said, smiling, as safe as any other artist in Songzhuang.

On the wall in front of us was a large photograph of a young-looking Chen beside a 75-year-old man. Both were bare-chested. The older man had one arm around Chen's neck; the other caressed his nipple. Chen Guang's determination to use art to break taboos had at one stage led him to have sex with 100 different people. This particular piece of performance art, he said, was all about politics. The older man was a history professor who had been a victim of almost every political movement sweeping contemporary Chinese history. During Chairman Mao's Cultural Revolution in the 1960s and '70s, he had been sent twice to labor camp and was prevented from earning a living because of his background. Hence, the elderly victim of one of the most shameful periods in China's history was physically embracing the young perpetrator of a different outrage. Yet, according to Chen, both were equally guilty, "We are all participants in building this society. If you are living quite comfortably, I believe you are guilty, almost like the religious concept of original sin."

In their own ways, Chen and the elderly history professor were among the few who acknowledge the past instead of turning away from it. Chen believes that amnesia is, for many, the easy option. "People find it very easy to forget, because there is no way to cleanse their consciences. China's political education forces you to forget what happened in the past—forget the bad things that the party did, and only remember the good things. For a collective, this is very destructive. You can only think about things that are beneficial to you. This makes people live like animals. In order to serve your own interests, you can do whatever you want to the culture or the environment."

Sitting in his apartment surrounded by half-built illegal buildings bathed in the white miasma of the smoggy pollution that regularly engulfs large swathes of northern China, this argument seemed convincing. Politics, he believed, was like the air in China. "If you can't breathe, you'll die. If you breathe, you'll be infected by these viruses. The air is so polluted, but who can't breathe?"

• • • •

Back in 1989, once Chen Guang's unit had finished cleaning up the physical reminders of June 4th, their next role was to serve as the public face of the suppression. For two additional months, his unit remained in Beijing, staying at a guesthouse in Qianmen close to the square. One of its main tasks was public relations; in groups of seven or eight, the soldiers performed a kind of victory lap, visiting schools and residential committees to recount their role in suppressing the counterrevolutionary riots. To Chen's surprise, they were treated like conquering heroes, given hyperbolic introductions by school principals, and personally thanked by the students.

Another duty, one that he hated even more, was taking part in police raids to capture "counterrevolutionaries." The soldiers were still carrying their rifles, and sometimes they were encouraged to use them to hit the terrified, cowering targets of their raids, who were mostly students. This was a necessary part of the propaganda campaign of intimidation that leaned heavily on wall-to-wall television coverage of armed police and soldiers rounding up "rioters," who often bore visible bruises as stark warnings of the cost of resistance. "At the time, we thought those people were definitely bad people," Chen said. "Only bad people would be arrested. Good people wouldn't be arrested."

What shocked Chen Guang most was the change in attitude toward the martial law troops. He detected no malice or fear directed at himself or his fellow soldiers despite their role in putting down the largest protests to shake Beijing in modern history. In fact, he was bemused by the fawning treatment they received from local residents, who often brought them presents of food and drink. "The residents suddenly changed to become really nice to the soldiers," he remembered. "I thought about this a lot at the time. It really confused me. Why was it like that? On June 4th, all the residents supported the students. So overnight how did they come to support the soldiers?"

Chen Guang struggled to comprehend how a swarming sea of Beijingers had stopped the PLA's advance with their own bodies, and now these same people were pressing gifts onto the same troops. He did not believe this about-face was motivated by fear, but rather by a deep-seated desire—a necessity even—to side with the victors, no matter the cost. "It's a survival mechanism that people in China have evolved after living under this system for a long time. In order to exist, everything is about following orders from above."

In his new sitting room, tucked carefully away in a desk drawer, Chen has kept the commemorative souvenirs issued to all who "quelled the turmoil." He took them out to show me. There was a small red linen-bound book titled *The Defenders of the Capital*, which contained pictures of rows and rows of soldiers rallying in the square, with the caption "We will always be the protectors of the people's interests." One photo showed two schoolgirls looking up adoringly at a martial law soldier while shyly caressing his rifle. There was also a gold-colored medal issued by the Central Military Commission depicting Tiananmen Gate superimposed on a star and a wreath above the words "Defender of the Capital." Then there was the wristwatch.

The care with which Chen Guang handled these mementos of glory and guilt sum up the contradictions that roil him. He knows that he will spend the rest of his life painting what has become the defining fact of his existence. As a taboo-busting artist, his aim has been to confront the Chinese people with the truth about Tiananmen. Yet how can he confront people about an event that many no longer remember with art that cannot be shown? There is no answer to this question.

2 :: Staying

Zhang Ming has become used to his appearance startling small children. Skeletally thin, with cheeks sunk deep into his face, he walked gingerly across the cream-colored hotel lobby as if his limbs were made of glass. On his forehead were two large, perfectly circular purple-red bruises, one above each eye. "Kids often think I have four eyes," he said with a puckish grin. Indeed, the unexpected visual symmetry of the garish circles was so discombobulating that several times during our long conversations, I found myself addressing his purple forehead orbs. The bruises were from *baguan*, or fire cupping, a Chinese medical treatment in which heated glass jars are adhered by suction to the skin to cleanse it of toxins. For Zhang Ming, this has been the only way to alleviate the splitting headaches that are the legacy of his seven years in jail.

Zhang Ming was number 19 on the list of 21 most wanted students issued by the Chinese government following June 4th. Ironically, he had once seen himself as the person least likely to become involved in the student movement, since he had not the slightest interest in politics. But, having been caught up in the whirligig of history, he can never disentangle himself from it. Like so many others who played prominent roles in the student movement, Zhang Ming remains, even after 25 years, in limbo. His attempt to leave his past behind failed; his body can never recover from the retribution meted out for his act of effrontery. His mind, too, constantly replays the events of 1989, endlessly searching for new answers to old questions.

Zhang Ming's first words to me were a request to help pin down the exact timing of the crucial Politburo Standing Committee meeting at the house of the paramount leader Deng Xiaoping on May 17, 1989, during which the decision was made to impose martial law. He wanted to ascertain whether a declaration criticizing Deng that he helped pen that same day could have been a factor that pushed Deng toward that decision. At that time, Deng held no party or government posts, even though he was still in charge of the military. In their declaration, which Zhang says was moderate in tone, the students had asked the 84-year-old Deng to withdraw from politics, so as to avoid repeating the same mistakes as Chairman Mao Zedong in his later years. Immediately after the students broadcast their declaration across Tiananmen Square, Zhang noticed demonstrators bearing banners painted with crude epithets attacking Deng. For years, Zhang has been gripped by doubts about whether those personal attacks against Deng had tipped the balance, pushing him to declare martial law. "If we hadn't pushed Deng Xiaoping into opposing us, there might have been other possibilities," he mused out loud. It is an exercise in retrospective futility. But for those who have been made to believe that they bear the historical burden of bloodshed, questions that cannot be answered or forgotten can only be repeated.

• • • •

In the early months of 1989, Zhang Ming was at the tail end of his degree program in automobile engineering at Tsinghua University. He was looking forward to beginning the job he had been assigned in Shantou, one of only five special economic zones established to attract foreign investment, where he thought he would enjoy more freedom. Safeguarding that job was at the forefront of his mind when the students began to gather in large groups, mourning the sudden death of the demoted party leader Hu Yaobang on April 15, 1989. As general secretary of the Communist Party, Hu had been a political and economic reformer who was removed by Deng in 1987 after being blamed for student protests in the winter of 1986 and 1987. Hu's popularity meant that the student commemorations for his death almost immediately tipped over into politically sensitive territory, with banners bearing veiled criticisms of Deng Xiaoping like "He Who Should Have Died Did Not, He Who Died Should Not Have." Zhang Ming didn't care. He was determined to stay away from trouble.

Two days later on April 17th, the students organized their first march to Tiananmen Square, as if drawn by the pull of history. At the forefront of their minds was the May 4th Movement of 1919—a tableau of which had even been memorialized in stone at the base of the Monument to the People's Heroes near the center of the square. At that time, 3,000 patriotic students had marched on the square to protest against the government's acceptance of the Versailles Treaty ending World War I, because it was to cede control over part of eastern China to Japan. The rowdy protest, during which the house of one pro-Japanese cabinet minister was set on fire, culminated in the protesters being beaten and arrested; one was killed. This march was the consummation of a period of cultural, political, and intellectual ferment that had begun in 1915. Its impact was perhaps best summed up by a young Mao Zedong who wrote in an essay, "We are awakened! The world is ours, the nation is ours, society is ours. If we do not speak, who will speak? If we do not act, who will act?" The idea of the intellectual elite serving as the nation's conscience was etched deep in their psyches as it was in those of their counterparts seven decades later.

For one more day, Zhang Ming managed to rein in his curiosity. On April 18th, he was persuaded to accompany a friend to the square, where several hundred students were trying to deliver a seven-point petition affirming Hu Yaobang's views on democracy and, among other demands, calling for freedom of speech and an end to restrictions on demonstrations. As Zhang and his friend returned to campus, they passed *Xinhuamen*, the Gate of New China, marking the entrance to *Zhongnanhai*, the old imperial leisure garden which now housed China's Communist leaders. Hundreds of students staging a sit-in had become angry and around midnight began trying to get into the compound by barging through police lines. Frustrated by the protesters' confrontational methods and lack of strategy, Zhang Ming stepped in to advocate a more tactical approach. Why not draft written demands or call for a meeting with government officials instead of wasting energy on so futile a showdown? That was how Zhang Ming became a student leader. From that moment on, there was no going back. That night, police beat and injured some students at *Xinhuamen*, further incensing them.

During the days that followed, Zhang helped organize massive student marches and a boycott of classes. He became involved in the students' own tortuous bureaucracy that aped the government's circles of power, with its endless and overlapping preparatory committees, dialogue groups, and federations, all of which rose and fell with ever-increasing speed as the movement gathered momentum. By the end, the internal hierarchies had become so entrenched that the most significant student leaders installed themselves at the Monument to the People's Heroes in the center of a series of concentric circles delineated by volunteers holding up transparent fishing lines. Each circle had its own checkpoint; Western journalists encountered half a dozen checkpoints protecting the self-appointed leaders from the rank and file. The internecine feuding among the students reached a frantic pace; one group was said to have changed presidents 182 times within the span of a few days. Some of the student leaders had their own bodyguards, and they had even instituted a system of censorship at the radio station they had set up on the square.

Zhang Ming was active at his university, as well as being a member of the Beijing Students Autonomous Federation, and his days were taken up organizing demonstrations, liaising between universities, and attending endless meetings at which the various factions jockeyed for advantage. The movement's turning point came on April 26th, when the government outlined its attitude toward the students in a front-page editorial in the *People's Daily*. The editorial took its tone from Deng Xiaoping, who accused a tiny minority of having ulterior motives to undermine the nation's political stability and unity by conspiring against the leadership of the Communist Party. When Zhang Ming saw the editorial, he knew that his future in Shantou was doomed. There was little left for him to lose; when the accounts were tallied by the officials, he would surely be seen to be on the wrong side of the ledger.

Tens of thousands of students made the same calculation, and the next day they marched in a mile-long column to the square. The sheer numbers overwhelmed the police. As the students passed *Xinhuamen*, where some had been beaten one week earlier, they chanted, "We are not afraid! We are not afraid!" In a year when failed price reforms had led to runaway inflation of 28 percent, the students won support from bystanders who were angered by growing income disparities, official corruption, profiteering, and nepotism, themes that were stressed in the early campus manifestoes sometimes even more strongly than democracy.

As the student movement swelled, Zhang Ming found himself trying to act as a restraining influence. Aged 24 and approaching the end of his last year at university, he was one of the older students. He advocated pushing for student demands that were concrete and achievable—such as specific reforms of the press—rather than grandiose demands for freedom and democracy. For his restraint, he was criticized by other students as a collaborator and traitor, in a pattern that was to continue beyond the square and into prison. One of the tragedies of discourse in China, Zhang believes, is that grey areas have been swallowed up by black-and-white moral absolutism. Rule by the emperor, or the strongman, has become the only mode of governance that people recognize: Obey or be crushed, for there is no alternative. Even the students, while clamoring for democracy, had become mini-dictators of the world that they had created with their wordy titles, petty denunciations, and fervid inner-court power struggles.

As the protests morphed into a wider movement encompassing workers and government organizations, even official work units like the Party's Central Committee Communist Party school, sections of the public security service, courts, and military began to take part in the huge demonstrations, marching proudly under banners announcing their identities. But from the commanding heights provided by a quarter-century of reflection, Zhang Ming's memories are not of giddy euphoria or oratorical debuts or the camaraderie of a "Woodstock of the mind." He does not evoke the excitement of the massive rallies or the historical significance of the student movement. That aspect—the sense of optimism, of exhilaration, of a moment when anything seemed possible—seems entirely absent from his memories, in contrast to the student leaders who fled into exile after June 4th. If he had felt any sense of hope, the memory of it has long since been excised. For Zhang Ming, the most vivid recollection from those seven weeks of demonstrations is a muscle memory—of bone-aching, brain-scrambling exhaustion. At one stage while riding his bike back to campus from the square, he was so tired that he kept nodding off to sleep even as he pedaled.

When the students launched their hunger strike on May 13th, he opposed it, fearing that it would alienate the reformers within the government, leaving the students politically isolated. But once the hunger strike had started, he led a team of students to support those in the square, where he stayed until after it was called off six days later. By then, Zhang Ming had begun arguing for the students to return to their campuses to focus their energies on starting an opposition party instead of continuing to colonize the square. The students had already become fragmented, however, with the more radical new arrivals from the provinces outflanking the more estab-lished student leaders from Beijing.

One particular memory still rankles even after all these years. On May 15th, Zhang Ming was barred from participating in nego-tiations between the students' dialogue delegation and three senior government officials. Although he had been designated by the stu-dents as one of their dialogue delegates, once he reached the meeting room, he found an unfamiliar student stationed at the door, vetting the views of the attendees. Zhang believed the students' demand for a withdrawal of the April 26th editorial was politically impossible, so instead he advocated requesting an emergency session of the National People's Congress. "Once he heard that, he was very an-noyed," Zhang remembered of the door guardian. "He said, 'All the students are united now. How could you bring up this demand at this time?' He wouldn't let me in. There was nothing I could do. We students couldn't fight each other." Even a quarter of a century later, the counterfactuals still nag at him: What if he had been allowed into that room? What would the official response have been had he been able to lodge his demand? Was there a chance, however tiny, that he might have been able to change the course of history?

As Deng Xiaoping edged closer to declaring martial law, the students tried to follow the official line of thought through back channels provided by some of their number whose parents were high-ranking government officials. When the martial law troops tried to enter Beijing on the evening of May 19th, Zhang Ming played a large role in coordinating the citizens' blockades that stopped the advance of the soldiers like Chen Guang. Zhang Ming's army of volunteers shuttled information about troop movements back to the student headquarters at Tiananmen Square, and he then relayed the details over the student radio station. "We reported where the army was, and we told people to go to block them. We also had money, so we bought supplies."

Toward the end of May, Zhang Ming fell ill, spending several days in bed with a high fever. But when the crackdown became inevitable, he was determined to return to the square to bear witness. "If I didn't go, my conscience would have haunted me," he said quietly. "Even today, my conscience is not at peace. On this, there's nothing I can do."

In the square that night, the loudspeakers were broadcasting a warning, over and over, that "a severe counterrevolutionary riot" had broken out, the first time the government was using these terms. The warning stated that rioters had savagely attacked soldiers of the PLA and had burned vehicles in an attempt to subvert the People's Republic and to overthrow the Socialist system, and it warned citizens to evacuate the square, "We cannot guarantee the safety of violators, who will be solely responsible for any consequences." The threats of violence were no longer implicit. At the time, Zhang Ming was huddled with the other students around the Monument to the People's Heroes as tracer bullets arced through the air, marking the steady progress of troops approaching along Chang'an Avenue.

Zhang watched the advance of the troops, moving through a hail of bricks and paving stones hurled by disbelieving and irate crowds. Some 25 years later, he is still moved to tears at the memory of what he saw, such as the sight of one young man being carried to an ambulance just outside the square, a red blossom spreading across his chest. "I had thought death would be terrifying, but he looked as though he were sleeping." Zhang remembers the tense wait while negotiations were underway for safe passage for the remaining students from Tiananmen Square. As the students straggled out of the square hand in hand, singing the "Internationale" and the Chinese national anthem, tears poured down their cheeks.

None of the student leaders died that night. The vast majority of those who were killed on June 4th were ordinary bystanders, citizens who had come out to see what was happening as the tanks rolled through the city to secure the square. Many were hit when soldiers fired indiscriminately into crowds on approach roads heading from the west toward Tiananmen Square. One of the sites of the worst killings was Muxidi, where troops even fired at the apartment block housing high-level government ministers, killing a high-level official's son-in-law, who was shot in the head when he switched on the light to enter the kitchen.

After leaving the square, Zhang Ming felt deep exhaustion numbing his limbs and paralyzing his mind. No longer caring about his own safety, he staggered along Chang'an Avenue until he saw a patch of grass outside the Cultural Palace of Nationalities. There he stopped, laid down, and instantly fell asleep, insensible to the tanks rolling past him. Local residents noticed the sleeping student on the grass and shook him awake, warning him that he would probably be arrested if he did not immediately leave, so he returned to his school.

Back at Tsinghua University on June 5th, he spoke at an emotional meeting in front of faculty and Communist Party members, who later helped build the case against him in court. The students called the suppression of the protests a military coup and even discussed whether they should take up arms against the troops. That afternoon, amid rumors that the PLA would enter the universities, the student leaders made the decision to flee.

Zhang Ming left Beijing with another student, heading toward the relative safety of Hong Kong, which was then still a British colony. They had the telephone number of Hong Kong activists who had promised to try to smuggle them to safety if they could get as far as the border. The two spent three weeks on the run, mostly sleeping under the flickering light of all-night cinemas, where no one asked for identity papers. Their first stop was the Beijing suburb of Tongzhou, from where they took a train to Shanhaiguan, where the Great Wall meets the sea. By then, Zhang Ming was a wanted man, a grainy black-and-white shot of his face appearing on a constant loop on television. But he never saw it since he was always on the run, continuing to travel by boat to Shanghai, then by train to Guangzhou.

On June 26th, freedom was almost within their grasp. The pair, together with two other students, was in the border city of Shenzhen, in a taxi heading toward a getaway boat that would carry them to safe waters when they were stopped by police. Zhang Ming was not carrying any identity documents, so he was detained. Other students, he commented acidly, who had links to Communist Party officials, were sprung from detention and helped to leave the country. Like most of those who ended up in jail, Zhang Ming had no family ties to the Communist aristocracy. He was sent to Beijing's Qincheng Prison, where major general Xu Qinxian, who had refused to deploy his troops, was also being held.

In January 1991, Zhang Ming was in the first batch of students to be sentenced for their role in what was now labeled a "counter-revolutionary rebellion." He was given three years in prison for inciting subversion against the people's government and attempting to overthrow the Socialist system. He remembers being surprised by his relatively light sentence. In line with the leadership's assertion that the students had been manipulated by behind-the-scenes "black hands", most of the undergraduate leaders received jail terms of four years or less. In the immediate aftermath of the crackdown, 15 people were sentenced to death, mainly for violence against the security forces. The earliest of those death sentences were passed just 11 days after June 4th. Harsher treatment was meted out to the older intellectuals and workers. Some of the longest sentences were given to three workers who had thrown ink-filled eggs at the portrait of Chairman Mao that hung on Tiananmen Gate and had been turned over to the police by the students; they received between 16 years and life. Despite the importance of his trial, Zhang Ming has retained no memories of it whatsoever. In the light of what was to follow, its importance has faded.

• • • •

Of his treatment in Qincheng Prison, Zhang Ming also has few memories. "It was the first time that I had ever even seen a proper toilet!" he laughed. "It was a prison for leaders!" The students were held together, and though they were occasionally placed in solitary confinement, Zhang Ming had few complaints about his treatment.

All that changed in April 1991 when he was transferred to Lingyuan Prison in the Northeast with 10 other political prisoners including Liu Gang, a graduate student who was number three on the most wanted list, and who had received a six-year sentence. Known to the outside world as Lingyuan Motor Vehicle Industrial Corporation, Lingyuan was a penal colony so vast that a Japanese visitor who spent two days touring it by car had still not seen the whole site. The prison-production complex produced buses, trucks, tractor-trailers, and vehicle components for export. It also held so many Tiananmen activists that it was given special recognition for its role as an "Outstanding Collective in Curbing the Turmoil and Suppressing the Counterrevolutionary Rebellion."

That world is one to which Zhang Ming is unwilling to return, even in conversation. Those days have passed, and there is no benefit in revisiting them. "Facts are facts," he announced firmly. "Talking about what happened is not conducive to my influencing more people within China." He had refused all earlier requests to describe how prisoners were treated at Lingyuan, fearing he would be tarred as a traitor and accused of "standing on the side of the U.S." Chinese people, he went on, believed that the West was interested only in human rights issues, and although human rights were important, the West should look at the bigger picture.

As he briskly skated over his time in Lingyuan, it was clear that the mistreatment had been vicious and immediate, beginning the very moment the 11 prisoners arrived at the jail, when one of them was assaulted with an electric prod for asking a prison guard for a light for his cigarette.

The 11 political prisoners chafed against the prison rules. They refused to memorize the 58 provisions of the "Rules of Conduct for Criminals Undergoing Reform," which prisoners are supposed to be able to recite by heart. It was, for Zhang Ming, an act of principle, as he put it, "I can serve my sentence, but my brain does not belong to you." As a lover of classical Chinese poetry, the idea of polluting his brain with prison guidelines was repulsive. It was also hypocritical, given that the jailers openly flouted their own regulations. Yet for the prison authorities, this mass show of insubordination set a dangerous precedent.

For a while, Zhang Ming refused to take part in compulsory labor—making matchboxes. He was a slow worker, and his daily quota sometimes necessitated 14-hour working days. He firmly resisted going into detail, and I stopped pushing, uncomfortably aware that failing as a journalist is preferable to failing in human sympathy.

To find out more, I dug up an old copy of an Asia Watch report detailing the treatment of those 11 political prisoners at Lingyuan. As I read the account, I felt a low pulse of shame at my attempts to excavate those long-buried memories. The report describes the consequences of the prisoners' refusal to memorize the prison regulations or to be tested on them. First, they were beaten by common criminals who were responsible for disciplining them. Later, Zhang and four others were put into solitary confinement cells, each measuring six feet by three feet. According to Asia Watch, "They were tortured continuously, stripped naked, held down on the floor and assaulted repeatedly with several high-voltage (varying from 10,000 to 50,000 volts) electric batons simultaneously administered to their head, neck, shoulders, chest, belly, armpit, inside part of the leg and fingers."

In November 1991, Zhang Ming finally went on his own hunger strike. He was one of 13 prisoners who refused food, demanding to be allowed to serve their sentences in their hometowns. They were also calling for an end to corporal punishment and the system whereby common criminals supervised political prisoners. This hunger strike was declared one of "resisting reform and even a prison uprising." Nine of the prisoners were punished; Zhang was again put in a tiny confinement cell, while those who continued to resist food were force-fed by tubes stuffed down their esophagi.

The inmates soon discovered that their only weapons were their own bodies, and the only resistance tactic at their disposal was the power to refuse food. The political prisoners developed a crude method of communicating with each other by tapping out English letters on the wall of the prison. When I asked why they had used English, Zhang Ming pointed out that Chinese characters can't be tapped out numerically. The code (one tap for A, two for B, etc.) was time-consuming, so messages were often cryptically abbreviated. Zhang remembered that once Liu Gang tried to get the others to take part in a hunger strike. Zhang could not understand what they were supposed to be striking over, so he refused, tapping out NO. Immediately Liu began tapping out a message, which Zhang painstakingly counted out: TRAITOR.

On New Year's Day 1992, eight of the political prisoners launched another hunger strike from their tiny solitary cells, this time demanding to be allowed to receive visitors. Zhang Ming wrote a poem on the prison wall, for which the Asia Watch report says he was stripped naked, beaten, kicked, and then left naked in the sub-zero temperatures for half an hour. The police commander told him, "It is my job to beat you. It is for your reform. So you want to stage a hunger strike? Go right ahead! Labor reform detachments aren't afraid of deaths! When one dies, we'll bury one. When two die, we'll bury a pair!" In mid-January, Zhang was tortured again, and when he took a bath, witnesses saw the scars and flesh wounds that the electric batons had left on his chest. Conditions were so bad in Lingyuan that Liu Gang described it as "worse than a concentration camp."

Though horrific, Zhang Ming's treatment was not unique. The exiled poet Liao Yiwu has published an autobiography about the four years he spent in jail after penning "Massacre," a stream-of-consciousness poem memorializing those who died on June 4th. Liao's For A Song and A Hundred Songs describes how his prison cell replicated the state bureaucracy outside, with a clear hierarchy of power governing almost all interactions inside the cell. In an act of gruesome creativity, a diabolical torture menu had been concocted that transposed the inmates' yearning for decent food with the harrowing torments of jail life. Thus "Noodles in Clear Broth" referred to strings of toilet paper soaked in a bowl of urine, which the inmate was forced to eat and drink. Another "dish," "Twice-Cooked Pork on an Iron Platter," required the enforcer to stab the inmate's back with bamboo sticks and spread salt on the puncture wounds. These areas were covered with adhesive bandages that, when ripped off, left the flesh on the inmate's back looking like cooked meat.

As I read the accounts of Lingyuan Prison in the Asia Watch report, I thought back to my conversations with Zhang Ming in the quiet lobby of the smart hotel in his hometown of Jilin in the Northeast of the country, while I drank Iron Buddha tea and he sipped milk. I realized the cruel naïvety of my clumsy questions about his prison years. For him to even think about the prison years had become a continuation of what he had resisted. For China's former political prisoners, there is no therapy. Contrary to the glib platitudes we hold dear, time cannot heal everything, especially irreparable physical and psychological damage. But those brutal prison years had taught Zhang Ming about the importance of strategy and one other key lesson that he would put to impressive effect.

• • • •

After being released from jail in the spring of 1991, Zhang Ming reinvented himself as a businessman, throwing himself into changing China through economics rather than politics. This was, after all, the overriding message of 1989: Politics is dangerous. Better to keep your mouth shut and make money. "After June 4th, Chinese people's political fervor disappeared, so they threw all their efforts into making money," one of China's most famous authors, Yu Hua, told me. "It became a crazy, money-making, materialistic era. It was like a pendulum that swung from one extreme to the other."

Getting rich had become glorious, and Zhang Ming wanted a part of that glory. To try to distance himself from the notoriety of the most wanted list, he changed his name to Li Zhengbang. His first foray into business was successful, perhaps too successful. He joined a company that was an early credit cooperative and also doubled as a real estate developer. As the company went from strength to strength, he decided to make a tentative foray back into the political arena.

He wanted a cause with popular resonance that would be judged safe by the authorities, so in 1995, he decided to start a foundation to commemorate the Anti-Japanese War, which is how the Chinese refer to the Japanese invasion of Northeast China in the 1930s and World War II. His company provided two million yuan [approximately $232,000] of seed money—then a huge amount—for the foundation, and initially the local authorities in the city of Wuhan gave him the go-ahead. But the project stalled when the local bank refused to grant approval, and the foundation was shut down before it had ever begun operation.

If that had been a warning signal, Zhang Ming was not paying enough attention. Two years later, his boss was imprisoned for the unlikely crime of "using capitalism to engage in politics." His boss had been politically active, too, but Zhang Ming still wondered whether their association had doomed him.

Subsequently, Zhang Ming moved to Shanghai and began helping a new boss build up a real estate conglomerate with subsidiaries in the auto industry, cell phone sector, and elsewhere. The company was extraordinarily successful and by 2002, its cash assets alone were worth 4.5 billion yuan [more than $600 million]. "We were too rich," Zhang Ming admitted, and that had attracted the authorities' attention. "They thought that our money was a threat to them."

In September 2002, Zhang Ming was arrested once again, this time on a charge of endangering public security by allegedly plotting to blow up a building. When the case came to court, that charge had been dropped and was replaced by accusations that he had "abused executive benefits." The trial was riddled with irregularities. A defense witness was refused permission to testify, while a government witness admitted his evidence was false, but disclosed that he had been threatened with a prison term of three to five years if he recanted. In the end, Zhang Ming was sentenced to seven years in prison. His boss, Sun Fengjuan, was given a four-year sentence in October 2003 for "falsely declaring registered capital and withdrawing the capital."

During his first prison term, Zhang Ming had muddled through with no strategy other than survival. This time, he was determined to risk even that in order to gain early release. In November 2003, Zhang Ming began yet another hunger strike. The prison authorities responded by tying him to a bed for 113 hours without access to a toilet, after which he was force-fed milk through a tube in his throat. At that point, Zhang Ming made a key compromise: He would not take any solids but he would drink milk in exchange for being untied from the bed. As he continued the milk diet, he lost a quarter of his body weight, which dropped to just under one hundred pounds.

By June 2004, his condition had become so precarious that nine exiled student leaders wrote an open letter condemning his treatment. It decried the political persecution meted out to their counterparts who had remained in China, "Following their release from prison, they never again had an opportunity to fulfill their potential. Sooner or later, the National Security Bureau would pick them up on some pretext and destroy everything they had worked for. Zhang Ming is a classic example." Were it not for the pressure generated by that letter, Zhang Ming believes he might well have died in prison.

In any event, it took another 21 months of fasting—except for milk—before he was released on medical parole. By February 2006, Zhang's condition had deteriorated so much that he was having heart problems and flitting in and out of consciousness. On March 6th, 2006, fearing he would die in jail, prison authorities summoned his parents to collect him. Zhang Ming's extraordinary willpower had triumphed, but at the cost of his own health.

What still sets him apart is that his self-imposed hunger strike has continued to this day. Wherever he goes, Zhang Ming carries a brown cloth bag, inside which half a dozen small glass milk bottles clink. He buys the milk directly from a farmer and then heat-treats it at home. Throughout our conversations, Zhang occasionally reached into his bag for a milk bottle, from which he took a small swig. His prolonged fast is not so much a matter of principle, he insists, but one of habituation. He can eat food, and sometimes does, although he says his body can no longer process solids. He believes that solid food exacerbates his many physical problems, and he enjoys the clarity of vision afforded by fasting. It is a tribute to the power of positive thinking that Zhang sees his way of life as an unexpected dividend of prison, rather than a continued punishment.

It has cost him dearly in his relationship with his parents, a retired physics professor and a schoolteacher, who have borne the brunt of his decisions. They only found out about his activism when they saw his photograph on television as one of China's most wanted. He had kept his role in the movement secret, knowing they would have tried to stop him. For his father, the physical shock of seeing his son demonized as a national enemy led to dangerously high blood pressure and a host of related health problems. The stress of the two trials and two jail sentences was compounded by the manner of his son's final release, emaciated and in critical condition, followed by his continuing refusal to take food. "I have a lot of conflict with my parents," he told me, grinning. "My mother and father sometimes say they want to give me a beating!"

Interviewing someone who does not eat presented a unique set of challenges. Breaking for mealtime or even a snack was no longer necessary, and the social crutch of sharing food had been whisked away. Zhang Ming was scrupulously polite and reminded me that we could move to a restaurant whenever I got hungry, but the intensity of our conversation—amplified by the weirdness of his purple four-eyed stare—made it difficult to break the flow. It seemed impolite, even uncouth, to eat in front of someone who was fasting. Added to that, there was the question of willpower. Faced with someone who has survived on nothing but milk for a decade, breaking for food within a matter of hours seemed like an act of weakness.

At first, I idly imagined it might be interesting to join his fast if only for a few days. Several hours later, dizzy with hunger and snitched on by my rumbling stomach, I abandoned that notion.

When I could bear it no longer, we drove to a small Shanghainese restaurant decorated with ornate silver and black wallpaper. I ordered as parsimoniously as possible. For once, the act of eating seemed out of place. In a country obsessed with food, where "Have you eaten yet?" is a common greeting, it is difficult to imagine anything more radical than not eating. Zhang even compared himself to an alien. "I'm not like anyone else on earth. I don't eat." For his parents, his decision to continue refusing solid food is a rebellion against everything they held dear.

The paradox of Zhang is that his uncompromising exterior masks a conciliatory nature. He attributes the success he has had in business to his ability to make concessions. "Without compromise, there's no way of moving forward. I'm still an idealist, but there's also a realist side to me, otherwise in China you wouldn't be able to take the first step." His heroes are not Nelson Mandela or Lech Walesa. Indeed, they are not even political figures. He reserves his most lavish praise for Steve Jobs, Bill Gates, and Warren Buffett, self-made businessmen whom, he believes, have exercised influence over people's lives in ways that politicians have failed to do. In this, Zhang is tapping into the zeitgeist. Across China, successful entrepreneurs are worshipped like sages for possessing the secrets to enormous wealth. Indeed, one of the most hotly anticipated cultural events in China in 2011 was the release of Walter Isaacson's authorized posthumous biography of Steve Jobs. A quarter of a million copies had been printed; every single one was snapped up within the first day of release.

Domestically, Zhang Ming invokes the name of Jack Ma, a former English teacher who started China's first Internet company in 1995. Ma now comes in at number 395 on the Forbes billionaires list, with an estimated wealth of $3.4 billion. The e-commerce giant he founded, Alibaba, has more than 24,000 employees around the world. Ma has married his business flair with patriotism, singing "I love you, China" on his last day as Alibaba chief executive, to become an inspirational icon among young Chinese. Ma has a religious fervor for small businesses combined with an unerring ability to deliver a pithy sound-bite. "Small and medium-sized businesses are like grains of sand on a beach," he famously said. "The Internet can glue them together. It can make them into an invincible force that is able to go up against the big stones."

Alibaba has been an empowering, democratizing force in the Chinese marketplace, leveling the playing field for small businesses by matching suppliers and buyers transparently, cutting out the need for personal connections. In a society where materialism reigns, bringing people power to the virtual marketplace affords Ma a measure of influence far beyond that of traditional dissidents penning political tracts that few will ever read. Ma himself has acknowledged the good fortune of his timing, telling Charlie Rose, "I think my father said, 'If you were born thirty years earlier you would probably be in prison because the ideas you have are so dangerous.'"

However, Jack Ma stepped into dangerous territory in 2013 when he endorsed Deng Xiaoping's suppression of the 1989 movement and compared this decision to his own behavior as CEO of Alibaba. He said, "As CEO of a company, whether it's the scandal involving Alibaba or the spinning off of [its online payment service] Alipay, at that moment you're like Deng Xiaoping during 'June Fourth.' As the country's highest policymaker, he wanted stability. It was necessary for him to make this cruel decision. It wasn't a perfect decision, but it was the most correct decision—the most correct decision at the time. At any time, a person in charge must make these kinds of decisions." Amid the storms of outrage from exiled Tiananmen activists who threatened to picket Alibaba's U.S. headquarters in Santa Clara, California, Zhang Ming's response was characteristically measured. He was disappointed Ma had bought into the official narrative that repression had been the only option, yet he advocated tolerance. "We should forgive Jack Ma," he said. "He's an influential person. We shouldn't alienate him, we should keep him on our side."

Indeed, had history been different, it is not impossible that Zhang Ming himself could have been another Jack Ma. With his Midas touch, backed up by the huge funds at his disposal, he had been perfectly positioned to ascend into the ranks of China's homegrown tycoons, had it not been for the Tiananmen stain on his record. Zhang suspected that his second prison sentence had been aimed specifically at preventing his ascension into the pantheon of tycoon gods. "If you do business, you can influence a lot of people. That's the reason why later on, they wouldn't let me do business, I think," he told me, with a shy laugh. Even now, he is still able to survive on his investments from that period, especially from the sale of a computer company back in 2001, which netted him a windfall.

Despite his two jail terms and the loss of two fortunes he had helped build, Zhang Ming harbors no bitterness about the course his life has taken. When I asked him whether he regrets becoming involved in the student movement, he shook his head. "You can't even think about that," he said. "You've already been through it. You just have to think about how you can make your heart more at ease." He professes to no longer have any political ambitions. "I have no ability to change China; I have no ability to change the world. The only thing I can change is myself."

• • • •

For Zhang Ming and the other student leaders who remained in China, the seven weeks of the student movement were a Rubicon that, once crossed, transformed their lives forever. The preordained career paths that ordinarily would have been theirs— the government posting, the academic career, or Zhang Ming's job in Shantou—were gone. After prison, the alternatives were vanishingly small.

After June 4th, the Communist Party launched a massive ideological campaign that lasted 18 months. According to secret documents, at least four million party members— a tenth of the total—underwent investigation into their roles during the unrest. Those who participated in the protests had to write long confessional accounts of their activities during that period, stating their support for the government's repression. Having already morally co-opted the academics in this way, the government then skillfully dangled financial incentives in front of them to try to buy their silence on sensitive issues. The compromises necessary for success in Chinese academia were laid out in a 2013 *New York Times* essay by author Yan Lianke. "It doesn't matter whether you are a writer, a historian or social scientist. You will be awarded power, fame and money as long as you are willing to see what is allowed to be seen, and look away from what is not allowed to be looked at; as long as you are willing to sing the praises of what needs to be praised and ignore what needs to be blanked out. In other words, our amnesia is a state-sponsored sport."

Even some of those who hoped to circumvent government control by starting their own businesses ran into difficulty. Back in 2004, I interviewed Zhu Hong, a journalist who lost his job after Tiananmen and who then tried to open a small bookshop. We met in a McDonald's, a favorite meeting place for dissidents, since the jaunty pop music and bustling atmosphere were thought to make eavesdropping harder. Zhu Hong was tense and jumpy as he told me how he had rented the space, built bookshelves, and even bought the books. Then the relevant government department refused to issue the proper business license, and eventually he had to abandon the scheme in which he had invested his life savings and all his hopes for the future. Administrative powers had become political tools, he said bitterly. "They can control everything. If you want to move on, I'm not saying you have to betray yourself, but you do have to abandon certain ideals."

A number of former student leaders who made those compromises benefited immensely from their first-mover advantage, according to Chen Ziming, the intellectual who was sentenced to 13 years in jail as one of the "black hands" behind the student movement. "I know for a fact that some of them are multimillionaires," he told me. "Their focus was re-centered. But while they are doing business, these people won't become involved in politics. They're afraid of political interference. They won't even admit to having been student leaders." But Chen Ziming believes that may change if the former protesters grow secure enough to raise their voices once more.

One salutary tale is that of Wang Shi, the chairman of one of China's biggest property developers. A former PLA soldier, Wang is a homegrown hero, with 11 million followers on *weibo*, China's version of twitter. His fame is not just due to his business acumen, but also due to his decision at age 60 to step away from his $16 billion-worth real estate behemoth to spend time at Harvard as a visiting research fellow. In 1994, he told the *Washington Post* that he had spent a year in prison after 1989 for encouraging his employees to take part in a march of solidarity. He made, he said, a public statement of regret. "I have a responsibility to my shareholders that is more important than politics," he told the *Post* reporter. "For the CEO of a big company to take his employees onto the streets for a political protest against the government, well, it really doesn't look very good." By 2008, however, he was denying through a spokeswoman that any of this had ever happened—the protest march, the year in prison, or the recantation.

As China's citizens follow their government's lead in airbrushing their own history, the Communist Party was also moving on. In 2001, it announced it would welcome capitalists into the party, dubbing them "advanced productive forces" in order to perform this ideological somersault. Since then, the party of the proletariat has become one of the richest political parties in the world, marrying wealth and political power to produce a system characterized by crony capitalism and widening inequality.

According to the *Economist*, the wealthiest 50 delegates to China's National People's Congress in 2014 controlled around $94 billion, about 60 times more money than their 50 richest American counterparts. The NPC currently resembles nothing less than a Chinese outpost of the Fortune Global Forum, replete with film stars, celebrity CEOs, and the "princeling" politicians descended from the Communist revolutionaries. One year, it was even scornfully nicknamed "Beijing Fashion Week," so ostentatious was the display of luxury labels sported by the delegates. Most pilloried was Li Xiaolin, the daughter of the Tiananmen-era Premier Li Peng who had been nicknamed "The Butcher of Beijing." Her outfit included a Chanel necklace and a salmon pink Emilio Pucci pantsuit reportedly retailing for almost $2,000.

One bold newspaper analyzed the professions of almost 3,000 NPC members whose five-year terms ended in 2012. By its account, just 16 were workers, 13 were farmers, and only 11 were official army delegates. Thus the party of the workers, peasants, and soldiers has become anything but that. In 2013, one-sixth of the members of China's legislative assembly, or National People's Congress, were chief executives, chairmen, or leading businessmen. Indeed, snagging a seat in the Great Hall of the People boosts a company's share price by about 3 percent. Thus China's Communist Party has managed to co-opt those it once reviled as "capitalist running dogs" by making the political process profitable.

• • • •

In November 2012, seven middle-aged men in black suits strode self-confidently onto a stage in the Great Hall of the People, positioning themselves in order of importance on numbers stuck onto the red carpet. As the cameras flashed, they managed to look both smug and ill-at-ease. The "Magnificent Seven," as they were immediately dubbed, represented the new political order.

Once a decade, China's leaders shuffle off the political stage, with varying degrees of reluctance, to be replaced by a younger generation of Communist functionaries. The new leader of the Magnificent Seven was Xi Jinping, the son of a first-generation revolutionary leader and therefore a "princeling." He had benefited from the decision of the departing party chief Hu Jintao to break with tradition and hand over all his positions of power simultaneously. For Zhang Ming, that single act was a political watershed, offering hope in the future of China's Communist Party. On China's social media, the verdict was less charitable: During Hu Jintao's decade in power, cynics said, his single biggest achievement had been stepping down.

The run-up to the transition had already been marred by China's most serious political scandal in decades—the precipitous downfall of another prominent princeling, Bo Xilai, then Communist Party secretary of Chongqing. Bo was a highflying star of the political world, a princeling whose charisma was second only to his boundless ambition. In Chongqing, he had carried out a high-profile campaign against organized crime, backed up by Maoist-style mass rallies singing songs lauding the Communist Party. His plummet into disgrace was precipitated by a failed attempt by his long-term enforcer and former police chief, Wang Lijun, to seek asylum in the U.S. consulate in Chengdu. His accusations proved to be the unraveling of the Bo clan, setting in train a series of events that culminated in the sensational trial of Bo's wife, Gu Kailai, on charges of murdering a British businessman, Neil Heywood, and then ordering Wang to lead the cover-up. Wang received 10 years in prison, and Gu Kailai received 15. Bo Xilai received a life sentence for bribery, embezzlement, and abuse of power, all charges he refuted forcefully in an extraordinary show trial.

Inside China, the case was watched with the avidity of a soap opera, tempered by massive cynicism. But Zhang Ming shrugged it off as unimportant. The key progress, he believed, was embodied in this new generation of technocratic leaders. As teens, these men had been "sent down" to the countryside to learn from the peasants, an experience that had left them with a better understanding of the lives of ordinary people. In terms of their priorities, he strongly supported their focus on upgrading the economy from traditional industries to creative ones. Real creativity, he believed, could not flourish in an authoritarian environment, so economic structural shifts should inexorably lead to more democratic workplaces. Like the government itself, Zhang espouses the idea that change should be evolutionary rather than revolutionary. By instinct, Zhang is a reformer rather than a rebel, with views so mainstream it is difficult to understand how he ended up serving two jail terms.

Even in 1989, the young Zhang Ming argued that the time might not be ripe to push for full democracy. As he tried to persuade his fellow students to abandon Tiananmen Square and marshal their forces, he told them a story. In the frigid climes of Northeastern China where he grew up, a popular wintertime delicacy is the frozen pear. Ordinary pears were traditionally buried under a layer of tree leaves until they were frozen solid. Once defrosted in cold water, the pear's crisp icy sweetness sings in the mouth. As a boy, Zhang Ming could not bear to wait for his pear to defrost, continually nagging his mother to speed up the process, by asking her, "Why don't you soak the pears in hot water?" Finally, she explained to him that this would spoil the pears. They had to be defrosted slowly, without hurrying the process. "A country is like that, too," Zhang Ming said he told his fellow students. "You can't save on time. If you hurry things up, you will ruin the pear."

• • • •

One afternoon, Zhang Ming drove me to the rural village where his mother had grown up. We passed the rows of cheerless utilitarian blocks left over from the days of state planning that have left Jilin stuck in a time warp, far from the fast-forward vision of modernity that has transformed other Chinese cities into endless canyons of grey steel and mirrored glass skyscrapers. Very soon, these squat buildings gave way to rolling hills with chartreuse rice paddies and fields of corn. His mother's village has now evolved into a small county town whose brick bungalows are topped by red roofs embellished with ceramic birds standing guard over their eaves. The market still consists of glum farmers squatting on the street selling haw fruits piled high on newspapers and misshapen chilies in hand-woven baskets.

As we cruised past, Zhang Ming told me the story of how his mother had fled this village at the age of 10 during China's civil war. With the sound of fighting coming ever closer, her whole family decided to flee to Jilin, which happened to be the nearest city, for shelter. At the time, they had no idea who was fighting whom; they were simply following their survival instincts. On arrival in Jilin, they discovered that the Communists were vanquishing the Nationalists.

The family stayed in the city, which soon fell under Communist rule. Then came a crucial moment upon which the fate of the entire family pivoted: The newly triumphant Communists asked Zhang Ming's grandfather about his own background. This could have been an opportunity for him to reinvent himself with a more politically acceptable past. After all, as a newcomer to the big city, he knew no one and no one knew him. Yet his grandfather could not bring himself to tell a lie about his status. "Landlord," he replied. Because her father was a class enemy, Zhang Ming's mother was not permitted to attend university, and the whole family was targeted during the Cultural Revolution. That single act of honesty doomed the family for decades.

• • • •

Over the years, Zhang Ming's path has been one of renunciation as he abandoned politics, then business, then paid work, and finally even the act of eating. As I pondered his continuing fast, I came across a passage by China scholar Orville Schell in his book *Mandate of Heaven* about the hunger-striking students. "The kind of passive resistance implicit in a fast was congruent with one other deeply ingrained aspect of traditional Chinese culture, the notion that when an upright official disagrees with a ruler, he should express his displeasure and then withdraw from direct action rather than form an opposition party to foment overt rebellion."

For his part, Zhang Ming cites the traditional Chinese religion of Daoism as one of his biggest influences, and in particular its principle of *wuwei*, which translates as "not doing" or "non-action," referring to a way of living in harmony with the outside world instead of trying to bend it to one's will. In Zhang's case, it seems a poignant antidote to an excess of youthful action.

Even his attempts to alleviate his many physical problems are redolent with symbolism. One day I received an excited e-mail from him, outlining a new breakthrough in his medical regime. Using cupping therapy on the forehead was highly unorthodox, yet it was proving to be the only way for him to alleviate the chronic pain resulting from the prison beatings. By trial and error, Zhang Ming discovered that cupping a certain point on the soles of his feet was also beneficial. In his desperate attempt to free himself from pain, he was now trying to purge his body quite literally from head to toe. "If I can't find a way to cure myself, I may not live very long," he told me one day.

Zhang Ming lives in an airy duplex apartment, the walls of which are hung with colorful art created by his wife, who is almost 20 years his junior. On one visit, she cooked a dinner of light vegetable dishes, and as we ate, Zhang Ming sat beside us, chatting and breaking his fast to try one small mouthful of cabbage. He was cupping his scalp with a small transparent plastic bulb suctioned to the side of his head, drawing up an enormous, angry purple bruise that was growing visibly larger as we ate. His wife smiled when I asked what it was like being married to someone who doesn't eat. "Very relaxing!" she replied, beaming. "I don't need to worry about his food at all!"

The pair had met online, and he had persuaded her to move to Jilin where the pace of life is more relaxed. They have defied China's strict family-planning guidelines to have two children and would like to have a third. Zhang Ming is a hands-on father who blogs almost daily about childrearing issues. His three-year-old son is a whirlwind of toddler energy with an infectious grin and an obsession for street signs, while his infant daughter is a placid beauty whose plumpness contrasts with her father's angular contours.

In yet another radical departure from usual life in China, Zhang Ming plans to home-school his children. He wants their world to be one of infinite possibilities, not a place where there is one right answer and many wrong ones. He wants to protect his children from autocratic teachers and playground dictators, fearing their innocence could be infected by the contagion of violence that runs through Chinese society—all the way down to the microcosm of the playground. In his own life, the refusal to conform has repeatedly been met by violence: the soldiers opening fire on people who did not obey orders to stay inside; the brutal prison beatings for his refusal to be brainwashed; even the petty violence of parents beating a disobedient child. Political power comes from the barrel of a gun, in Chairman Mao's words, and violence has become the ultimate solution.

Ever the businessman, Zhang still has a few projects underway. He is investing in a traditional teashop hidden away in a modern high-rise apartment with views over the entire city. In this refuge, he envisions sipping tea and learning how to play the *guqin*, a traditional Chinese instrument similar to a long, horizontal harp. He has also invested in a small startup company, funding an inventor who has designed recyclable ceramic floor tiles that fit together like jigsaw pieces to provide under-floor heating. The company is based in a disheveled apartment block across town.

When we visited, another angel investor opened the door for us—Zhang's business partner, a woman in her mid-50s with smudged makeup, wearing a grey, bejeweled nylon blouse. She brewed us green tea in tiny ceramic cups, which I gulped down greedily, while Zhang Ming warmed his bony hands on the miniature cups despite the stifling weather. One room was fitted with the beige honeycombed ceramic tiles that emanated a toasty Turkish-bath kind of warmth. Zhang's business partner had been trying to get the tiles featured on a Chinese television show, where inventors have 90 seconds to pitch their products to a panel of entrepreneurs. She was optimistic about their chances, declaring, "I've been reviewing the tapes of all the past shows. None of the other products are nearly as good as ours." She had decided to invest all the profits from her clothing business into the floor tiles, which she described as "revolutionary."

Later, she gave me a lift to the cavernous train station, which was so new that access roads had not yet been finished. As she nosed her expensive white SUV through the muddy puddles of the dusty parking lot, I asked her what she thought of Zhang Ming. "He's a good person, regardless of his involvement in the student movement," she replied. "He was young then, and over-enthusiastic. If it happened today, he wouldn't take part in it again."

Somewhat surprised, I asked, "Is that what he said to you?"

"Look at how much he's suffered," she replied. "He's paid a huge cost for his actions. Surely he wouldn't make the same choices again?"

From her perch in the soft leather seat of her plush SUV, the cost-benefit analysis was too obvious to bother stating: The students had lost out in every way. Their intentions had been good, but their actions might have unleashed unthinkable chaos on the country. The government had done what was necessary to regain order, and the winners had been the ordinary people who kept their heads down, followed the rules, and were now enjoying the fruits of their hard work. Such has become the default position in today's China.

At home Zhang Ming doesn't talk about what happened 25 years ago. His wife was just four years old in 1989. The events of that year remain outside her line of vision. They are not even on the periphery. It is as if none of it had ever happened. "She didn't experience it," he said bluntly. "You can talk to her about art or music, or about things that she wants to hear about. But she doesn't care about things she's not interested in."

The generation gap is illustrated by their childhood heroes. Zhang Ming's generation grew up on stories valorizing sacrifice in the service of the country. As a child, he loved to hear the story of Huang Jiguang, a soldier during the Korean War who became a national hero when he sacrificed his life by using his own chest to block the machine-gun slit of a dugout manned by American troops. Growing up worshipping such role models—willing to give up their own lives for their country—became one factor that encouraged the students, who saw themselves as galvanized by patriotism, to stay in the square right up until the very last minute.

Zhang's wife's generation worships a different breed of icons: the heroes of the boardroom, the innovators, and businessmen. The creation myths the younger generation embraces are the stories of struggle from grinding poverty to unimaginable wealth. Death plays no part in their legends; the aspirational young are only interested in success stories. These little emperors are the first generation to enjoy the luxury of selfishness. From birth, their entire families have orbited around the sun of their precious only child.

Zhang Ming has no illusions about how young people today see the Tiananmen protests. His wife and her friends have no interest at all in his role in the protests, or how the government sent soldiers with guns and tanks to clear the square. The reason they do not like to talk about 1989 is not because it is a politically sensitive topic or because it makes them uncomfortable. It simply does not register.

Casting about for a parallel, Zhang Ming remembered how a Red Army soldier had visited his primary school class to describe how hard life had been. The old man spoke of the endless mountain passes the soldiers had trekked over, the crippling physical exhaustion, and the unthinkable deprivations they had suffered. He had brought along a dumpling partly made of chaff, which he shared with the children to help them "taste bitterness and think of the sweetness of the present." Zhang Ming remembers being repulsed by both the dumpling and the old soldier. His life had nothing to do with their lives. It was ancient history. "That's like me talking to my wife about '89," he said simply. "It has no impact. I'm like the Red Army soldier."

3 :: Exile

Wu'er Kaixi's essay collection was stacked in the New Releases section of the Taipei bookshop, piled alongside the latest release from Taiwan's former President Lee Tenghui. Glaring from the cover was his face, still familiar albeit older, plumper, and chastened by a quarter-century of exile. During the 1989 protests, Wu'er Kaixi had been a skinny, scruffy, charismatic 21-year-old, always center stage, often grasping a bullhorn as he chivvied, hectored, and hustled, his voice hoarse from shouting. Two and a half decades later, as he strode into a hipster cafe in Taipei, he brought with him the low thrum of superannuated celebrity. The old cockiness, however, was still there; when I told him about his book's prominent placement, he grinned and quipped in fluent English, "Well I'm glad the bookshop thinks I'm presidential!"

Wu'er Kaixi was the brashest of all the student leaders, always in the limelight. His unerring instinct for showmanship created some of the most dramatic moments of the movement. During the students' hunger strike, he went straight from his hospital bed to meet Premier Li Peng in the Great Hall of the People. Sitting in an overstuffed chair dressed in his blue-and-white striped hospital pajamas, clutching an oxygen tank, Wu'er Kaixi interrupted the premier's paternalistic address to the students, chiding him for waiting so long before deigning to meet them. This bold assertion of equality by a pajama-clad student electrified television viewers accustomed to seeing state leaders treated with fawning servility. It turned Wu'er Kaixi into a household name, and eventually number two on the government's most wanted list.

Of all the tragic figures of the movement, Wu'er Kaixi was the most mesmeric, and after fleeing into exile following June 4th, he became the one most distracted by the enticements of the West: the party-ing, the bars, the women, the credit cards, the media appearances. He stayed at Harvard for several months, and eventually graduated from the Dominican College in San Rafael, California, working variously as a garage mechanic in Los Angeles, a busboy in San Francisco, and a radio talk-show host in southern Taiwan. He married a Taiwanese woman and settled in Taipei, working as a political commentator and managing an investment fund. Now divorced with two teenage sons, Wu'er Kaixi has struggled with the growing irrelevance that over-whelms political exiles. "We don't have a battlefield. We don't have a stage," he admitted wearily, accepting that tilting against China's growing political and economic might is an increasingly quixotic task.

Why, then, had it taken him so long to write his book? "I will give you a long answer of excuses, pretend excuses," he said, with a deep, low chuckle. "But the real reason is being lazy." He regards this book—a collection of essays, many about Taiwan—as a gift to his adopted home. The time had not yet come for his own personal memoir. "I need to get some more things done before I write about my own life," he maintained. "The Tiananmen thing is the first page. It's not a book yet."

• • • •

Wu'er Kaixi tasted politics young, becoming a Little Red Guard at age seven. It was the tail end of the Cultural Revolution, Mao's decade of chaos, and the Little Red Guards imitated their older namesakes, whose aim was to "Destroy the Old World, Build a New World." The Red Guards were initially university students who terrorized their institutions with the aim of destroying the "Four Olds" —old customs, old culture, old habits, old ideas—and tar-geting counterrevolutionaries. As a Little Red Guard, Wu'er Kaixi learned the art of protest at school, taking part in mass rallies that were a tiny simulacrum of adult politics, at which he shouted slogans, belted out revolutionary songs, and painstakingly copied posters criticizing Deng Xiaoping. Later, Wu'er Kaixi became a Young Pioneer—wearing the red neckerchief symbolizing the blood shed by the martyrs of the revolution—and then finally joined the Communist Youth League.

Unusually for a student leader, his parents were both ethnic Uighurs, members of a Turkic minority group from Xinjiang province, which borders Pakistan, Afghanistan, and other countries. Both were true believers in Communism so neither practiced the Muslim faith, unlike most Uighurs. Wu'er Kaixi's father had been an itinerant ox herder who at age 14 was fast-tracked to receive an education in Beijing. During Wu'er Kaixi's childhood, his father's job was to translate works by Marx, Lenin, and Chairman Mao into Uighur. During the Cultural Revolution, while his son was reenacting the political tumult at school, the father was hounded almost to the point of suicide. Despite this, he continued to work at the state-run publishing house, where his rise through the ranks was stopped only by his son's involvement in the 1989 protests.

Wu'er Kaixi's mother also worked for the Central Minorities Publishing House in Beijing, and the family lived in "Xinjiang block" with the other "publishing-house Uighurs." As a child, Wu'er Kaixi idolized the military—then, every little boy wanted to be a soldier—and his favorite game was to dress up in a tiny navy uniform complete with a cap embroidered with a golden anchor. His best friends Erkhim and Ilshat wore their own miniature army and air force uniforms, and the trio would play at war. But there was an undercurrent of petty racial prejudice in Beijing, and when Wu'er Kaixi was 16, his parents, to his horror, decided to move back to Urumqi, the capital of Xinjiang.

It was there that Wu'er Kaixi's activism was born with the launch of an ambitious student newspaper. By the third issue, the paper was selling beyond the gates of his own school. Its biggest draw was Wu'er Kaixi's biting editorials, which became more daring until he castigated a boorish teacher for beating students and reading their mail. Prophetically, the newspaper's name was *Chutouniao* or "The Bird that Sticks Its Neck Out" which comes from a Chinese proverb stating: "The bird that sticks its neck out gets hit the hardest."

Indeed the newspaper's third issue, containing Wu'er's criticism of the teacher, was its final one, and the bird that had stuck out its neck—Wu'er Kaixi—was summarily expelled from school.

At his next school, Wu'er Kaixi kicked his activism up a level. He lobbied for students to be allowed to work part-time, and he persuaded them to donate some of their income to a local orphanage. When he visited the orphanage, he was so horrified at its state of disrepair that he wrote a letter of complaint to the province's top official, the party secretary of the Xinjiang Uighur Autonomous Region. This set off alarm bells, and Wu'er Kaixi was summoned for a warning by the head of the Communist Youth League. By then, however, the all-important university entrance examinations were looming, so Wu'er Kaixi changed gears, channeling all his energy into studying. He devised a system whereby he slept just five hours a night in three separate shifts to maximize his study time. That hard work won him a spot to study education administration at the country's best teacher training college, Beijing Normal University, giving him his ticket back to the capital.

That was how Wu'er Kaixi became the 1 percent at a time when the universities excluded 99 percent of the population. The simple act of being accepted into a university elevated ordinary teenagers into the "proud sons of heaven," separating them from the rest of the population. After matriculating, Wu'er Kaixi found that the older students viewed the freshmen as shallow, materialistic, and self-involved. Back then, he joked, students fell into four categories: the disco-dancers, the mahjong-players, the money-makers, and the TOEFL-takers whose only aim was to study overseas. In the spirit of the age, Wu'er Kaixi was having the time of his life, going out at night, dating girls, making money, and only just scraping by in his coursework. Politics was far from his mind. But when Hu Yaobang died on April 15th, 1989, everything changed. "All our shut-down senses were wakened at that moment. We became very political overnight."

• • • •

Wu'er Kaixi likes to reminisce about the early days of the movement when he was—in his own words—a "general" with unrivaled authority over his army of students. He was one of the earliest student leaders to emerge, bursting onto a stage that he little imagined would set him on the road to a quarter-century of exile. His debut came two days after the death of Hu Yaobang when hundreds of students gathered on the campus of Beijing Normal University to mourn the late leader. Crowds of youngsters huddled together, mute with nervous anxiety, each waiting for someone else to be the first to speak out.

For Wu'er Kaixi, stepping forward was a split-second decision driven not by politics but by disgust at this collective failure of courage. "I didn't want to hide in my own shell like a turtle," he remembered. So he spoke out, loud and clear. "My name is Wu'er Kaixi. I am a Beijing Normal University education administration student, in the class that joined in 1988. I live in dorm 339." By giving out his own personal details, Wu'er Kaixi was not only defying the authorities; he was also ensuring that his name—with its distinctive Uighur inflection —would be the one everyone remembered from that moment onward.

He found the spotlight again just a day later at the same student sit-in where Zhang Ming became involved in the movement. Typically, Wu'er Kaixi thrust himself into a leadership role, front and center. As he put it, "When a leader was called, I was the one who stood up." He appeared in front of the crowd of students and asked them to write down the sentiments they felt but dared not say out loud. Then he read them aloud with a humorous running commentary, illustrating his characteristic mix of impetuosity and drama.

In those early days when the movement was still coalescing, Wu'er Kaixi saw himself as both director and producer of the whole show. A couple of days after the sit-in, he posted a communiqué at Beijing Normal University, calling for a class boycott and a student rally. He had little idea of what to expect and was staggered when thousands of students from other schools began trickling onto the campus before the gathering. The government was watching, too; it took only a couple of hours from the moment he tacked up his first poster for his father to be summoned from the Central Party School, where he was attending training sessions, to rein in his wayward son. His father spent the day trudging from one dorm room to the next in search of his boy; the son spent the same hours dodging his father, desperate to avoid any act of overt disobedience.

At the ordained time of the rally, Wu'er Kaixi could hardly make his way through the mass of students—tens of thousands of them—gathered on his school's campus. In order to be seen above the crowd, he hoisted himself onto the highest structure he could find—some asymmetric bars for women's gymnastics—and sat on the top bar, his legs braced wide against the lower one. For lighting, he asked volunteers to shine flashlights on his face. For a sound system, he created a human megaphone, enlisting nearby students to echo his words at a shout for those at the back. An estimated 60,000 students were present at the rally. It was a moment of cinematic significance; the single, spot-lit figure emerging from the dark crush of bodies. When he looked down, he happened to spot his own father standing before him. His father had aged a decade.

• • • •

There could only be one destination for this teeming mass of students on the eve of Hu Yaobang's funeral. The students marched out of the gate, school by school, in five columns flanked on either side by picket lines of student marshals wearing red armbands.

On arriving at Tiananmen Square, Wu'er Kaixi ordered the students to link arms and walk across the huge expanse, driving all other occupants ahead of them out of the square. This hastily conceived gesture symbolized the students' desire to maintain the purity of their movement, perhaps fearing that participation by non-students could open them up to accusations that they had been infiltrated by "black hands."

That night they camped on the square. The next day, April 22nd, as China's leaders gathered inside the Great Hall of the People for Hu Yaobang's funeral, thousands more students flooded the square. The service was broadcast live through speakers into Tiananmen for the students, who became angered when the hearse bearing Hu Yaobang's coffin left the hall through a backdoor, bypassing them.

Gathered at the bottom of the steps to the hall, the students were led by Wu'er Kaixi in chants of "Dialogue! Dialogue! Li Peng, come out!" As the wait for the Premier lengthened, three student representatives ran through the lines of armed police stationed in front of the hall and up the steps, where they knelt in supplication, the scroll of their seven-point petition held high above their heads, in the ancient gesture of the loyal commoner imploring for the mercy of the emperor.

This searing moment of political symbolism gained poignancy as the minutes ticked past. For half an hour, the three students remained on their knees in a move that began as an act of defiance but became one of despair. Some of the students began to cry as the extent of their abandonment by their leaders became clear. For Wu'er Kaixi, kneeling was a feudal gesture that betrayed the passivity and weakness he abhorred. "I felt I was commanding a battle, but kneeling was not part of my plan," he told me. The students far outnumbered the soldiers, and he had hoped to use the strength of numbers to intimidate. Instead, by kneeling, the initiative had been ceded to the Communist leaders shut inside the hall. Wu'er Kaixi described his reaction as one of disgust. "I didn't know if I can command a troop of 30,000 or 40,000 crying people. That is something I am incapable of!" As self-appointed "commander" of that night's action, Wu'er Kaixi issued the last order to the students to withdraw from the square to return to their schools.

• • • •

As the movement gathered momentum, Wu'er Kaixi was everywhere. When the students established the Beijing Students Autonomous Federation, he became its president within days, after the original choice was ousted in a vote. When a dialogue delegation was established, Wu'er Kaixi was a member. He met foreign journalists and held press conferences, firmly establishing himself as a major player. He remembers the euphoria of those days; when the students heard their calls for dialogue being echoed by Communist Party General Secretary Zhao Ziyang, they felt that momentum was on their side, "Even at university, when the college president saw me, he was shaking my hand like shaking [the hand of] the future national leader, or something like that. We were winning. We were winning the battle."

Another student who emerged early on in a prominent role was Wang Dan, a bespectacled, cerebral history undergraduate from Peking University whose "democracy salon" had invited prominent political thinkers to campus the previous year. Wu'er Kaixi, in contrast, downplayed the role of political theory. Shortly after fleeing into exile, he stated, "Chinese rock and roll influenced students' ideas more than any of the theories of the aging intellectuals on democracy." One song that became an anthem for students, partly due to its overt nationalism, was "Descendants of the Dragon" by the Taiwanese singer Hou Dejian, who camped out with the students and helped negotiate their departure from the square on June 4th. The square became a stage for rock concerts by Hou and other musicians. In the U.S.-produced "Gate of Heavenly Peace" documentary, Hou said that rock music—inspired by the West—had become a form of liberalization. "When someone takes part in a rock concert, that kind of crazy feeling is all about self-liberation and about self-expression."

When I asked Wu'er Kaixi whose idea the hunger strike had been, he pointed his thumb toward his chest and said, "Yours truly." The idea was born during an inedible meal of fried cucumber and beef attended by Wu'er Kaixi, Wang Dan, and four other friends. As they complained about the dismal food, the idea of a hunger strike took shape. It was a deliberate strategy to escalate the movement, which was ebbing away as students began defying the class boycott to return to school. Once the hunger strike started on May 13th, white-coated medics began running through the square, ferrying fainting students on stretchers to hospitals. This vision of the country's youth sacrificing themselves for its future shook many who until then had not been involved, and brought more than a million ordinary citizens into the square.

The world's media played along; the telegenic students' struggle for freedom and democracy pitted against their Communist overlords was too good a story to spoil with nuance. In her autobiography *Red China Blues*, Canadian journalist Jan Wong describes catching one hunger striker red-handed with yogurt in his backpack. When confronted, he told her, "Snacking is okay. It's not really food." Wong reported the yogurt story but admitted that she never really told the whole truth about the hunger strike, which was, she wrote, "like a game at first, with students dramatically fainting on cue and the world's media pretending they really were starving themselves."

Nobody was playing the game better than Wu'er Kaixi, whose fast was interspersed with dramatic fainting spells that he blamed on a mysterious heart ailment. So confident was he that he even enlisted a Western journalist to help him cheat, betting that his charisma would save him from being outed. Wu'er Kaixi summoned Associated Press reporter John Pomfret in the dead of night and asked him to drive to an outdoor market to buy him food. "I can't get it myself," Wu'er had explained, "If anyone sees me, it will hurt the movement." In his book *Chinese Lessons*, Pomfret described the scene as Wu'er Kaixi secretly sated himself, "After pork with noodles, he moved on to shredded chicken with noodles, bell peppers and ham with noodles, and noodles in soup—all slurped down at full volume next to me." It took 16 years for Pomfret to write about Wu'er Kaixi's duplicity.

When I asked Wu'er Kaixi if this was accurate, there was a long pause. "He shouldn't have written that," he said reluctantly. "It was unfriendly."

"But was it true?" I asked.

There was a very long pause. Then he tilted his chair back and sighed deeply.

"No comment," he said, all of a sudden looking very tired.

• • • •

Shortly afterward, Soviet Premier and Communist Party General Secretary Mikhail Gorbachev began his landmark visit to reopen party-to-party ties with China under the glare of the world's press, which had come to cover the summit but was glorying in the students' occupation of Tiananmen Square. By this point, the limits of Wu'er Kaixi's authority had become painfully apparent. He had hoped to clear half the square for Gorbachev's welcoming ceremony in a move that he saw as a goodwill gesture to demonstrate

the rational patriotism of the students. No sooner had he managed to persuade the students to move than the empty space filled up again—this time with civilian supporters and more radical students.

As the conservatives inside government clashed with the reformers over how to deal with the snowballing movement, the students too had atomized into different interest groups with varying agendas. One rare instance of consensus was reached at a meeting at the end of May when the students reached a unanimous decision to withdraw from the square. But even while the agreement was being announced, it had already begun to unravel due to objections from students who had not been at the meeting. Though the students were calling for democracy, they were unable to implement democratic principles within their own ranks, with the idea of the minority yielding to the majority utterly ignored. Wu'er Kaixi came to this bitter realization while he was still based in the square, telling an interviewer, "One of the things which I have realized is that consciousness of democracy is inseparable from the environment and the people. Just as I said in the past, the greatest obstacle to reform in China is its population of one billion and its 5,000-year history."

By this time, Wu'er Kaixi was actively seeking an escape route. Again he called upon journalist John Pomfret for help. Pomfret drove him to the home of a Scandinavian diplomat, where Wu'er Kaixi inquired about political asylum, or even the possibility of sneaking into the diplomatic pouch. "Where am I going to go?" he asked the diplomat, according to Pomfret's memoir. "I'm too young to go to jail." After the crackdown, Pomfret was expelled from China, accused of protecting the leaders of student groups and using illegal methods to get state secrets.

On the night of June 3rd, Wu'er Kaixi gave a final speech to a crowd of more than 10,000 students at his university. "Tiananmen Square is ours, the people's, and we will not allow butchers to tread on it," he told them defiantly. "We will defend Tiananmen Square, defend the students in the square, and defend the future of China." Returning to the square, he took another emotional oath devoting his life to protecting Tiananmen, "I may be decapitated, my blood may flow, but the people's square will not be lost. We are willing to lose our young lives to fight to the very last person."

In the event, Wu'er Kaixi left the square before the students' final withdrawal. As troops began to gather, he was smuggled out in the back of an ambulance packed full of casualties. As the ambulance drove away, it was flagged down by people carrying another seriously injured student, who was then crammed in beside Wu'er Kaixi. The student had been shot in the head. "I will never forget that I left Tiananmen Square holding on to a dead body," Wu'er Kaixi later recalled. The ambulance took him to a hospital, from where he began his long journey into exile.

When the most wanted list was issued, Wu'er Kaixi was number two. Wang Dan was number one. Wang Dan decided that he could not take life on the run, so he returned to Beijing where he was captured and sentenced to four years in jail. He was re-arrested in 1995 and given an 11-year sentence before being released on medical parole to the United States.

On the run, Wu'er Kaixi's recognizable features became an impediment. With his girlfriend Liu Yan, he hid in friends' houses, hospitals, and temples as they wended their way toward Hong Kong, just as Zhang Ming was doing. They contacted the underground railroad known as "Operation Yellowbird," which had been set up by an unlikely alliance of Hong Kong's pro-democracy politicians, celebrities, gangsters, and Western diplomats. Operation Yellowbird took its name from an ancient proverb: "The mantis stalks the cicada, unaware of the yellow bird behind." In the immediate aftermath of the crackdown, 7 of the 21 most wanted students managed to escaped China, mostly with the help of Operation Yellowbird, which during its lifetime brought some 400 dissidents out of China.

Wu'er Kaixi's escape was probably Yellowbird's most expensive operation, costing around U.S. $75,000. Hong Kong's democracy activists relied on their underworld connections—including one of the "Five Tigers" of the infamous Sun Yee On triad—to use smuggling routes to bring the students out of China. In Wu'er Kaixi's case, the first two attempts failed; the waves were too high for the speedboat to get close to the shore, and then army patrols scuppered the plans. The gangsters who operated the smuggling routes demanded payment of $25,000 for each attempt, regardless of its success.

Finally, after almost a week of waiting, Wu'er Kaixi and Liu Yan were driven to an isolated oyster farm. They were told to stay there until they saw two long flashes of light across the water. Upon seeing the light, they should swim towards it. They waited and waited until, just as they were about to give up, they saw the flashes. They waded out to sea in their jeans and sneakers, and swam out toward their new lives outside China.

On arrival in Hong Kong, Wu'er Kaixi was kept cloistered by nervous British officials who allowed him to issue a single statement. Video of that moment shows him white with exhaustion, lips trembling, accusing the Chinese government of being "bestial fascists." While he was in Hong Kong, he became close to one of the donors who had funded his escape, the Madonna of the Chinese-speaking world, pop superstar Anita Mui. When she died, he was permitted to attend her funeral in 2004 in Hong Kong, which by then had returned to Chinese sovereignty under an agreement that allowed it to keep its freedoms intact for 50 years. By then, so great was Wu'er Kaixi's longing for his home that he made a pilgrimage to the border. As the border guards watched, he poked his fingers through the wire fence. "My fingers went back to China," he said ruefully.

• • • •

Even within China, Wu'er Kaixi had always been an outsider. His real name is Uerkesh Davlet. As a Uighur growing up in Beijing, he had felt like an alien. But by the time his family moved to Xinjiang, he saw himself as a displaced Beijinger. This sense of otherness prepared him for his long years of exile in the United States and Taiwan. Back in April 1989, he told the Associated Press, "I look at my status as a minority in this country of Han people as a bonus.... We have an expression in Chinese: 'The onlooker sees the game best.' I think I see the problems of the Han better because my blood is different."

Yet exile has been particularly punishing for him, cutting him off from his community and deepening his sense of banishment. In 2009, he was forced to watch from afar as ethnic riots wrenched apart the city of Urumqi where his parents still lived. Almost 200 people died—mostly Han Chinese—in pitched battles between Han and Uighur, and more than a thousand were injured. The immediate cause of the riots was the police decision to shut down a peaceful demonstration about social injustice. The underlying cause, however, was Uighur anger over their own marginalization by incoming Han Chinese who dominate the government and the economy. The riots led to several days of ethnic unrest, during which Uighurs were forced to hide from thousands of Han Chinese patrolling the streets with clubs and shouting, "Exterminate the Uighurs!" When foreign journalists were bused on an organized tour to the scene of the violence, they were besieged by hundreds of Uighur women and children complaining about the arbitrary arrests of their male kin.

During those tense days, Wu'er Kaixi was unable to contact his family in Urumqi. Indeed, Internet communication between the province and the outside world remained shut off for 10 months after the riots, showing the willingness of China's rulers to use technology as a tool of control. As Wu'er Kaixi wrote in the *Guardian* newspaper, the government was sending a zero-tolerance message, "The government response to the Uighur explosion of frustration that sparked this crisis—for having become politically oppressed and treated as a minority in their homeland—was to label them 'separatists' and 'terrorists' and to shoot them." It marked a dangerous deterioration in the already fractious relationship between the governor and the governed. "China has, in effect, declared war on an oppressed minority group within its own borders," he wrote.

Since then, the anger and dissatisfaction have mounted further, reaching a point whereby Uighurs whom Wu'er Kaixi knows—even the young, college-educated beneficiaries of Chinese rule—have become entirely disillusioned with their lot. The mood is one of bitterness and rage, as people talk of even dying for their homeland. "I think the Chinese government is extremely nervous about Xinjiang nowadays," he told me. "They have very good reason to be nervous." But Wu'er Kaixi has resisted involvement with the Uighur movement in exile, arguing that his role as a democracy activist will ultimately benefit Uighurs, as well as Han.

In 2011, Wu'er Kaixi passed a milestone: He had now spent more time in exile than he had in his homeland. Since 1989, he has not been permitted to see his aging parents, unlike most other exiled student leaders, who were either allowed to slip back in quietly or whose parents were given passports allowing them to visit their children abroad. Negotiations over Wu'er Kaixi's own return broke down almost a decade ago, though he tried to offer up his silence as a bargaining chip. Meanwhile, his parents have not been issued passports. Their son's activism is one factor, their ethnicity is undoubtedly another; given recent ethnic tensions, few Uighurs or Tibetans are granted passports to leave the country. This means that Wu'er's two teenage sons have never met their grandparents, who are both in their 70s. For Wu'er Kaixi, the pain of this forced estrangement has built over the years. "What I cannot swallow is the fact that I am in this position of being bullied, and I do not want to give into that."

He hit his nadir in 2007 when a typhoon in Singapore grounded his flight. As he waited for the howling winds to pass, he watched a Chinese film called *Blind Mountain*. It tells the story of a young female college graduate who is trying to earn money to pay for her brother's education when she is sold as a bride. Her buyer then rapes her as his mother holds her down. For Wu'er Kaixi, the movie was a distillation of all he most despised about his homeland. It seemed to him that ordinary people were no longer merely acquiescing to the system, but rather actively becoming part of that system. Suddenly he started to question whether it was worth devoting his life to China. "I paid my dues. If I feel I have a responsibility for the democracy movement, I believe I have done more than average people. If I have to pay some price for fame—my God, I think I paid that too."

Fixating on these thoughts, he watched as the whole world flocked to Beijing's Olympic Games and the Communist Party basked in the golden glory of its success. Then the financial crisis reshuffled the world order, hastening China's progress to become the world's second biggest economy. Suddenly, the doors that had once been open to him—to the offices of decision-makers and heads of state—were slammed in his face. "I felt betrayed by the Western democracies. We became an inconvenience," he spluttered, shaking his head as if he still couldn't believe it. "We were heroes, for God's sake, we were on the right side. [It was a] clearly well-documented movement. We were the leaders and received in a grand gesture by the free democratic world."

• • • •

As the 20th anniversary of the killings approached, Wu'er Kaixi decided not to give up on China, but instead to try to claw his way back onto that stage in order to remind the world what kind of values the Chinese government holds. He also desperately wanted to see his parents again, even if it had to be through the bars of a prison cell. So he hatched a plan that he saw as answering his obligation to himself. "I wanted to throw myself into prison as a protest against China, against Western democracies: to use myself as a reminder, cast myself as a stone into otherwise tranquil waters."

His plan was to fly to Macau, the only place on mainland soil where he could visit visa-free with his Taiwanese passport, and once there surrender himself to the authorities. Though decades have passed, the most wanted list has never been rescinded, so he imagined it would be impossible for the central government in Beijing to ignore such a prominent fugitive from justice. In his mind's eye, he pictured himself inside a Chinese courtroom forcing a public discussion about the 1989 crackdown, or in a prison cell finally serving his time.

As he explained his thinking, it was clear that the years he had spent in the freedom of exile while his fellow students sat in jail now seemed less of a deliverance and more like an added burden. "When I'm with Wang Dan, I always feel like I owe him something," he told me. "We were both student leaders. We were good friends, still are. But he served his term. I didn't. I feel I owe a lot of people." The families of those who died that night weigh the heaviest on his conscience, and he imagined that serving a prison term would somehow redress the balance. "I'm the captain of a sunk boat, and I survived. That's not something I can brag about. Before I serve my prison terms, I don't know how I can face those people."

On arrival in Macau, it was clear that the mainland authorities had no intention of putting Wu'er Kaixi in jail. He was denied permission to enter the territory and kept in a holding cell overnight.

Spending the 20th anniversary of the killings in detention gave him some slight comfort, he admitted. "I'm happier that I'm in a detention room than being anywhere in the world holding a candle. It's a slightly better way to commemorate." The next day he was put on a flight back to Taipei.

Despite this setback, he decided to stick with the strategy. In 2010, he had hoped to fly to Beijing from Tokyo, but his air ticket was cancelled. So on the 21st anniversary of June 4th, he tried to force his way into the Chinese embassy in Tokyo as an act of protest. He was arrested by the Japanese police and held for two days before being released with no charge. In 2012, he decided to hand himself over to the Chinese Embassy in Washington, D.C. This time, the doors were locked and the staff did not respond to telephone calls. In late 2013, Wu'er Kaixi made one more attempt, flying to Hong Kong, where he again tried to turn himself in. He was promptly sent back to Taiwan.

He also wrote a public appeal with five other Tiananmen exiles, including Wang Dan, imploring China's leaders to let them go home. "We believe that returning to one's motherland is an inalienable right of a citizen. As rulers, you should not deprive us of our most fundamental human right because of differences in political views between us and you." There was no official response. Yet the very narrowness of their demands, the gradual shrinkage of their ambitions over the years, contained within it a world of despair and disillusion.

Beijing's cold shoulder sidestepped confrontation while underlining the impotence of the exiled dissident. Like football players on the bench, the overseas activists have been removed from the field of play, limiting their ability to change the game. Begging to be let back in and shouting from the sidelines only serves to underline their futility. An editorial in the *Global Times*, a Chinese state-run newspaper, rubbed this in, stating, "Pro-democracy activists have almost been marginalized and consequently feel lonely. The Western world has shown less support for them than for Chinese separatists and, furthermore, many young Chinese people have never heard of them."

Beijing has effectively neutered Wu'er Kaixi, turning his grand gestures into little more than grandstanding. Such criticism is familiar territory for Wu'er Kaixi, yet he takes it on the chin: For exiles, he believes, narcissism is a necessity rather than a luxury. "I have met with many dissident leaders around the world. We are all more or less *zilian*. It's kind of required—to be self-involved—to be a martyr."

• • • •

One evening, I accompanied Wu'er Kaixi to a television interview at the headquarters of the *United Daily News*, a Taiwanese newspaper that had started producing video for its website. As our taxi rolled up to the gate, a grizzled guard glanced inside. "Is that Wu'er Kaixi?" he asked, recognizing the famous face. Wherever he goes, Wu'er Kaixi generates double-takes as people struggle to place his features. He appears regularly as a political commentator on Taiwanese television, but when I asked one prominent editor to gauge Wu'er Kaixi's influence on Taiwan's political scene, he caustically replied, "None at all."

In the building's lobby, an anxious producer was pacing with the look of a man wondering how on earth to fill the looming half-hour hole in his program. When he spotted Wu'er Kaixi striding in, his expression was a mix of utter relief and awe. He pumped his hand, beaming with relief. "I'd like to have my picture taken with you later!" he told Wu'er Kaixi eagerly. "I was in high school in 1989. I watched everything! I even had a T-shirt with your face on it!"

Upstairs in the state-of-the-art studio, the urbane host was waiting anxiously, wearing a smart blue shirt and a grey tie. As Wu'er Kaixi clomped onto the set in his casual sandals, camouflage shorts, and a washed-out grey polo shirt, anxiety hovered in the air. Upon entering, Wu'er Kaixi thanked the host with unusual humility, "This is a very rare chance to have a one-on-one," he told him. In the gallery, the air of apprehension seemed to solidify into unvoiced accusations. But as the producers began their countdown, Wu'er Kaixi visibly gathered himself up. The minute the remote-control camera began rolling, the old commanding presence was back. The segment length was 12 minutes, and he gauged the timing impeccably, working up his indignation to sound off with a final emotional denunciation of Taiwan's President Ma Yingjeou's capitulation to China's Communist leadership. It was good television, sandals or no.

After the commercial break, the host asked Wu'er Kaixi to respond to the widely voiced criticism of the failure of the dissident movement in exile. "We should be ashamed of ourselves," Wu'er Kaixi answered frankly. "We really haven't done a good job." Quoting another exile, he admitted that they had "found heaven, but lost the earth." Indeed, once they had made it overseas, the Tiananmen students discovered generations of earlier political exiles of whom they had never heard, leading to damaging internecine squabbles over resources and an atomization of their ebbing influence. As Wu'er Kaixi was talking about the moral equivalence of condemning the exiles for their lack of unity while rushing to do business with the Chinese government, the young producers in the galley were focusing on more superficial matters. Eyes fixed on the wall of screens, they were discussing a shot that had flashed by of the two most wanted student leaders two decades on: a plump Wu'er Kaixi sitting next to Wang Dan, who had transformed himself from a skinny, bespectacled geek into a suave university lecturer. Perhaps not even realizing she was talking out loud, a young female producer muttered, "Wang Dan looks so much better nowadays."

By the time the interview was over, it was half past eight. Outside the studio, the young producer thanked Wu'er Kaixi politely, but did not mention the photo opportunity he initially had been hankering after. In any case, the next guest had arrived and had to be ushered into the studio in the two-minute interval. We had not eaten for many hours and as we got onto the subway, Wu'er Kaixi noted that I must be hungry, and he apologized. He was, he said, trying to control his weight, since people criticized him for it all the time. The weight gain was partly due to steroids that he took for asthma. "I don't think it's anybody's business but my own," he said. "But people say it doesn't look good. Exiled dissidents are meant to suffer."

Do you ever get bored of being on television? I asked him. "No," he said, "that's what I do." Television was, as he saw it, the only stage open to him now. He and the other exiled leaders had been practically children when they left China, completely unschooled in the ways of the West, and they had just witnessed wholesale murder. They probably should have been receiving therapy. Instead, they were received with bouquets, red carpets, and the adrenalin shot of cameras everywhere they went. They were adored and invincible until suddenly one day, the new exiles realized that the cameras and the adulation were all gone, and they were alone, marooned in a new land without even the ability to make themselves understood. The tides had changed, and they were the flotsam of an earlier age. The media were their only allies, yet Wu'er Kaixi, for one, knew all too well how fickle those allies were.

• • • •

While I was in Taipei, this media cycle was repeating itself for the latest celebrity dissident, but at the warp speed of the social media age. This time, the focus was on the blind legal activist Chen Guangcheng who was on his first trip to the island since his dramatic escape from the mainland one year earlier. Chen was a self-educated lawyer who had exposed family-planning abuses, including forced abortions, by his local government in Linyi in the province of Shandong. For this, he was first put in jail on the trumped-up charge of "assembling a crowd for the purpose of disrupting traffic," and then remanded into the prison of his own home, where his whole family was kept under jail-like conditions and subject to brutal beatings. Despite his blindness, Chen managed to escape by scaling a wall in the dead of night and managing to flee to the refuge of the U.S. Embassy in Beijing, despite breaking his ankle during the escape. After protracted high-level political negotiations, he gained passage to the United States to take up a year-long fellowship at New York University. At the time of his Taiwan trip, Chen was embroiled in a new controversy, having accused New York University of bowing to Chinese pressure in not extending his fellowship.

I went to see the two exiles appear together on a panel about human rights. When I stepped out of the elevator, I was greeted by a crescent of expectant photographers, their cameras raised shot-ready, then lowered with disappointment when I was the only one emerging from the lift. When Chen finally arrived, he was greeted by a burst of applause and a fawning receiving line of dignitaries. As he took his place at the top table, the semicircle of photographers kneeled in front of him, genuflecting to this latter-day icon of suffering. Wu'er Kaixi sat at the end of the table; no photographers were at his feet.

The symposium mainly consisted of a bevy of stout, elderly lawyers declaiming earnestly about the importance of human rights, while the journalists played games on their cellphones. Early on, there was a moment of intense embarrassment when one of the elderly lawyers forgot that Chen Guangcheng was blind. "Tell us, what you have seen in these 18 days of travel?" he asked sycophantically, before scrambling to recover from his mistake. "Of course you can't see, but tell us all the things you experienced while you have been here, even if you were unable to see them?" This awkwardness was compounded by Wu'er Kaixi who, clearly unwilling to miss an opportunity to plug his essay collection, ceremonially presented a copy of his book to the blind lawyer.

When he finally spoke, Wu'er Kaixi jerked the journalists out of their torpor with another spirited attack on the Taiwanese government. He also spelled out the differences between the two generations of dissidents, even as he praised Chen Guangcheng for his work defending citizens' rights. "To do such specific, such pedantic work is not as interesting as a student movement, with its several million people on the streets. It's not a grand dream of changing the entire system. If you could succeed in that, it would have a greater influence. But the noble mission of rights activism is to change the world in a very specific, very grassroots kind of way." In 21st-century China, to advocate changing the entire system is to lay oneself open to charges of inciting subversion of state power. In today's climate, even the simple act of rights protection—trying to ensure that local governments respect citizens' rights as enshrined in China's own laws—has become politically suspect.

To see the two exiles together was like being at the beginning and end of a circle, watching the ambitions of the new exile balanced against the weariness of the old. Afterward, with a certain degree of schadenfreude, Wu'er Kaixi commented that within the

exile community, the consensus was that little could be done to prevent Chen Guangcheng from destroying himself. He understood
what it was like to be plunged into exile, he added. After all, when he
first arrived as the darling of the media, he had completely ignored
all advice.

"So what advice do you wish you could have given your younger
self?" I asked him.

"To shut up!" he said, with a big rollicking laugh. "Stop talking!"

• • • •

In exile, many of the Tiananmen students went into academia, depriv-
ing China of some of its most prominent intellectuals. Others became
businessmen and entrepreneurs, running their own funds and setting
up tech companies. The younger students tended to find it easier to
adapt than the older exiles, some of whom still struggle to communicate in English after decades overseas. Several turned to religion, including one of the most famous faces of the movement, Chai Ling,
who had styled herself as the commander-in-chief of the Protect
Tiananmen Headquarters. On her website, she now cites her proud-
est accomplishment as "becoming a Jesus-follower." After gaining an
M.B.A. from Harvard Business School, she founded an Internet company, followed by a charitable organization called "All Girls Allowed"
dedicated to ending China's one-child policy. In 2012, she announced
that her Christian faith had allowed her to forgive the Chinese leaders
who had ordered the suppression and the soldiers who had carried it
out. "I understand that such forgiveness is countercultural," she wrote.
"Yet it is only a small reflection of the forgiveness that Jesus gave, and
I was filled with peace when I followed him in forgiving."

Chai Ling's statement outraged many other exiles, particularly
in the light of her prominent role in the student movement. It was
her change of heart that had led to the collapse of the agreement to
withdraw from the square at the end of May 1989. The very next day,
she asked a young American to record "her last will and testament,"
words that later aired in *The Gate of Heavenly Peace* documentary.
She said, "The students keep asking, 'What should we do next? What
can we accomplish?' I feel so sad, because how can I tell them that

what we are actually hoping for is bloodshed, for the moment when the government has no choice but to brazenly butcher the people. Only when the square is awash with blood will the people of China open their eyes. Only then will they really be united. But how can I explain any of this to my fellow students?"

For this, she was pilloried. In her recent autobiography, she lays out her defense, arguing that she had simply been trying to communicate her concern that an inevitable crackdown was getting closer, and that she had been misunderstood. She believes the government response had been decided long before. "Even if we had abandoned the square before June 4, some other event would have triggered the massacre." In Chai Ling's eyes, the very act of asking whether an earlier withdrawal from the square might have prevented the killings implies that the students bear some responsibility for the loss of life. "The victims were presented as villains and their sacrifices were laughed off as foolishness."

For his part, Wu'er Kaixi—who clashed repeatedly and publicly with Chai Ling back in 1989—attributed her words back then to an excess of emotion rather than any Machiavellian scheme to engineer a crackdown. Like her, he is wary of any reevaluation of the students' actions. "At this point, we should stand very clear," he told me. "One hundred percent, it's the government's responsibility. How would it make it right for us to say maybe we are also responsible for a certain percentage of this result? To me, logically, this is so wrong. Morally, it's very wrong. We are discrediting those who died. We are dishonoring them." Thus, the struggle for control over the past stretches into exile.

Wu'er Kaixi was referring in particular to recent doubts by his fellow leader Wang Dan over the hunger strike they staged on Tiananmen Square to escalate the movement. In an e-mail to me, Wang Dan spelled out his reservations, writing, "I don't think the hunger strike itself was mistaken. I think the timing of the hunger strike could have been more strategic. After the sit-in, we should have withdrawn from the square. This is just a reflection on the specific method, rather than a criticism of the whole movement itself." Given the different forces at play, even regret—that most human of instincts—has become politically loaded.

In the documentary film *The Gate of Heavenly Peace*, Wu'er Kaixi offered an off-the-cuff summary of what the students had wanted: "Nike shoes. Lots of free time to take our girlfriends to a bar. The freedom to discuss an issue with someone. And to get a little respect from society." Today, none of these are out of reach for young Chinese people who revel in the ability to buy designer sports shoes online and drink at bars offering lychee martinis, "Hooters"-style waitresses, and even pole-dancing. It is a world of materialism, consumerism, and entertainment unimaginable to the students of 1989.

Yet the political causes that the students wrote about in their hunger-strike declaration—"widespread illegal business dealings by corrupt officials; the dominance of abusive power; the corruption of bureaucrats; the fleeing of a large number of good people to other countries; and the deterioration of law and order"—remain not merely unresolved but *worse* than in 1989. The corruption cases that make the headlines today feature billions of dollars rather than millions. A campaign against rumor-mongering has placed new controls on speech and online expression, punishable by prison. Meanwhile, citizens are being arrested for simply trying to protect the rights afforded to them by law. Wu'er Kaixi is confident that this tightening political noose will make ordinary Chinese realize that the cost of delaying political reform now outweighs any perceived dangers from undertaking reform.

As he put it, "In 1989, the drive that put us on the street was that we felt despair, we felt hopeless about our future. That kind of despair—that kind of hopelessness—exists in China today in a different form, but perhaps clearer than 1989." Though Chinese youth have a reputation for being apolitical, he is confident that they, too, could experience the same overnight awakening as his generation of disco-dancers, mahjong-players, money-makers, and TOEFL-takers. "When they are given a chance to be idealistic again, I bet they are going to take that chance."

4 :: Student

Feel Liu was almost tripping over his numerous shopping bags, so keen was he to visit the June 4th Memorial Museum, which had temporarily been set up inside a building at a university in Hong Kong. "Feel" was his English name given to him by an English teacher from Sichuan, ostensibly because his grades were so good that he "had a feeling" for English. Rushing up to the yellow-vested volunteer manning the door, he asked whether he had to register his name in order to enter. No, he was told, just go straight in. Did it matter that he wasn't a student at the university? No, he was told, it's fine. Did they realize that this kind of material was banned in China where he lived? Yes, he was told, but here in Hong Kong, we can still show what really happened.

Feel collapsed into a seat in a row of chairs that had been set up in the room, arraying his purchases on the floor in front of him, and then proceeded to watch an 11-minute film on the student movement. He concentrated intently, his eyes growing wide with disbelief. When it was over, he watched it a second time. In between, he carefully unwrapped his new iPhone and plugged it into the wall beside him to charge it so that he could snap pictures of everything he was seeing. I happened to be standing behind him, and after his second viewing, I asked him what he thought of the film. "This is the first time I've seen any of this, even though I'm already a college student," he replied. "In the classroom, the teachers have mentioned it in passing, but they don't want to talk about it. They're scared." From a teacher's perspective, no good could come of teaching about the "events of 1989"; it was best left untouched.

"I think the Chinese government is very good at covering things up and cheating people," he said bluntly.

"When did you start to think like that?" I asked.

"Right now, just as I'm watching this," he replied. "In the past, when I was trying to join the Communist Party, I thought its behavior was very upright. There may have been a few things that weren't quite so fair, but on the whole its behavior was very good. However, watching this, I realize how very little I know, particularly about the Communist Party."

Feel was a 22-year-old marketing student visiting the Special Administrative Region of Hong Kong on a shopping trip from mainland China. He had bought shiny peacock-blue Adidas trainers—at a third of the mainland price—as well as his precious iPhone, also at a considerable discount. He stroked the screen lovingly as we talked. "I have to like this. I've invested everything I have in this phone." His shopping bags also contained brand-name cosmetics for a friend, but mostly they were packed with food and water that he had brought with him from mainland China to save money.

Feel had come to Hong Kong not just to shop, but to experience all its differences from the mainland. He had been wandering around the campus of the university to see how it compared to his own school back in China. He had even made a special trip to the pharmacist to inquire about the different brands of condoms; such directness about sex was impossible inside mainland China. "The way of thinking here is very open," he enthused. "It gives you the feeling that you dare to speak out, dare to do stuff, dare to criticize and dare to think."

As he was walking down the street, Feel was astonished to be accosted first by members of the *Falungong* sect, which is banned inside China as an evil cult, and then immediately afterward by *Falungong* opponents. He had slipped literature from both groups into his bag, and when I spoke to him he had already dipped into the "Nine Commentaries on the Communist Party," a *Falungong* publication that offers a blistering condemnation of Communist rule. Feel just wanted to know more although, he added quickly, he was unlikely to oppose the government in any case. He wasn't political, after all; he was someone who pretty much went with the flow.

• • • •

In the West, the iconic image of Tiananmen is that of "Tank Man," a slender man in a white shirt and black trousers, facing down a column of tanks on Chang'an Avenue. The picture was taken on June 5th, one day after most of the killings. In each hand, the young man clutches a plastic bag, as if he had been on his way home from a shopping trip when he made a spontaneous decision to challenge the state's military might. Footage shot from the balcony of the Beijing Hotel shows how the man had positioned himself well in advance of the arrival of the long line of tanks barreling down the avenue toward him. When the first tank maneuvered to avoid him, he defiantly moved into its path again. When it ground to a halt in front of him, he clambered up onto the tank and had an exchange with a soldier who had peeped out of the hatch. One unconfirmed report said that Tank Man had shouted, "Turn around! Stop killing my people!" The footage shows him being hustled off by three unknown people; it is unclear whether they are security forces or supporters trying to protect him. Despite years of effort, no one has ever been able to ascertain what happened to the man, or even learn who he was.

How many young Chinese today know about Tank Man? In a crude experiment designed to test the limits of Chinese censorship in the Internet age, I took the photo of Tank Man to the campuses of four Beijing universities whose students had been instrumental in the 1989 movement: Peking University, Tsinghua University, People's University, and Beijing Normal University. I was curious to know how many of today's Internet-savvy students would recognize the photo. The students I spoke to are the crème de la crème, the best-educated students in China, yet the vast majority of them looked at the photo without the slightest flicker of recognition. "Is it in Kosovo?" one astronomy major asked. A student pursuing a Ph.D. in marketing hazarded a guess, "Is it in South Korea?"

"I feel that it looks a bit like Tiananmen Square. But it isn't, is it?" asked one student doing postgraduate work in education at Beijing Normal University. Out of 100 students, 15 correctly identified the picture; two of whom had never seen it before but had guessed correctly. In fact, the number of students who mistakenly believed it to be a photo of a military parade was higher at 19, than those who recognized it.

Of those students who identified Tank Man, a couple had a visceral physical reaction, gasping and literally shying away from the picture. One young Beijinger, with whom I had been chatting in English, involuntarily cried out, "Oh my God!" A couple of students who claimed not to recognize the photo betrayed themselves by their reactions. "This is a sensitive topic," one young man at Peking University offered nervously. When I asked him if he would talk about it, he replied, "I think I cannot," and then left, almost at a run. Another undergraduate showed the makings of a party official with his careful response, "This picture maybe is related to a counterrevolutionary incident, which was two or three years after my birth in the last century."

I was surprised to find how readily I, too, had internalized Chinese censorship. Confronting these young students with the picture of Tank Man felt like an act of heresy—as if I were lobbing an ideological grenade onto the orderly, treelined campuses. I became so nervous that someone might report me to the police or university security that I made a point of talking only to solitary students, calculating that a single student would be less likely to report a foreigner to the authorities. Despite the journalist's credentials that allowed me to operate in China, I became paranoid that I might be detained for simply showing the picture of Tank Man.

I need not have worried. My informal survey revealed the degree to which the party has asserted its hold over the minds of China's brightest youth. Indeed, several students who identified Tank Man defended the government's actions. "I think the country's reaction was a bit extreme," one young English major at People's University argued. "At the time, the country had its own reasons for crushing the turmoil. New China had just been established, and had undergone so many destabilizing events. If at that time, turmoil were to break out, it was very likely the regime might fall. Lots of foreign powers had been using this turmoil to try to overturn the government of China." She believed that the government had shown laudable restraint in permitting the protests to continue for so long and only taking action after "foreign reactionaries" had begun to stir up trouble. She was quick to point out that her understanding of the "events of 1989" had not come from official channels but from her own extracurricular reading.

"All countries have their own dirty laundry," reflected another self-possessed young woman studying entrepreneurship at Tsinghua, in fluent English. "I know a lot of people blame our government. Actually they have really done something to be blamed. But the thing is to consider if another party rules our country what would be the outcome? Maybe it won't be as desirable as people thought. With the current status, we have to be grateful for the things they have done for us." The government had acted in the interests of the majority, she believed, and those countries that condemned China's reaction should look to their own records. "There is no real freedom of speech in other countries," she said, neatly deflecting any blame by launching into accusations against others in a move straight from the playbook of China's propaganda apparatus.

One young medical student was perched on a shiny motor scooter outside a student canteen, wearing a luxury watch and an ostentatious black-and-white T-shirt featuring the intertwined Cs of the Chanel logo. "I don't think it's reliable," he pronounced, peering closely at the photo. He mused on the large number of faked pictures online and the sophistication of digital photo-editing tools. "Photographs cannot be relied upon to prove anything. I think it's very likely this is fake," he concluded. With that, he donned a pair of expensive designer shades, revved up his motor scooter, and swooped off, turning a few female heads with his departure.

In the immediate aftermath of June 4th, China's students did not swallow the government's version of events quite so readily. Perhaps that was not so surprising given the crudeness of the government propaganda, which sometimes even reversed television sequences to make it appear as if the troops had only opened fire after the demonstrators had turned violent, obscuring the fact that those throwing stones were doing so in retaliation to gunfire. Indeed, one survey carried out in 1990 by the Hangzhou Electronic Research Institute found that only 2–3 percent of students surveyed "deeply believed" the Party's version of events. At that time, there was almost no access to the Internet. Now, every student can go online. Yet the propaganda apparatus has laid the groundwork so well that most students simply have no interest in questioning the government's version of events.

• • • •

Feel had never seen the Tank Man photo. Before traveling to Hong Kong, he had tried to look for information about June 4th on the Internet, but he didn't know how to use a Virtual Private Network (VPN) to bypass the government's controls, and so had discovered little. He told me this when I took him up on his invitation to visit him at his college in the south of China, a couple of hours by bus from Hong Kong. The ride there was extremely comfortable, whizzing along in an air-conditioned cocoon past a jumbled amalgam of emerald-green palms, pink-tiled three-story houses, and urban sprawl, all crisscrossed by endless grey ribbons of highway from the recent infrastructure binge—some of which had been abandoned half-finished.

For lunch, Feel chose a fast-food restaurant whose color scheme was dominated by virulent orange. He was polite but subdued, nothing like the exuberant young man I had met a few days earlier. He even made an attempt to excuse his behavior in Hong Kong, saying that he had not felt quite himself; it was too unfamiliar, too crowded, and he had been rather tired. Now he was back to normal. I had enjoyed chatting with Feel in Hong Kong because of his openness, and I was taken aback by this new air of detachment, which continued to build as we approached his school.

During the hour-long bus journey from the city center to his campus, he peppered me with questions about money: How much does it cost to see a film in Hong Kong? Did my husband and I have a joint bank account? How much did I pay every month for my phone bill? His concerns were purely materialistic, as if finances were the major factor determining happiness.

The bus jolted through the city, whose suburbs were still rather quaintly named after the villages they had long since outgrown. Outcroppings of skyscrapers rose up between the enormous factory buildings and gigantic government offices. As we finally appeared to be nearing the edge of the city, we glided into an area that looked more like Silicon Valley than China. Manicured bushes and trees lined the smoothly paved roads, and on both sides shiny new building complexes appeared through the lush trees, though the quacking noises from nearby duck farms were a reminder of just how recently all this had been countryside.

Feel's college was located in a recently built academic hub that houses an estimated 80,000 students, testimony to China's push to invest in higher education; the number of colleges and universities has doubled in the past decade. In 1989, just over two million students were engaged in higher education. By 2012, that figure had tripled to almost seven million. Some things were unchanged, however. I spotted a sign at one university plaza that encapsulated the restrictive nature of campus life: "Work Place: It is forbidden to sit or lie down, to stop, to play or to make noise."

Feel's idea of a good time was to invite me to sit in on a two-hour class in marketing. We scurried up the steps of the classroom building into a huge auditorium to watch the lecturer giving a PowerPoint presentation on the importance of after-sales service ("Don't forget: customers are your source of capital"). I sat in the back row and took copious notes out of habit, until I noticed that I was the only person in the entire class bothering to do so. Most students had not even brought a pen or notebook with them, and many spent their time surreptitiously texting or playing games on their cell phones beneath the desks. One young woman in the front row was videoing the entire double session on her phone; she was the only person making any attempt at record-taking.

After a while, I became distracted by the slogans on the students' T-shirts. My favorite, which read "Wicki Wacky Woo," was emblazoned in bright letters on the chest of a young man. Two rows ahead of me sat another student whose T-shirt identified him as a member of "Class Two Unremitting Marketing World."

Feel sat next to his friend Moon, whose glasses were endearingly patched together with adhesive tape. The teacher valiantly tried to engage the class, forcing them to role-play by taking on the parts of salespeople and customers. An exercise in praising the customer proved to be an uphill struggle. One reluctant participant—who had admitted to the class that his interpersonal skills were poor—could not think of a single compliment to pay his neighbor. After an uncomfortably long silence, he had a sudden inspiration, "You've got a nice cell phone!"

Earlier, I had asked Feel whether he liked reading. "Yes," he had replied earnestly. "I like watching videos." I asked what he had read recently. He spent a long time thinking about this before saying that he could not remember the last time he had actually finished an entire book. He had only managed to read halfway through the inspirational autobiography of the Olympic badminton champion Lin Dan. It was on the shelf in his dorm room, along with just one other book that was not part of his curriculum—a double biography that outlined the strategies for success used by two homegrown business icons, Tang Jun, known as the "king of migrant workers," and Alibaba's Jack Ma. The tagline on the book read, "Success can be replicated. Every person can be a successful person."

Success preoccupies these students, and for them money is the only yardstick for measuring achievement. They will be entering the job market at a time when an expansion of higher education has collided with a dearth of job opportunities in an economic slowdown. According to one poll, merely 35 percent of recent graduates have found work. Feel and Moon, both the first in their families to go to college, know that failing to find a job would devastate their parents who have invested years of toil in their education.

Feel was preoccupied with trying to find an internship for the next year when he was supposed to be getting some work experience. A position in a leading company would help build his network of contacts and give him an advantage in the cutthroat job market. Hanging over him was the other alternative: the school-mandated placement, which would leave him spending a year stacking shelves in a supermarket, a position at the very bottom of the marketing pyramid with a correspondingly low salary. The expansion of higher education has eroded the upward mobility once conferred by the simple possession of a degree, and as in most areas of life in today's China, those with the right *guanxi* —the most expansive Rolodex— will prevail. Feel knew that his connections were not ideal, but he was a striver determined to better himself.

He already had an income stream. Having studied his parents' transport business, he had set himself up as a middleman, helping factories find university students to work over the summer break. The factory hours were long—10 hours a day—and the pay was low—around $1.30 per hour—but food and lodging were included. There were always students willing to sign up. Judging by the advertisements plastered around the dorms, Feel was not the only one engaged in this line of work. Enticements included pointing out that the factories had karaoke rooms, ping-pong tables, and canteens offering three dishes and one soup at every meal. For this work, Feel negotiated a fee of around $30 for each student he himself recruited or $8 per head for workers that subcontractors had recruited on his behalf.

Factory life was not for Feel himself. He had once tried working on an assembly line in an electronics components factory, but he lasted only a couple of weeks. He needed something more interesting. His biggest challenge now, he judged, was finding the right job. Unlike his parents' generation, Feel was not willing to put up with a job he did not like. "If it's suitable, then maybe I could do it a whole lifetime," he said. "But maybe after a while, it might get a bit tiring or I might not like it, then I might quit." Feel found it difficult to understand why the older generation had been willing to put up with such hard graft when there were easy pickings to be had elsewhere. "Why should you be a migrant worker and be tired and suffer your whole life? As a boss, you just need to make a few telephone calls, and you can earn 10 times as much. Everything depends on yourself and your own abilities."

For Moon, the son of farmers, the situation was quite different. When he was 10 years old, his parents had left him, his brother, and their farmland under the care of their own parents, and had gone off to find factory jobs in order to earn enough to finance their boys' education. "They really know how to eat bitterness, how to suffer," Moon told me as he dug into an enormous bowl of meat stew in the university canteen, which resembled a hipster coffee shop combining industrial chic with red-and-white Chinese motifs. "We are lazy compared to them."

Moon's life has become unimaginable to his parents, who in the past two years have not had the means or time to leave their jobs to visit him at college. He spent his school holidays touring the countryside by bike with friends, sleeping in cheap hotels or at friends' houses. For his family, a number of reforms over the past decade, including the elimination of agricultural taxes, the provision of nine years of free education, and the introduction of social security, have markedly improved the quality of their lives. From Moon's standpoint, change has been tangible and positive. "Society is getting better, from one set of leaders to the next. The system and our education are all slowly getting better."

Indeed, China accounts for three-quarters of the global decline in poverty in the past 30 years, lifting more than 600 million people out of poverty since 1981. For students like Feel and Moon, these are more than statistics; they are the stories of their lives.

But even within their own circles, there is a visible wealth gap. When we arrived at their dorm room, which housed four students, young men were lounging on the beds and chairs, each inside their own virtual world: some watching videos, others chatting online or playing games on their smart phones. They scattered as we came in, but a quick scan of their various electronic devices was revealing. Feel had far more electronic paraphernalia than the others, including a computer, his brand-new iPhone, and an iPad clad in a smart pink-leather case. One of his roommates had an entry-level cell phone; a single piece of clothing was hanging in his cupboard.

The evening's drama was a dorm inspection by officious student monitors with clipboards who were checking for illegal kettles or hotplates that could interfere with the building's electricity supply. It was supposed to have been a surprise, but Feel had already been tipped off that the inspectors were on their way and had managed to hide his own kettle and hotplate. He devoted his energies to trying to intercede for a female friend whose kettle had already been confiscated. "She's weeping in her dorm room," he said, lying shamelessly. "She's really upset. Maybe you could just give it back?" But the clipboard lady was unmoved, pushing her glasses up her nose and demanding a written statement of self-criticism from the offender. Self-criticism echoes the Chinese legal system itself by emphasizing the acceptance of guilt and a show of repentance as key steps in the punishment process, even for such minor transgressions as possessing an illegal kettle.

During an evening stroll round the campus, Feel and Moon proudly pointed out the enormous library and the sports facilities. It was a balmy, humid evening, and almost all the students were outside, practicing their hip-hop moves by the running track, doing soccer drills, or simply strolling about and chatting. Feel tried to flirt with a marathon runner who beat a quick retreat, shouting over her shoulder, "When did you break up with your girlfriend? I'm not talking to you!" Campus life was accompanied by the shrill chirps of cicadas and the bellows of water buffaloes from the adjacent farms, which acted as a constant reminder to students of the lives to which they would return if they didn't work hard enough.

• • • •

The students' ignorance regarding 1989 is hardly surprising considering the efforts made to expunge the "Beijing Spring" from the official version of history. Most high-school textbooks take a simple approach by entirely neglecting to mention it. At the undergraduate level, the textbooks used by history majors devote a paltry few pages to June 4th, though these contain what French academic Michel Bonnin calls a "monumental historical untruth." I found the inaccuracy repeated in identical passages of two separate books— *The History of the People's Republic of China* and *A New Edition of Chinese History*—though nominally written by different authors.

The passages follow an explanation of the larger context, claiming that the imperialist Western world was "trying to make socialist countries abandon the socialist route" while the general secretary of the Communist Party, Zhao Ziyang, had neglected the struggle against "bourgeois liberalization." Both textbooks zero in on the editorial that appeared in the *People's Daily* on April 26th labeling the student demonstrations as part of a plot designed to "negate the leadership of the CCP and the socialist system." "After the editorial was published," according to the textbooks, "and due to the increased political and ideological education of the students by Party organizations at all levels, many realized the nature of the struggle. The situation at higher educational establishments in Beijing and other cities began to stabilize." The statement is not merely untrue; it represents the polar opposite of what actually happened. The editorial enraged the students, sparking the largest demonstrations to that point and breathing new life into the movement. Protests opposing the editorial were held across the country, including in the cities of Shenyang, Dalian, Shijiazhuang, Jinan, Kunming, Shenzhen, Yinchuan, and Guilin, none of which had previously seen any protests.

On the behavior of the military, one textbook praises the "extreme patience and tenacious persuasion of the martial law troops" while clearing the students from the square. As for the fact that soldiers opened fire on unarmed civilians, the same textbook says that these actions were taken in self-defense, since "the heads of the illegal organizations instigated some people who did not understand the truth to construct blockades at some crossroads to stop the army trucks. There even emerged some serious incidences of rioting in which army trucks were set alight and PLA soldiers killed. As the soldiers were in a situation that was no longer tolerable, facing savage attacks from thugs, they were forced to implement necessary self-defense tactics."

Textbooks aside, the taboo surrounding June 4th means that it is almost never referred to in public institutions. Over the years, visiting dozens of mainland museums, I have found only one overt reference to the suppression. It appears in a memorial honoring police martyrs inside Beijing's Police Museum, an imposing granite building fronted by Ionic columns and crammed with fascinating, if gory, glimpses of police life: fountain pens that magically transform into guns; a suspiciously clean grey hold-all that purportedly once held a dismembered corpse and had been discovered on a luggage rack on the Beijing-to-Dandong train; the handcuffs worn by an unfortunate police chief when the Red Guards turned against him during the Cultural Revolution.

On the third floor is the Memorial Wall to the Martyrs, a spectacularly ugly 25-feet-high red sandstone wall relief dedicated to policemen who died in the line of duty. Cubes of red stone and enormous pairs of eyes jut from the wall. One pair of eyes is framed by large square spectacles, making the wall resemble a garish advertisement for an optician carved in stone. A number of hands also protrude from the wall holding, variously, a pistol, some handcuffs, and a flower.

On top of a glass display case housing a police helmet and a gold wreath are two folders with leather pages listing the details of the police martyrs honored here. Among them are—as the English translation puts it—two policemen "killed by ruffians on June 4th 1989 while performing a mission" and a third who was mortally wounded that night. The explanation in Chinese adds the information that the policemen were "killed by ruffians while performing the mission of pacifying the 'political storm.'" Reading between the lines, those who know what happened will find the alternate universe of the student movement and its brutal repression. But for today's young people, who may not know what happened, parsing the lines of this bland account yields almost nothing.

• • • •

The great forgetting is not just limited to campuses. It has happened in homes around the country, too. Parents who knew about or took part in the protests now want to protect their children from learning about what happened. Some go to extraordinary lengths to shield their offspring by lying or withholding information. One example is the artist Sheng Qi who, in the aftermath of the suppression, hacked off his own little pinkie with a meat cleaver as an act of protest. It was, he says, a moment of madness, but one that came to form a basis for his art. One series of his artwork entitled "Memories" features photos of his mutilated hand holding old black-and-white pictures, including one of himself as a chubby infant in a Mao cap.

Yet Sheng Qi has still not told his 12-year-old son why he chopped off his own finger. Whenever his son asks him what happened, he jokes that he lost his finger on a bus. His son knows that he's lying, Sheng Qi admits, but he has decided not to tell him the truth until he becomes an adult. "I'm always thinking of some story, because he's still a little kid. I want to protect him."

Paradoxically, the Chinese government's success in enforcing collective amnesia and whitewashing its own history may now threaten its control over information. Many of those too young to have lived through Tiananmen are completely ignorant about what happened, indeed dangerously ignorant from the government's perspective. On a couple of occasions in recent years, young media workers have even failed to recognize Tiananmen-related material and thus have neglected to censor it.

One example was a tiny classified advertisement that was printed in the lower right-hand corner of page 14 of the *Chengdu Evening News* on June 4, 2007. A single line long, it read, "Paying Tribute to the Strong mothers of the June 4th victims." Chengdu rights activist Chen Yunfei told me that he had placed the ad, which had been accepted by an ad agency worker who had been unaware that "June 4th victims" had any special significance. When she called him back to ask what the date meant, he told her that it referred to the anniversary of a mining accident. After the newspaper was published, Chen Yunfei was detained for a day and then placed under close surveillance for six months. Three editors at the paper were demoted, and the advertising agency was dropped. All of them were paradoxically victims of both the success and failure of government censorship.

The next year, the *Beijing News* fell afoul of the censors when it printed an iconic June 4th shot of a bicycle cart driver frantically pedaling two young men to hospital as they lay on a wooden pallet, their pale shirts drenched in blood. Simply captioned "The Wounded," it was one of four photos accompanying a profile of Liu Heung Shing, the Pulitzer Prize-winning photographer who had captured that moment. Rather more aptly than intended, the accompanying article was titled, "I Used Photographs to Record the Journey China Has Taken."

According to a U.S. Embassy cable released by Wikileaks, a senior editor at the paper attributed the mistake to the ignorance of editors too young to recognize the picture. The editor tellingly admitted that he himself had failed to realize what the photo was until he started receiving telephone calls about it. The editor described "a wave of fear and anger" sweeping the newsroom over the possibility of punishment, though senior journalists at the paper had "an interest in reviewing the Party's taboo on media commentary on 1989." The leaked cable concluded by saying that the editor and others "are hoping the case will become a test case that will lead to a change in the ground rules for covering Tiananmen, but conceded this is unlikely." Indeed it remains unlikely; the ground rules are still unchanged.

It took a full two decades after 1989 before a state-run media outlet intentionally broke the official silence. On June 4, 2009, an article titled "Prosperity Tangible along Chang'an Avenue" was published in the *Global Times*, an English-language tabloid belonging to the *People's Daily*. It wrote, "Twenty years after the June 4 Tiananmen Incident, public discussion about what happened that day is almost nonexistent in mainstream society on the Chinese mainland." So complete has been the vacuum of information that even the acknowledgement of such a void constituted a step forward.

One other major discussion of June 4th appeared in an opinion piece in the *China Daily* in 2011. Entitled "Tiananmen Massacre A Myth", it blamed "black propaganda" by the Western media for the "so-called Tiananmen myth," opining that "Tiananmen remains the classic example of the shallowness and bias in most Western media reporting, and of government black information operations seeking to control those media. China is too important to be a victim of this nonsense."

• • • •

The only place on Chinese soil where the events of June 4th are publicly commemorated is Hong Kong, with a huge public rally, as well as a smaller, symbolic 64-hour-long hunger strike held by students every year. The student encampment is often incongruously located in the courtyard of a smart shopping center in the tourist district of Causeway Bay. When I dropped by, several dozen sweating students wearing white headbands were slumped on camping mats on the ground, typing madly on their cell phones and photographing each other. Their almost total silence was a vivid reminder of how social media is changing the act of protest; the pithy tweet is fast displacing the rousing, impassioned speeches of yesteryear.

The students' choice of location was guided by the driving power of economics. They were aiming to catch the eye of passing mainland tourists—now the territory's top spenders—and distract them from their shopping missions for long enough to educate them about their own country's recent history.

Sure enough, as I chatted with a young student who had been fasting for over 40 hours, a couple of inquisitive mainland tourists struck up a conversation. Neither of the mainlanders knew one another, but both had timed their trips to Hong Kong specifically to attend the candlelit vigil. Like Feel, they were hungry for knowledge, though they had managed to figure out how to bypass China's strict Internet controls. One was a middle-aged civil servant, a small man in his 40s, who had first begun dreaming of attending a vigil in Hong Kong almost a decade earlier. He had intended to come with friends, except that one had missed his train and another had been prevented from leaving his hometown by police who had discovered his intentions. The civil servant had been part of the 1989 student movement in his hometown. He told me he had come to assuage his own conscience; when he thought of those who had died or served time in prison, he said, their voices clamored in his head. "That year we took to the streets together. Those of us who were killed are dead. Others went to prison. Don't any of you care? Have you all forgotten or will none of you speak out about this?"

Despite vociferously condemning the Chinese government's violent repression of the protesters and its subsequent cover-up, the civil servant had continued to work for the same government for the past 20 years. "How can you cope with that contradiction day after day?" I asked. He squirmed, fiddling with his expensive camera, as he explained that at the time of his graduation, almost all university students had gone on to government careers. It was embarrassing, he acknowledged, but he couldn't blame himself too much. Like them, he also needed to earn a living. Besides, he went on, in his career he was working for the general good, avoiding participating in "anything evil." Yet, within five minutes, he was describing how he had spent almost six months seizing land from farmers for a government project. The compensation for the farmland had been far too low, he conceded, so some of the villagers had attacked and injured his boss. At least they hadn't blamed him personally.

The younger mainlander, meanwhile, was smirking contemptuously while the older man offered this justification. When I asked the younger man how he had funded his expensive French university degree, it was his turn to look embarrassed. His parents had paid for it, he told me, from the salaries they earned as a policeman and a government official. This conversation brought to mind the assertion by the jailed Nobel peace laureate Liu Xiaobo, who was imprisoned for 20 months after June 4th as a "black hand" behind the student movement, that China has entered an age of cynicism "in which people no longer believe in anything and in which their words do not match their actions, as they say one thing and mean another."

Now more than ever before, these contradictions are called out and mocked in social media, which thrive despite the government's attempts to muzzle them. At the time of writing, China had almost 600 million Internet users, ensuring that memes go viral before the censors are able to delete them. The authorities' natural reflex has been to simply clamp down, banning sensitive words on *weibo*, the Chinese equivalent of Twitter, and deleting postings as quickly as possible. Every June 4th, the authorities' level of paranoia can be charted by the increasingly lengthy lists of banned words. Terms deemed sensitive enough to be forbidden include "today," "tomorrow," "that year," "special day," and "sensitive word." On the 2012 anniversary, censors moved to ban any references to the Shanghai stock exchange after an extraordinary numerological coincidence led it to fall 64.89 points, numbers that when spoken in Chinese spell out "June 4th, 1989."

In the run-up to the anniversary, sensitive images are also often scrubbed from the Internet, including birthday cake candles featuring the numbers 6 or 4; photos of chrysanthemums, which are traditional flowers of mourning; anything with the slightest similarity to a tank, including Lego tanks, cartoon tanks, or tanks made out of mahjong tiles; and, in 2013, even yellow rubber ducks. This stemmed from an artistic installation by a Dutch artist who had floated a gigantic yellow rubber duck in Hong Kong harbor. That theme was then adopted by Internet wags who recreated the Tank Man picture substituting yellow rubber ducks for tanks. The censors moved in quickly but not quickly enough, proving the limitations of old-school censorship in a new media environment.

On the square itself, the authorities have also betrayed the depth of their anxieties by attempts to stymie open reporting. On the 20th anniversary of June 4th, the authorities experimented with a new tactic: the "Umbrella Men" of Tiananmen Square. Plainclothes policemen ostentatiously shielding themselves from the sun with open umbrellas were sent to wander around Tiananmen Square with clear orders to disrupt foreign journalists' work by inserting themselves and their umbrellas between the reporters and their cameramen. The result was a surrealist ballet between the weaving reporters and the pirouetting umbrellas of the security apparatus. Given that all other reactions were suppressed, the Umbrella Men themselves became the focal point of the television dispatches, serving as an unwitting symbol of the government's deep insecurity.

Major political meetings held in the Great Hall of the People have also elicited extreme security measures that have tightened over the years to ensure that no acts of resistance might sully the square. Prior to the big party meeting at which the new leadership was unveiled in 2012—the 18th Party Congress—pigeon owners were forbidden from allowing their birds to fly, while model planes were also banned from Beijing's skies. Taxi drivers were instructed to remove the window cranks so that passengers could not open the car windows. A memo was even circulated warning taxi drivers to be on their guard lest passengers try to throw "ping-pong balls bearing reactionary messages" out the windows.

In this climate, the category of "reactionary message" seems to cover a multitude of content. I myself was censored on *weibo* after tweeting one short sentence. I had simply written "I am in Hong

Kong," after which I posted an icon of a candle burning. Almost immediately, I was sent a warning that my post had been "made confidential" so that only I could see it because "this *weibo* is not suitable to be made public." Soon after that, the candle was removed from the list of available icons to ensure that nobody else could post such an incendiary picture.

• • • •

Feel loved using *weibo*, but had no interest in tweeting anything political. He liked using it to chart his moods, favoring such inspirational maxims as "Take it slowly, and don't be in a rush. Although it's very difficult, I can make it." These were interspersed with his darker thoughts, offered at moments when he was clearly struggling. "My willpower is immature. It's very difficult to achieve what I want." For Feel, *weibo* was not a political platform; it was a tool of self-actualization.

The longer I spent at his school, the more I noticed the difference between Feel-in-Hong-Kong and Feel-at-College. He was nervous to the point of twitchiness, not because of embarrassment at my presence, but due to an instinctual wariness as he tried to police his own words. In Hong Kong, he had been temporarily liberated to speak freely—to "dare to speak out," in his own words. Back at his school, the situation was more complicated. His self-control was a matter of self-preservation; nobody had warned him to mind his words. He knew without being told what was expected of him.

There were glimpses of the old Feel, but only brief ones. He admitted he had felt depressed since returning to China. He was worried, he said, that mainland students' creativity was being stifled, though he would not elaborate on this. Moon, who had not been exposed to Hong Kong's noisy plurality of views, disagreed. His reference point was the lives of his parents, who came from the generation that had required official permission to get married, change jobs, have children, apply for a passport, and travel overseas. From Moon's perspective, there was no comparison. "We are certainly freer than our parents' generation, and our lives are better than theirs," he stated, as he happily cracked his way through a pile of sunflower seeds.

For all its modern facilities, their college is relatively isolated, with few opportunities to socialize with students from the neighboring schools. "Does it remind you of prison?" Moon had asked me jokingly. Until that moment, it hadn't even occurred to me, but afterward, I could not escape the image of the identical dorms stacked on top of each other, factory-farming China's youth into dependable, self-regulating citizens.

Feel had already tried to join the Communist Party. For him, the benefits were manifold, though the most compelling was an increased chance of getting a government job. Joining the party was little more than a rite of passage since his grades were good and he was deputy class monitor. All excellent students joined the Communist Party, he told me in a tone that made it clear that such a statement was self-evident. But this year, his grades had dipped disappointingly, and his application had not been approved. He feared there would not be many more chances to join the party while at college, though he hoped he would still be able to join after starting work. "It's the trend. If everybody thinks the Communist Party is doing a good job, then why not join?"

Such pragmatic views are common among young Chinese, who tend to see party membership as a canny career move because it brings social mobility, not to mention the possibility of material gains due to greater proximity to power. The popularity of the Communist Party at home is such that it signs up a new member every 10 seconds on average. It is the world's largest political party, with 85 million members at last count, outnumbering the entire population of either Egypt or Germany. In fact, if China's Communist Party were a country, it would be the world's 15th most populous. Despite its burgeoning ranks, the party is selective, rejecting six new members for every one it accepts. And it is far from the gerontocracy that outsiders imagine, with more than a quarter of its membership below the age of 35.

Judging by the numbers, few potential party members are dissuaded by the snowballing cascade of scandals, each more absurd than the last, whether it be the rail minister with his epic comb-over and 18 mistresses, the county traffic chief who arranged for 14 of his relatives to get government jobs, or the policeman who owned

192 separate properties. On the contrary, such preposterous stories could make party membership all the more attractive to China's youth by suggesting that it might be the first rung on the ladder to unimaginable wealth, power, and sex. I once asked a 15-year-old schoolgirl in Yunnan what she dreamed of doing when she grew up. "I want to spend time with corrupt officials," she answered. "The more corrupt they are, the better. Because they're the ones who know how the world works." Morality aside, it was difficult to argue with the logic of her argument.

The idea of the robber-baron official as an aspirational figure was further cemented by a video that went viral because it unwittingly exposed the spiritual bankruptcy of Chinese society. It stemmed from an innocent question that a reporter from the outspoken *Southern Metropolitan News* had asked some kindergartners: What do you want to be when you grow up? He filmed a video showing an adorable procession of starry-eyed, gap-toothed kids who stated their various ambitions to be a teacher, an artist, an astronaut, and a firefighter who helps people. Then a six-year-old girl appeared onscreen, her face pixelated. "I want to be an official," she answered sweetly. "What kind of official?" the reporter asked. There was a long pause, and then she replied: "A corrupt official. Because corrupt officials have lots of things."

Even Feel had a pragmatic reason for wanting to join the party. One of the benefits of membership, he believed, was that it offers certain protections to party members who commit crimes, including the fact that party members might not be handcuffed in public like ordinary criminals.

When it came to the events of 1989, Feel was the first to admit that he didn't really understand what had happened. "What I say is blinkered," he told me, as he unwittingly reflected the extent to which those events have been consigned to history. "If I had been alive at the time, or if I were an archaeologist or a historian, then I'd have the right to speak about it." After reflection, he was skeptical about the accuracy of what he had seen in the June 4th Museum in Hong Kong, wondering whether the curators had chosen to present a selective view of history. So loyal was he to a system that had served him well that he wondered whether he should even be *trying* to find out more. The Communist Party must have had good reasons for not being more open about what had happened, he thought. What it had done had turned out to be necessary for stabilizing the country and propelling it to become the world's second-largest economy. Even if it had made mistakes, the party had shown through its subsequent achievements that it deserved the people's trust and understanding. "If the government really was wrong," Feel confidently concluded, "then it's already in the past, and people will understand what they did."

5 :: Mother

Memory is dangerous in a country that was built to function on national amnesia. A single act of public remembrance might expose the frailty of the state's carefully constructed edifice of accepted history, scaffolded into place over a generation and kept aloft by a brittle structure of strict censorship, blatant falsehood, and willful forgetting. That's why a five-foot-tall, 76-year-old grandmother poses enough of a threat that an escort of state security agents, at times as many as 40 strong, has trailed her to the vegetable market and the dentist.

"They knew you were coming," were Zhang Xianling's first words to me, delivered with a welcoming smile as she swung open the door of the tidy ninth-floor apartment in a drab high-rise block. She spoke lightly, as if she were commenting on the weather or the price of pork. Zhang Xianling resembled nothing more than the archetypal Chinese grandma, a stoutly comforting presence with her short, tidy, grey hair, roomy slacks, and bright blue zip-up cardigan. But her appearance did nothing to mask her redoubtable personality and extraordinary resilience.

The local police station had called, she explained, to ask whether she would be going out that morning, and was she, by the way, expecting a visitor today? A foreigner perhaps? With a gleam of satisfaction, she confessed that she had told her interlocutor she was expecting the friend of a friend, someone who might be a "foreign

Chinese person" or perhaps even a "Chinese foreigner of some sort," a neat summary of my mixed racial heritage. Her approach, deploying equal quantities of directness and obfuscation, has been refined over two decades of contact with the state security apparatus.

A retired aerospace engineer, Zhang's background condemned her to pariah status from the moment the Communists "liberated" China when she was 12. She was descended from a family of high-ranking Qing dynasty officials, the eighth generation to have lived amid the moldering splendor of their ancestral home, a maze of traditional buildings and landscaped gardens the size of 11 soccer fields in Tongcheng in Anhui province in the eastern part of the country. When I asked her how big her family's quarters were in those pre-revolution days, she could only make a rough guess—perhaps 70 or 80 rooms or thereabouts—but she did remember that she had to walk across seven courtyards to get from her family's living quarters to the main entrance. By the time she was 15, the whole compound with its ancient buildings was occupied by the People's Liberation Army, and her family was sent to live in an old grain warehouse.

Her status as part of the landlord class made her a passive participant in China's political movements under Communist rule, during which landowners were demonized as class enemies. She was often a spectator, occasionally a victim, but never a protagonist, feeling that she was not worthy to participate. So great was her sense of original sin—of having, by dint of her birth, grown up exploiting the blood and sweat of ordinary people—that at age 15, she penned a work of self-criticism as long as a novel. Nowadays, however, the open letters she signs are a very different kind of written work. Together with Ding Zilin, a frail but iron-willed former professor of aesthetics at People's University in Beijing, she has transformed herself from victim to activist to moral giant, whose very presence invokes the wrongdoing of the state.

The two women were brought together by shared tragedy after their teenaged sons were shot and killed in Beijing as the night of June 3rd turned into June 4th. They became the founding members of the Tiananmen Mothers, a pioneering group of relatives of those killed that has become the closest thing to a political lobby in China. Their demands are summed up in three simple words, each of which poses a direct challenge to China's Communist leaders: truth, compensation, and accountability. Every year since 1995, they have marked the opening of the rubberstamp legislature, the National People's Congress, with a letter restating their demands. In early June, they write another petition, reminding China's leaders of the anniversary they have done their best to expunge. By 2013, the Tiananmen Mothers had submitted more than three dozen letters. They have never received a single reply.

In addition to being lobbyists, the Tiananmen Mothers have also become detectives, working to compile a list of the victims of the army's onslaught. They have painstakingly confirmed the identities of more than 200 victims who were killed in the crackdown. Zhang Xianling takes pleasure in the small deceits she perpetuates in the pursuit of truth, combining terrier-like tenacity with quiet dignity. But her aptitude for sleuthing is grounded in personal pain; her first quest, which tempered her ability to get beyond her own fear and break through the wall of silence, was to discover exactly how her own beloved son had died.

• • • •

We met at Zhang Xianling's apartment in one of the anonymous utilitarian buildings that make winter in Beijing a canvas of unremitting bleakness. Each time I visited, I was surprised anew to see that the building was actually pink, so well did it blend into the surrounding greyness. Its location on the campus of China's finest music conservatory somewhat alleviated the ugliness, with snatches of music shimmering through the air and students bustling to class clutching unusually shaped instrument cases. Zhang's husband, Wang Fandi, is one of China's foremost teachers of the *pipa*, a traditional instrument similar to a six-stringed banjo. Inside their spotless living room, Wang's *pipa* hung from a stand in one corner below a black-and-white photo of him playing it and looking like a dashing Chinese Fred Astaire. Behind the dining table was a bookcase neatly stacked with books, tape cassettes, and medicine bottles. Perched at eye level on one shelf was a small framed photograph of

Wang Nan, the 19-year-old son they lost, grinning as if he had not a care in the world.

Taking down a shoebox, Zhang unearthed photo after photo of her dead son. In all but one, he is smiling. Teetering on the brink of adulthood, he laughs happily, his eyes shining behind his glasses, cheeks reddened from drinking beer at a friend's birthday party. He was, she said, the kind of boy who loved singing even though he wasn't very good at it; the kind of boy who would carry Thermos flasks of hot water upstairs for his teachers every day, without ever having to be asked. Pictured next to his two serious older brothers, he looks straight into the camera, his expression the very personification of hopeful innocence. As a six-year-old, his eyes crinkle with delight as he sports a huge gap-toothed grin.

However, in the very last photograph ever taken of him, Wang Nan's expression is serious. The picture was taken at military camp in May 1989, and he is wearing a camouflage jacket, a People's Liberation Army cap, beige trousers, and cloth sneakers, with a machine gun casually propped over his shoulder. That year, camp was compulsory for his class; Wang Nan had been as enthusiastic about it as he was about everything else and he was delighted when the soldiers gave him an army belt as a gift. In the photo, he looks like a child playing at being a soldier.

The next thing his mother produced was a tissue-thin white receipt, similar to those grudgingly dispensed by sour-faced shop assistants in state-run emporia. But this receipt was headed "Notice of Death." Beneath that was a box marked "Name of the Deceased," next to which someone had written Wang Nan's name. Under "Reason of Death," someone had scrawled "Shot Outside and Died." Stamped on the form is the official seal of Huguosi Chinese Medicine Hospital. This tersely worded invoice from the bureaucracy of death marked the official end of the life of a young man.

• • • •

In 1989, Wang Nan had received an unexpected kind of political education during his half-hour bus rides between his home near the university district and his school, not far from Tiananmen Square.

Craning out of the bus window, he watched, fascinated, as the bus passed marching students, their banners held high and their fervor for a different kind of future spilling over. As an aspiring photojournalist, he had a ringside seat to history. During his lunch break, he took to rushing to Tiananmen Square to take photos of the student encampments, begging his mother for extra money when he ran out of film. Zhang Xianling tried to warn him not to get too involved. "Don't get too enthusiastic," she cautioned. "Student movements are always used by people."

But by mid-May, Wang Nan had plunged fully into student politics, organizing his high-school classmates to take part in a huge march in support of the hunger strikers. It was typical of his character, his mother noted, that while he led the teenage marchers, he also warned them against shouting the more extreme slogans like "Down with Li Peng!" referring to the unpopular premier.

On the night of June 3rd, family friends came over to the apartment for dinner. As they ate, the main topic of conversation was how the government would clear the students from Tiananmen Square. "Mum, do you think they'll start shooting?" Wang Nan had asked. "Impossible!" she had replied, arguing that China's Communist government had never yet opened fire on its own people, despite the turmoil of the Cultural Revolution.

Later that night, Wang Nan hand washed some of his clothes in a basin. He slept in a separate room in an adjacent building that was visible from the family's apartment, and had been given to them by a quirk in the system of apartment allocation. Before going to bed, he asked his mother to hang out his clothes if the sun were shining the next morning. "I never imagined that would be our last exchange," Zhang Xianling wrote in an essay titled "In Order to Record the Historical Truth," that she composed on the 15th anniversary of her son's death and posted on the Tiananmen Mothers' website. "How could I know that he would never see another sunrise?"

That night, when the shooting began, she could not believe at first that real ammunition was being used. Her disbelief turned to fear as the hours ticked by and gunfire continued to rattle. Looking out of the window to her son's room, she saw his light on and assumed that he was at home. Nonetheless, she slept little, worrying about what was happening on the streets. It was only the next morning when she headed over to Wang Nan's room that she discovered his bed had not been slept in. He had left a note. It read, "Mum, I've gone to find my classmates."

Later, she heard from a neighbor that Wang Nan had slipped out in the middle of the night, wearing military clothes and a red motorcycle helmet, his schoolbag slung over his shoulder. He did not return home that day. Zhang Xianling kept an endless, terrifying vigil, fear colonizing every molecule of her being. Friends came to sit with her and tried to calm her, suggesting that maybe Wang Nan had been arrested. Her husband and other relatives had already begun to visit the capital's hospitals in search of their son. In total, they went to 24 different hospitals. They didn't find Wang Nan, but they saw corpses wrapped up in sheets, dozens of them, in the corridors, including an old lady with bound feet. For 10 endless days, Zhang Xianling received no news of her son.

In fact, her husband was keeping the biggest secret of his life from her. He had been told of their son's death on June 6th, but he had not dared to break the news to his wife, so terrified was he of the depth of her grief. For eight days, he had kept silent, worrying, as he watched her disintegrate, that the truth would destroy her. Zhang Xianling believes that the effort of suppressing his own pain literally broke her husband's heart, leading to the chronic heart disease that has plagued him ever since.

On June 14th, ten days after the killings, Zhang Xianling received the telephone call for which she had been waiting. A staff member from her son's school informed her that a corpse similar to her son in age and appearance had been brought to Huguosi Chinese Medicine Hospital. It had been sent to this small, obscure hospital, she was told, because the mortuaries elsewhere were all full. She went to identify the body. It was her son. A single bullet had ripped into his forehead and emerged behind his left ear, denting his red helmet. His head was bandaged. Someone had tried to stem the bleeding and save his life.

She needed to know how her son had been killed and who had bandaged his head. First though, there was an agonizing wait before Wang Nan's rotting corpse could be cremated. Even in death,

China's bureaucracy had its hold. The family waited one more week before gaining permission for the cremation on June 22nd. On arriving at the crematorium in Babaoshan Revolutionary Cemetery, Zhang Xianling noticed that, more than two weeks after the night of the killings, the forecourt was still filled with vehicles delivering corpses.

Initially, she feared that her grief would destroy her, and that she would choose to do nothing to arrest the precipitous slide of her sanity. Her hair had turned white in the week after her son's body was found. "From that day onward, all my illusions were shattered," she wrote in her essay on the group's website. Then she resolved that her rational side would prevail, and she would channel her pain into a more productive activity. She needed to discover how her son had spent his last hours. After all, he had died in the cause of recording history. So she would force herself to live in order to record the history of his death. If she had been hoping that this would be the first step on a journey toward closure, in fact it took her in the opposite direction.

• • • •

The first witness Zhang Xianling tracked down was a taxi driver who had been near the northwest corner of Tiananmen Square at the intersection of Nanchang Street and Changan Avenue at 1:30 in the morning when the soldiers began to shoot. As the bullets flew, he saw a young man rush forward to take photos. That young man, who turned out to be Wang Nan, was immediately hit and fell to the ground. Several bystanders ran forward to help him but were blocked by the troops, who refused to allow anyone to reach him. After a while, he was dragged to the side of the road by solders. Seeing his face, an old lady dropped to her knees and begged, "He's only a child! Please let us save him!" In reply, a soldier turned to her and said, "He's a rioter. If anyone dares take one step toward him, I'll shoot them."

At that point, two ambulances driving down Nanchang Street were stopped by the soldiers. A doctor got out of one of the ambulances, but was stopped by the troops from helping Wang Nan and two other civilians who had also been shot. The ambulances eventually retreated, leaving the wounded civilians bleeding by the side of the road. This was later confirmed to Zhang Xianling by two other eyewitnesses.

It took her another eight months before she was able to find out what had happened next. The first tip was that someone surnamed Wu had phoned her son's school on the morning of June 4th to report his death. In the phone call, Wu had dropped some clues that eventually led her to identify him as an intern at a Beijing hospital. She tracked him down and wrote to him, asking him to contact her. She did not expect to hear back. Then suddenly one day in January 1990, he turned up at her home with some colleagues. He had brought Wang Nan's house keys and his school ID card.

He told her how, along with two other colleagues, he had decided to volunteer medical support on the night of the crackdown. The three of them had followed in the slipstream of the soldiers. They reached the intersection where Wang Nan had been shot at 2 a.m., half an hour after he was wounded. He was lying by the side of the road, unconscious but with a faint heartbeat. The three interns had asked the soldiers for permission to take Wang Nan and the two other wounded civilians to the hospital, but they were forbidden from doing so. They had only one bandage left, which they used to bind Wang Nan's head. They began artificial respiration, but he had already lost too much blood. He was certified dead at 3:30 a.m. The two other civilians also died by the side of the road.

The interns offered to take the bodies to a hospital where they could be claimed by relatives. Again, the troops prevented them, even threatening the medics with arrest. Before leaving Wang Nan's body, Dr. Wu had pocketed his student ID card to ensure that his parents were informed of his death. At 6 a.m., Dr. Wu called Wang Nan's school to report his death.

The bodies were left lying where they had been shot near the gate of a school, now called 161 High School, on Chang'an Avenue, abutting Zhongnanhai, the compound where the country's top leadership lives. Zhang Xianling pieced together what happened next from the school's night watchman, who said that just after daybreak

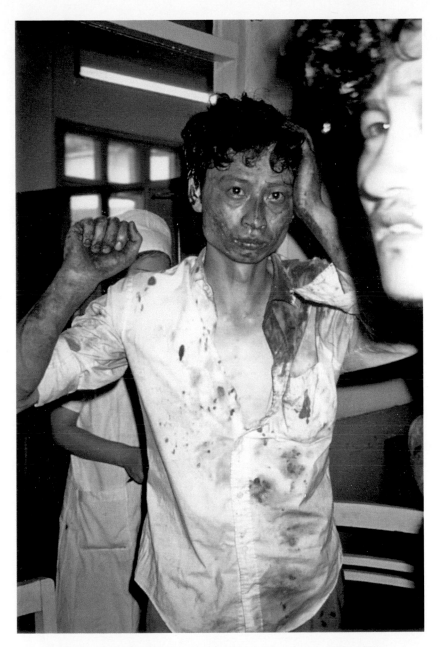

A victim of police brutality clutches his injured head as he waits to receive medical treatment in Chengdu on June 4, 1989. According to official statistics, 8 people were killed and 1,800 injured in Chengdu in clashes with police. This little-known episode has not been written about before now, and these pictures taken by Kim Nygaard have never before been published.

Angry protesters face off against riot police in Chengdu's Tianfu square on June 4, 1989. The pictures Kim Nygaard took (on right) at a Chengdu clinic show the prevalence of head wounds in a vivid illustration of the police strategy of using their batons to target protesters' heads.

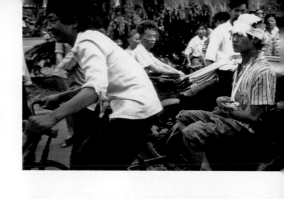

The protest movement spread far beyond Beijing, but that has been largely forgotten. These photos from mid-May show citizens thronging the streets of Chengdu bearing banners with slogans including "Power Belongs to the People." Students later occupied Chengdu's Tianfu Square, staging a hunger strike at the foot of the Chairman Mao statue.

Thousands took to the streets of Chengdu on June 4, 1989 in a brave protest against the killings in Beijing. The authorities used tear gas and stun grenades to try to disperse the marchers, but fighting broke out. Police were massively outnumbered and were forced to withdraw to government buildings, which were attacked by crowds, as in the middle left picture. Overnight, the city was plunged into chaos, with angry citizens setting fire to government property.

This photo, known as Tank Man, by AP's Jeff Widener, is the iconic representation of the Tiananmen movement in the West. Yet in China, few young people can even identify it, so deep is the chasm of knowledge surrounding the events of 1989. Out of 100 Beijing university students, only 15 recognized this shot.

A photo taken by soldier Chen Guang shows flames licking through Tiananmen Square, as soldiers burned all reminders of the students' occupation. This was taken on June 4, 1989 after the students had left the square. It—like the picture overleaf—shows the square inhabited by martial law troops, whose only task was destruction. Overleaf, the troops are clearing the steps to the Monument to the People's Heroes, which had been the students' headquarters.

Soldier-turned-artist Chen Guang still remains gripped by the events he witnessed as a member of the martial law troops clearing the square. The commemorative wristwatch featured in his triptych was given to soldiers to celebrate their role in suppressing the student movement. His sketch of tanks in front of Tiananmen Gate is based on a photo he took in 1989.

Chen Guang pictured in his former studio. Below is one of his photos showing food being airlifted into Tiananmen Square to feed the hungry soldiers billeted in the Great Hall of the People. His vivid memory of gnawing hunger in the days immediately follow- ing June 4th is borne out by official PLA accounts of the crackdown.

Zhang Xianling is a founder of the Tiananmen Mothers, a pressure group consisting of relatives of those who were killed on June 4, 1989. Her nineteen-year-old son, Wang Nan, was shot in the head; a fact noted on his death notice, which states "Shot Outside and Died" as the reason for his death. It incorrectly lists the date of his death as June 3, 1989. After being shot, Wang Nan died by the side of a road, after being denied medical assistance or transport by ambulance to hospital. His body was perfunctorily buried by martial law troops in a flowerbed near the entrance to a school, in the bottom left picture. His rotting body was disinterred days later, after it began to smell.

Clockwise from top left: Bao Tong was the highest official to be jailed in 1989, spending seven years in solitary confinement. He lives in Beijing under strict surveillance.
Zhang Ming was number 19 on China's Most Wanted list. He is still suffering the physical effects of two prison terms.
Ding Zilin is the public face of the Tiananmen Mothers, photographed in front of a pedestal holding the ashes of her seventeen-year-old son.
Former student leader, Wu'er Kaixi, who fled into exile in 1989, being interviewed by a Taiwanese newspaper.

A photograph taken by Chen Guang showing troops and tanks lined up in front of Tiananmen Gate. The Gate of Heavenly Peace had reverted to become the Gate of Heaven's Pacification.

soldiers had knocked on the school gate. They had asked to borrow spades and then proceeded to dig a shallow grave in the flowerbed beside the school entrance. That was where Wang Nan's body was peremptorily buried, along with the two other nameless victims killed by troops that night.

Rain began to fall on the morning of June 4th and continued sporadically. By June 7th, a stench was emanating from the shallow grave, and the clothes of the dead had begun to poke up through the newly turned muddy soil. The school was scheduled to reopen in five days, so the fact that decomposing corpses were clearly buried in front of its entrance posed a major problem. The school authorities contacted the local police and the health department, which sent people to dig up the three bodies. Because of his age, his army clothing, and his military belt, Wang Nan was mistaken for a soldier, so his body was sent to a hospital instead of being immediately cremated as an unidentified rioter. For this small mercy that saved her from a lifetime of uncertainty, Zhang Xianling remains grateful.

But she was appalled that her son had lain dying on the street while being refused treatment or even human comfort by the very soldiers who had shot him. "Even in wartime, it would be unprincipled not to let an ambulance treat the injured," she wrote in her essay. "But on Beijing's Chang'an Avenue, the government not only used tanks and guns to shoot people, it didn't allow the wounded to be saved. Are they human?"

For Zhang Xianling, each new piece of painstakingly uncovered information brought added torment.

"I try not to think about it," she told me. "If I think about it, I'm unable to sleep for several days," admitting that the night before my first visit, she hadn't been able to stop herself crying as she looked for material about Wang Nan. "I'm sure he spent his final hours in a lot of pain. I remember in one of the earliest articles I wrote about my child that I described him as he lay dying on the ground, and maybe he was thinking, 'Mama, I'm really cold. I'm really cold.'" Her voice had dropped to a whisper. "When I think about that, I still get very sad."

But that process of discovery changed her. "I started to have doubts about the Chinese Communist Party. I began to have a lot of questions about the principles that had been poured into my brain for decades, and that spurred me to study and to think," she wrote. "I slowly travelled out of my own personal pain. And I channeled this pain into a kind of bravery for finding the truth, for seeking justice. It supported me as I walked along this difficult road. The pain of mourning a child can never fade from one's memory, but sharing others' pain can lessen one's own pain." Along this road, her constant companion and inspiration has been Ding Zilin, whose 17-year-old son was shot in the back by the PLA.

• • • •

The two founders of the Tiananmen Mothers were as different in looks as they were in character. Ding Zilin was frail and slender, emanating grief as she moved stiffly around the apartment that had become the last resting place of her son Jiang Jielian. Her home in Beijing's university district was an airy flat decorated with elegant traditional Chinese furniture and carved totem poles used as hat-stands. An oil painting on the wall captured her son as a tall, lanky young man with a strong chin and a confident smile, waving a banner and wearing the red marchers' headband of which he had been so proud—and with which he had been cremated.

He had been frozen in time in a photo on the next wall, marching for eternity hand-in-hand with fellow students from his school. Like Zhang Xianling's son, he too had been enthusiastic about the movement, and had organized students from his school to march in support of the university students. My eye was drawn to a paper sign held up by one of his fellow marchers, its thick black calligraphy written with a traditional ink brush but bearing a very un-Confucian threat to China's rulers: "You will fall from power, we will still be here!" As if in rebuke to such youthful confidence, the photo looked down upon the engraved pedestal holding the ashes of Ding Zilin's serious, broad-shouldered son.

At the lowest point in their lives, Ding Zilin and Zhang Xianling found each other. They had been put in touch by an official from the Jiusan Society, a Communist-approved Potemkin political party whose membership of intellectuals and scientists included both of their husbands. In an irony that the Communist Party is unlikely to appreciate, this rubberstamp party, set up to foster the illusion of political plurality, was the catalyst for the formation of the Tiananmen Mothers, which went on to become a political force in its own right as one of the first and most prominent grassroots groupings outside the Chinese government's control.

At the beginning, the two families grieved together. Ding Zilin was in a worse state, physically incapacitated to such an extent that she could only move about her apartment by groping her way along the walls. On the night of June 3rd, she had spent two hours trying to persuade her son not to go out. Eventually, he locked himself in the ground-floor bathroom and snuck out the window. Less than three hours later, he was dead, a bullet through his back. Ding Zilin felt she had failed to protect him. Death was in her thoughts always; she hoarded sleeping pills. Then one day, Zhang Xianling and her husband bicycled over to visit, and gradually the two women began to discover a new purpose.

In 1991, they gave their first interview to the U.S. network ABC, describing how their sons had died. It was an act of bravery, the first time anyone inside China had gone public with a detailed account of a June 4th death, and both knew that there would be consequences. Both were subsequently warned against speaking out; Zhang Xianling was told that her husband might be barred from traveling abroad for concerts. She was so scared that she decided to stop giving interviews. "I'll keep on searching for people," Ding Zilin remembers her saying, "But when it comes to handling external stuff, you be the front line, and I'll be the second line. If anything should happen to you, I'll take up the slack." In Zhang Xianling's mind, this was also a pragmatic move to ensure the group's existence, since there was no point in both of them being detained. The concomitant risks of their campaign mean that the Tiananmen Mothers are overwhelmingly female, partly due to the economic necessity for the men to safeguard household incomes by staying away from politics, and partly, Zhang Xianling believes, because of the driving power of a mother's love.

"I respected her decision," Ding Zilin told me simply. Since that day, Ding Zilin has become the group's public face, braving surveillance, detentions, harassment, forced retirement, accusations of treachery, and expulsion from the Communist Party after 32 years of membership. During the long years before Zhang Xianling was ready to speak to the media again, Ding Zilin alone bore the burden, backed up by her husband, who was forced into retirement soon after she was.

Ding Zilin has borne her responsibility with extraordinary fortitude given her physical frailty and emotional vulnerability. Every mention of her son makes her voice thicken and tears spring to her eyes. Yet she has continued to force herself to excavate her anguish on a daily basis to keep the Tiananmen Mothers' mission alive. The Mothers have worked to compile a list of names of those killed by the government troops, an act that challenges the Communist Party's monopoly on information. Though Ding Zilin began this work almost immediately, the women were spurred into real action after hearing Premier Li Peng speak during a televised press conference in 1991. When he was asked if the government would release a list of the names of those killed in 1989, he replied, "The family members of the dead are reluctant to have their names disclosed because they view the event as an anti-government riot. We must respect their wishes." Zhang Xianling was seized with white-hot rage. She immediately telephoned the duty manager of the television station. "I heard Li Peng's answer," she told him. "That's a barefaced lie. My child died on June the fourth. I don't think it's harming my image. I demand that name-list is released." She left her contact details at the station, but no one ever called back.

Since then, the Mothers have tracked down 202 victims, each with their own story. It has been a painstakingly slow process hindered by silence, stonewalling, and the remodeling of Beijing into a modern city. Often the women would receive leads in the form of names and addresses, yet on arrival at the designated spot, they would find the entire neighborhood razed to the ground, its inhabitants scattered without a trace.

Over time, worries about government retribution and the profound taboos surrounding June 4th had solidified to such an extent that some families would rather disown their own offspring than admit they had been killed that night. Zhang Xianling was shocked by one phone call in particular, with a husband and wife, both teachers, who had moved to Guangzhou after their son's death on June 4th. She had been hoping to confirm the details of what had happened to their son, but the boy's mother refused to speak.

"Her attitude to me was fine, but she said, 'We don't want to bring this matter up. We're living a nice life. We don't want to talk about this stuff.' Then the father said, 'What's all this about?' I heard his voice by the phone. The mother said, 'She's asking about so-and-so—their son. Then the father grabbed the phone and said, 'It's none of your business. We have a good life! Don't give us any trouble!' And he hung up."

Such a reaction mirrored the wider reality in the post-Tiananmen years of suppression. For the majority, the tanks and guns removed any safe options except one: to stop talking about the past; to allow material gains to trump all else; and to become silent accomplices to the cover-up. Forgetting is a skill that older Chinese are practiced in, with the net of history stretched so wide that whole decades sometimes fell through the gaps. As time passed, the siege mentality built a closed, paranoid world that Zhang compares to that of the mafia, "Those in the mob have a similar kind of feeling. They've been terrorized. So they are afraid. Their sense of self-preservation is stronger than their sense of justice."

That was even true within Zhang Xianling's own family. To begin with, her two other sons were reluctant to come home. She understood that they needed to distance themselves for the sake of their own futures.

"They're still alive and they need to live in this system," she told me. The system would punish them for their blood ties with Wang Nan, whose posthumous label as a "counterrevolutionary rioter" put a black mark in his brothers' files, limiting their employment options in certain government and academic circles.

The ripples from Wang Nan's death even touched China's top leadership; Zhang Xianling's younger sister was married to one of the most powerful men in China at that time. Ding Guan'gen had reached the heady heights of alternate Politburo member, one of just 16 men who could attend Politburo meetings. More importantly perhaps, he was bridge partner to Deng Xiaoping, the paramount leader who was at that time chairman of the Central Military Commission. This relationship was widely believed to explain Ding Guan'gen's decade-long stint as the party's propaganda chief from 1992 to 2002.

Ding Guan'gen was shaken by Wang Nan's death, though at his funeral, he tried to shift the blame. "How could we have been so unfortunate?" he asked Zhang Xianling. "How could Wang Nan have died? Why weren't you watching him?" Later, his way of showing sympathy was to paint Wang Nan's death as an unavoidable cost of Communist rule. "So many people died under the Communists!" He would tell Zhang, reminding her of the cruel fate of Liu Shaoqi, the former premier hounded to death in 1969 during the Cultural Revolution. "His family doesn't bear a grudge against Chairman Mao's family! In fact, they have good ties now. This isn't just about your family!" Zhang Xianling listened in silence. By 2004, when her activism had stepped up a notch, her sister stopped talking to her. When Ding Guan'gen died in 2012, Zhang did not attend his funeral.

The events of June 4th remain so taboo that, merely by raising them, Zhang Xianling and Ding Zilin sometimes made themselves targets. In one incident, Zhang Xianling used a subterfuge—pretending to return a handkerchief and some money—to track down a young man who had died. She managed to get confirmation from the neighborhood committee that he was "the one who was shot." But when she found his apartment, the brother of the deceased began berating her, shouting angrily, "What right do you have to come looking for me after all these years?"

Fear of trouble, fear of chaos; these were the levers that China's leaders used to justify their repression, and afterward, playing on fear of the unknown served to convince many that the violence had been necessary, especially with the retrospective knowledge of the three decades of double-digit economic growth delivered by continued Communist Party rule.

Most of the time, though, the elderly women were welcomed, in part because they function as a traditional support group, disbursing funds received through donations—sometimes as much as $800 a year—to families that are destitute or burdened by medical expenses. More often, though, the support is emotional, allowing families the chance to unburden themselves after years of secret anguish.

• • • •

Their mission has forced the Tiananmen Mothers to face off against the full power of the state security apparatus, which has steadily expanded in the post-Tiananmen years. Just five days after the crackdown, when Deng Xiaoping congratulated the troops at the Great Hall of the People, he made it clear that in the future, protests should be nipped in the bud. "From now on, we should pay attention when handling such problems. As soon as a trend emerges, we should not allow it to spread."

With those words, the "era of stability maintenance" was born. According to available figures, starting in 2011, China has spent more on domestic stability than on its military. For local officials, maintaining internal stability means ensuring that there are no large protests, no troublesome dissidents, and no petitioners lodging complaints about local government behavior. In management-speak, "maintaining stability" has become one of the success criteria for officials' careers; squelching dissent—by whatever means necessary—is rewarded with promotion, while failure to do so can end a promising career. Extra funds are disbursed for stability maintenance, making the incentives for repression political, personal, and financial.

For the Tiananmen Mothers, the first major crisis came as Beijing hosted the United Nations World Conference on Women in 1995, when Ding Zilin and her husband were detained. Zhang Xianling had vowed to be the second line of defense, but she had little idea what to do next, having no contacts within the foreign media. To avoid being monitored by police, she called a meeting with other Tiananmen Mothers on top of a hill in Zizhuyuan Park in northwest Beijing. There, they drafted an open letter calling for Ding Zilin's release that they posted to President Jiang Zemin. Ding

Zilin and her husband spent almost six weeks in detention, accused of "economic irregularities," until a lobbying effort spearheaded by Hillary Clinton, then the First Lady of the United States, who attended the Beijing's Women's Conference, secured her release.

In 1998, the authorities froze a donation of around $6,500 sent by Chinese students studying in Germany. One lesson China's leaders had learned from the collapse of the Soviet Union and its Communist satellites involved the impact of non-government organizations, especially those with support from outside. Fear—even paranoia—about such outside groups was to have very direct consequences for the Tiananmen Mothers. They were outraged by the freeze put on their funds, so they wrote a letter to the minister of state security. But so secretive was the ministry that they could not find its physical location, even though Zhang Xianling and an elderly Tiananmen father spent hours wandering the streets of Beijing looking for it. Though state security agents listened to their telephone calls and monitored their computers, trailing them to doctors' appointments and keeping them under house arrest, they never managed to find the offices of the ministry that ordered this treatment.

In 1999, the group submitted a legal petition to the Supreme People's Procuratorate, a body similar to a public prosecutor, accusing Premier Li Peng of having committed crimes against humanity. They never received an official response. That year, some of the mothers began holding a memorial on June 4th at Wan'an Cemetery, a public cemetery located on the western outskirts of Beijing, where the ashes of some of the victims have been interred. Most years, uniformed policemen drove Zhang Xianling and her husband to the graveyard in a police car. At the cemetery, the Mothers have learned how to pick out the dozens of plainclothes policemen mingling in the crowds, whose only job is to monitor just over a dozen mourners.

Even this most personal of acts has been made political by the government's interdictions. One memorable year—1998—Zhang Xianling managed to hold her own small remembrance at the exact spot on the sidewalk outside the school where her son had died. The next year, she was prevented from leaving her apartment. When I met her more than a decade later, she talked about the prospect of being able to mourn her son at the place where he died, using the dreamy language of fantasy. "I'd like to go at eight or nine in the evening. If no one were watching me, I'd go at night. I'd pour some liquor onto the ground, then I'd scatter white flower petals there on the ground."

However, someone will always be watching her. A closed-circuit camera has been installed near the school's entrance, trained on the exact spot where her son's body was exhumed from the flowerbed beside the school gate. It is a camera dedicated to her alone, waiting for her in case she should ever try again to mourn her dead son. "That's the action of someone with a guilty conscience," she said.

Such is the moral vulnerability of China's Communist leaders that this simple act of memory is deemed a threat to stability. The power of the mothers' bereavement is perceived as such a threat that their mourning needs to be corralled and monitored to protect the rest of the population from their grief. None of this has been lost on Zhang Xianling, who summed up her situation with typical brio, "Such a great, glorious and correct party is afraid of a little old lady. It shows how powerful we are, this group of old people, because we represent righteousness. They represent evil. So they're afraid of us. We are not afraid of them."

• • • •

Under the steady guidance of these elderly women, the Tiananmen Mothers has grown into a political and moral force similar to the Mothers of the Plaza del Mayo in Argentina. By capitalizing on the unwillingness of the authorities to repress those who have already suffered so much, the Mothers have carved out a small space, which they have slowly expanded, broadening their focus to human rights and political issues. Some of the mothers, particularly the founding members, regularly sign petitions, such as the landmark Charter '08, which was a bold manifesto calling for political reforms—including an independent legal system, freedom of association, and an end to one-party rule. Among certain dissident circles, being included among the original 300 signatories was a badge of honor. Ding Zilin was the 12th name on the list, Zhang Xianling the 13th. "Such an unlucky number!" she chuckled.

They were asked to sign by Liu Xiaobo, the writer who was awarded China's first Nobel Peace Prize. The act of collecting these signatures—along with six articles he had written—became the cornerstone of the 11-year prison sentence he was given in 2009 on charges of inciting subversion of state power. It is a measure of the Tiananmen Mothers' stature that Liu himself had spent years lobbying for them to be awarded the Nobel Prize. Days before he was detained in 2008, he was still trying to figure out ways to nominate them. This was something that Ding Zilin had opposed vigorously. "Xiaobo, you can't do that! It's too dangerous!" she had told him. "You know that if you promote us, the Tiananmen Mothers can't support the historical burden of the Nobel Prize." She also feared what would happen to Liu should the Tiananmen Mothers actually win. She believed that the Communist Party felt it was already indebted to the Tiananmen Mothers, owing each of them a life for those killed in 1989, and so was less likely to visit retribution on them. "But they already hate you," she warned Liu Xiaobo. "What would happen if a hundred times more hate and madness were to fall on your body?"

Ding Zilin spoke about Liu Xiaobo with the exasperated familiarity of a mother complaining about a stubborn child. Their bond, she has written, goes deeper than a blood tie. Her husband, Jiang Peikun, had been one of Liu Xiaobo's thesis advisors back when he was making his name as a brash, abrasive literary critic taking on the world. Many an afternoon, he would be in their apartment debating with her husband when their son returned home from school. But her relationship with Liu Xiaobo has been by turns fractious and fractured.

I asked Ding Zilin what kind of influence Liu Xiaobo had had on the Tiananmen Mothers, and whether their ideas had been shaped by this man who has become one of China's preeminent intellectuals. Somewhat to my surprise, she cut me off. "I'm sorry. Liu Xiaobo didn't have any influence on me." He's not like me, she went on. "He likes the limelight too much." Zhang Xianling remembered only Liu's social awkwardness, his stuttering and brusqueness. Neither seemed to rate his essays very highly—Ding Zilin dismissed him as being too prolix, too cocky, though she admitted that his attitude toward the Tiananmen Mothers was one of humility and reverence, both words she did not readily associate with him.

To Liu Xiaobo, a writer obsessed with the concepts of responsibility, repentance, and redemption, the very existence of the Tiananmen Mothers may have seemed a personal reproach. He had played a key role in getting the last students to leave Tiananmen Square on June 4th. He was partway through a hunger strike that he had started with three others on June 2nd, yet he—like all the most famous activists—had escaped the crackdown without a scratch. After the killings, he was even said to be in high spirits, joking, smoking nonstop, and even riding a bicycle around the city as if to taunt the authorities.

On June 6th, Liu was knocked from his bike, forced into a van, and taken to prison. He subsequently spent 18 months in Qincheng Prison, where he described himself as having been "deathly bored." While still in prison, in September 1989, Liu Xiaobo gave an interview to Chinese state television in which he asserted that nobody had died in Tiananmen Square. He later wrote that he had decided to appear on television because exiled leaders like Wu'er Kaixi were exaggerating the bloodshed on the square to build themselves up as heroes. Liu knew the authorities would use footage of his words in their propaganda campaign, and he knew it would damage his reputation, but at the time, he felt it was his responsibility to history.

It was only on his release from prison in 1991 that Liu discovered that his own teacher's son had been killed that night. Moreover, Ding Zilin had seen his interview and was enraged by his willingness to make such a sweeping statement. "It's alright to say that you didn't see anyone dying," she told me, her voice still knife-sharp with anger, "but how can you say nobody died on the square?" After his release, Liu visited the flat of Ding and Jiang to mourn their son's death. As he knelt in front of the pedestal containing the ashes, he wept for having let down this boy. He then went out to buy flowers to place in front of the pedestal. Ding saw this as an admission of his own wrongdoing and forgave him. But she still felt bitter. After all, Liu Xiaobo's hunger strike—derided in Mayor Chen Xitong's report as a "farce"—was partly aimed at allowing the intellectuals to snatch back some of the initiative, and the publicity, from the students. Undeniably, it had been part of the escalating spiral of tensions that ended up unleashing the PLA onto its own people. Ding Zilin believed Liu Xiaobo shared some moral responsibility for her son's death; had he persuaded the students to leave the square earlier; had he not called a hunger strike; had events somehow played out differently, perhaps her boy would still be alive.

Her anger hit home. On the second anniversary of the killings, in the foreword of a poem for Jiang Jielian, Liu Xiaobo wrote, "In the face of your death, living is a crime, and writing this poem for you is an even greater shame."

The poem was in itself a self-criticism:

> I alive
> and with my share of infamy
> have not the courage, nor the right
> to come bearing flowers or words
> before your seventeen-year-old smile

In an essay dating from 1991, Liu Xiaobo wrote, "When we look at those 'Tiananmen Mothers' who so tirelessly persist in seeking justice for victims, can elite survivors like us not show a bit more compassion, a better sense of equality and justice, by being sure that moral credit goes to those people who suffered far more than we did, and to whom such credit in the first place rightly belongs?"

Liu also turned his pitiless glare onto the other student leaders and activists, whom he chided as being "opportunists large and small" especially when viewed against the quiet dignity of the Tiananmen Mothers. "Why is it that we scarcely hear the voices of the people who paid the heaviest prices, while the luminaries who survived the massacre can hardly stop talking?"

Ding Zilin, for one, was not impressed. She felt that Liu's effusions were self-serving, especially given the number of essays he was churning out. Her attitude toward him was harsh, she admits. After he was released from a later prison term, Ding Zilin refused to see him for several years, despite his repeated pleas that he should be allowed to make an apology to her. Besides her frustration at what she saw as his insincerity, she feared the consequences of his refusal to stop writing excoriating criticisms of the Communist Party. She repeated to me what she had told him: "I gave you the chance to voice a self-criticism. I accepted your empty words. I accepted your tears. I accepted your foolish kneeling in front of my son's ashes. I accepted all of this and forgave you. So why did you go on writing these essays?"

On Liu's Nobel Peace Prize, both women are plainspoken. "I would never have imagined it," said Zhang Xianling bluntly. The prize was a gift from the Communist Party, they both believe, sealed by the 11-year jail sentence he received in 2009. He is a creature defined by his defiance of the party. And so, as Zhang Xianling points out, are the Tiananmen Mothers. "If the Communist Party hadn't repressed the Tiananmen Mothers, we wouldn't be here today. If after the killings, they had apologized and resolved the issue legally, we probably wouldn't exist. All of this is created by them."

• • • •

Zhang Xianling's own crisis came in March 2004 when she was detained, along with two others. It all happened, she explained, because of the T-shirts. Some supporters in Hong Kong had sent her three boxes of T-shirts printed with Tiananmen Mothers' logos. Before she even managed to open them, two policemen and three plainclothes security agents had swooped into her apartment and presented her with a summons. As she was led downstairs, the sight of three police cars in the courtyard made her realize that the trouble she had always feared had literally arrived on her doorstep.

She was taken to a police detention center, which she describes as "a three-star bed and breakfast" for interrogation. She was photographed, fingerprinted, and handcuffed. "The righteous always suffer," she told them indignantly, invoking South African President Nelson Mandela, who spent 27 years in jail. Take off your belt, the police told her, ignoring her words, and take off any clothing with buttons or metal fastenings. The charge against her, she was told, was inciting subversion of state power, a catchall offense often used against dissidents. Far from scaring Zhang Xianling, this news awakened her mordant wit. "I said, 'Wah! You guys have given me too much credit. You think a little old lady like me can subvert state power?'"

The crux of the issue, as she discovered during her interrogations, appeared to be the T-shirts, which preoccupied her interrogator, Officer Tian. "He said, 'You might wear those T-shirts and go to protest, and let some foreign journalists take pictures.' I said, 'Wow! Officer Tian, that's a great plan! We didn't even think of that. We should have invited you when we were planning. We don't even know any foreign journalists. Maybe you can find some for us.'"

For four days and three nights, she remained in police detention as the authorities tried to construct a case. One other Tiananmen Mother had been detained in Beijing, as well as Ding Zilin who was being held in the city of Wuxi. Prospects were looking dim, especially when reports by the Xinhua news agency claimed Ding Zilin had confessed that the women had "conspired with overseas forces to evade Chinese customs and state security laws." But the detention of the three Tiananmen Mothers sparked a flurry of international condemnation that led to their release without charge.

Like the waning and waxing of the moon, the cycles of repression and relaxation have become a constant backdrop to Zhang Xianling's life. Her response has been to wage her own public education campaign on her watchers. On the 20th anniversary of the crackdown, when three shifts of people a day were sharing the watching responsibilities, she decided it was too good an opportunity to miss. She photocopied two articles she had written and distributed them to all the policemen and plainclothes agents, telling them, "You guys are the ones watching me, but you don't know why you're watching me, do you? I'll give you this information so you know why." She discovered that some of them had no idea what had happened on June 4th, and one—a young female student from the Police Academy—even abandoned her post in disgust after discovering the reason she was there. "There is nothing we can do about this," another watcher told her. "We were sent here by our superiors. They're all messed up. Their brains are all addled."

The resources expended on watching Zhang Xianling and some of the other mothers made her wonder just how messed up the system really was. This feeling was magnified when she and her husband experienced a security maintenance innovation: the enforced holiday. A police officer had approached them with an order couched as an offer: The security forces were spread too thin to watch them properly, they were told, so would they mind taking a short trip? It was an Orwellian kind of holiday, since they were accompanied by a police officer as they traveled to the southwestern province of Yunnan. The officer ate meals with them, stayed in the same hotel, and paid all their bills. When meeting others, they passed him off as a friend because they thought telling the truth might embarrass the police officer and cause him to lose face.

For Zhang Xianling, it was yet one more example of the colossal waste of public funds, though she realized that by using just one person to watch them all week, the local authorities were able to reassign many others to the task of watching other potential threats to stability. She was, nonetheless, outraged. "I'm just one person, but how many other people are there in China under the stability maintenance system? It wastes the money made through people's blood and sweat."

In 2009, the Tiananmen Mothers received an unexpected overture from a relatively low-level policeman. He approached several members to ask whether it might be possible that the issue of compensation be dealt with on an individual basis, rather than as a group. They turned the offer down flat, seeing it as an attempt to buy their silence. Zhang Xianling believes that money has clouded people's consciences in China. It has taken her group a quarter-century to track down just over two hundred victims, but she believes that if money were on the table—government compensation to families of the victims—the result would be entirely different. "If the government told everyone to register, saying victims of June 4th will be given compensation, then they'd sprout up like spring bamboo after the rain, saying, 'Oh my family has! Oh, my family has!'"

• • • •

Twenty-five years later, perhaps the greatest challenge facing the Tiananmen Mothers is the simple passage of time. At least 33 of their members—a full fifth of their complement—have been claimed by heart attacks, strokes, cancer, and other illnesses. The depredations of old age, depression, and caring for elderly spouses have eaten away at their spare time, leaving precious little energy to expend on the diminishing leads to track down new members. There is no way of sugarcoating the hard truth that a quarter-century of effort has not produced any change in the Chinese government's stance; if anything, it has hardened its position.

In 2012, the desperation born from two decades of profound grief gained its first victim. Seventy-three-year-old Ya Weilin had been one of the party faithful, spending his entire life working for China's nuclear industry. He had even named his son Aiguo, or "Patriot." Patriot died after being shot in the head by soldiers as he was returning home from shopping with his girlfriend. After that, Ya Weilin became an active participant in the Tiananmen Mothers, signing all the petitions and waiting for a response. But over time, he had lost hope.

Zhang Xianling had last seen him at Chinese New Year four months before his death. He was gloomy and dispirited, asking her whether she thought the Tiananmen Mothers would ever win any kind of resolution from the state. She had assured him that it was just a matter of time. Even to her ears, that mantra, uttered so confidently in the years following the crackdown, was sounding increasingly hollow. But he had concurred, muttering, "You have to keep on living." At the time, she had taken the words as a standard response, though afterward, she realized they may have been a cry for help.

By the end of May 2012, he had been dreaming of his son, Patriot, for days. His wife had already found a note he had written about the bleakness of passing 23 years without justice. She knew his state of mind, but she also knew that she could do nothing. On May 24th, 2012, he said goodbye to his wife, and then walked downstairs to a newly built underground garage beneath his housing complex. There he hanged himself. It was the group's first protest death, timed shortly before the anniversary for maximum publicity. The group issued a stunned statement, "We want to cry but have no more tears; we want to tell the world but have no more words."

Cognizant of their mortality, the Tiananmen Mothers have begun their own internal power transition, bringing younger members—widows of the dead rather than parents—to the forefront to try to prolong the group's longevity.

• • • •

For the past quarter-century, campaigners in Hong Kong—which hosts the only annual June 4th vigil on Chinese soil—have made their primary demand a reappraisal of the student movement. They are calling for the Communist Party to overturn its verdict on the 1989 movement as "counterrevolutionary," and instead endorse it as patriotic. Such an approach is controversial, since it not only recognizes the Communist Party's legitimacy, but also appoints it as historical arbiter.

While the mothers support the Hong Kong campaigners, privately they say that they believe such an approach is feudal in its insistence that redressing wrongs is the preserve of the ruler. "I think due to China's long feudal history, many people look too much to the 'imperial court,'" Zhang Xianling told me. "They always hope for an enlightened leader, or an honest general, to bring about another Golden Age. That's not going to happen. This is not an imperial age. We are our own masters. The people are their own sovereigns, yet you turn to the Communist Party as an emperor. Isn't that kind of thinking a bit behind the times?"

In their open letter marking the 24th anniversary of the crackdown, the Tiananmen Mothers seemed to invoke the "power of the powerless," as christened by the Czech dissident-turned-President Vaclev Havel. "Even though the authorities pretend to see and hear nothing, they cannot ban this kind of appeal month by month, year by year. The appeal gets passed down through the Internet, media, and the people. It simply cannot be banned, suppressed, deleted, or blocked."

Despite this long-term prediction, this letter, titled "Hope Fades as Despair Draws Near," is noteworthy for its bleak mood, reflecting the dashed hopes that the incoming President Xi Jinping might undertake political reform. "What we see, precisely, are giant steps backwards towards Maoist orthodoxy," the mothers wrote, in a reference to President Xi Jinping's warning that repudiating Chairman Mao would cause chaos. Their damning conclusion is that "Mr Xi Jinping categorically does not care about the tens of millions of lives of his fellow countrymen."

Back in 1989, both Zhang Xianling and Ding Zilin had assumed it would only take a couple of years before the official verdict on the demonstrations as "counterrevolutionary riots" was reversed. To them, it was so black and white that they assumed it would be in the party's interest to deal with it quickly. There was also a precedent. In April 1976, demonstrations in the square following the death of Premier Zhou Enlai were initially dubbed "counterrevolutionary riots" but then reassessed as "patriotic" two years later after Deng Xiaoping took over the reins of power.

Over time, however, it has become clear that China's subsequent rulers remain too dependent on the legitimacy derived from Deng to consider any kind of reappraisal of the student movement, especially given the continuing survival of so many of the key decision-makers. "It's possible that before I leave this world, I won't see justice," Ding Zilin told me, "but as long as I am alive and have strength, I can't abandon it." It is a view shared by Zhang Xianling, who in her dotage appears to be mustering energy to continue the struggle. "Now I'm more mentally prepared. It's a war of attrition. As long as I'm alive, I'll still be doing this." Her aim, she told me, was to be like Song Mei-ling, the widow of China's Nationalist leader Chiang Kai-shek, who lived to 106.

The possibility that their struggle could lead to jail is a risk that all the members of the Tiananmen Mothers have long faced. Though their struggle carries fewer risks now than it did at the beginning, it is still a hazardous path. "When you're fighting against such powerful organs of the state, there are bound to be sacrifices," maintained Zhang Xianling. "I was ready. Even now. Some people say the darkest time is just before dawn. I hope the darkness doesn't fall on me. But if it does, I'm ready."

• • • •

Within China, the Tiananmen Mothers are a tiny band of aging campaigners, a miniscule island among an ocean of people who have never heard of them or, increasingly, of the killings on June 4th. In Hong Kong, however, they are rock stars. In the run-up to the 2013 anniversary, Zhang Xianling had been scheduled to accompany her husband to the territory for a *pipa* competition. Getting ready for the trip, she had even gone to the trouble of getting her hair permed. But the day before she was due to travel, she was forbidden from leaving the country. After I attended the June 4th vigil in Hong Kong in 2013, I began to get an inkling of why the central authorities might have been nervous about her presence on the island.

Hours before the vigil was due to start, thousands upon thousands of people were streaming into the large Hong Kong park where it was to be held. They sat obediently in lines, clutching their candles expectantly, quietly studying leaflets with background information about the events of 1989. On one side of the park hung a big orange banner exhorting people to "Support the Tiananmen Mothers," and dotted around the park were stalls selling T-shirts for aid to the mothers or collecting donations for them. The latest T-shirt design was a typically in-your-face Hong Kong motif, featuring a line of tanks being stopped by an elderly woman clutching a bunch of flowers. The words read, "Don't let the Tiananmen Mothers Resist Alone." More popular still was the Tiananmen Mothers T-shirt from the previous year that was sported on thousands of young chests.

Just minutes before the rally's official opening, the sky darkened and a violent thunderstorm exploded above the park, knocking out all the electrical equipment. Despite the fact that there was no sound system, despite the driving rain extinguishing the sputtering candles, and despite the thunder cracking overhead and the lightning zigzagging through the sky, the crowd stood firm, shouting, "We will never forget!"

After about 15 minutes, the waterlogged vigil was canceled because of the electrical storm, though small clumps of people remained behind, singing anthems in the rain. As I sloshed past a stall selling Tiananmen Mothers T-shirts, it suddenly occurred to me that I should take a couple back to China as a souvenir for the group's founding members.

When I dropped them off at Zhang Xianling's house, she was visibly delighted. "I haven't seen one of these in years!" she declared. "After the incident when we got detained because of the T-shirts, no one dared send us any more." Then I took out my camera to show her pictures of the rally, and she stopped talking for a while. "Wah! So many people!" she finally said, her voice filled with wonder. "That's amazing! I had no idea so many people would be there." In fact, due to the driving rain, the organizers put the numbers at 150,000, some 30,000 fewer than the year before, though police estimates were lower.

I was surprised. "Haven't you seen pictures on the Internet?" "My Internet is too slow," she replied. "And it's monitored, so you can't really see foreign websites. And I don't speak English, so it's hard to visit overseas sites." In fact, her computer was so decrepit that a fan was trained on the hard drive in the hot summer months to prevent it from overheating.

I told her about the banners for the Tiananmen Mothers and the thousands of people wearing their T-shirts and clutching candles, the solemn atmosphere of high emotion, and all the mainlanders I had met at the vigil including a government official, and she became quieter than I had ever seen her, as entranced as if she were listening to a fairy tale. Finally, smiling broadly, she said, "So there is hope after all!"

As I got up to take my leave, she declared that she wanted to give me something. Ignoring my protestations, she rummaged around in a cupboard and presented me with a woven bracelet of tiny colorful beads and a chestnut silk jewelry bag. As I walked down the dark corridor toward the lift, I could hear the echo of her voice diminishing behind me. "Thank you!" she was calling after me. "Thank you! Thank you! Truly you have given me a wonderful gift."

6 :: Patriot

Gao Yong felt his excitement mount as he climbed the stairs out of Beijing's Liangmaqiao subway station. He joined the river of people flowing toward the exit, gathering in pace and resolve as they got closer to the roaring crescendo of angry chants pulsating down the boulevard. He was heading to join the largest protests to take place in mainland China since 1989. A similar roar was echoing across more than a hundred Chinese cities. The marchers—mostly young people—were not, however, calling their own government to account; rather, they were rallying in support of its foreign policy.

This self-righteous anger is part of Tiananmen's legacy, for it was born of the Communist Party's use of nationalism to shore up its shaky mandate after 1989. Since then, the biggest street protests permitted by the authorities on the Chinese mainland, including the 1999 demonstrations against the NATO bombing of the Chinese embassy in Belgrade and the virulent anti-Japanese demonstrations in 2005, have been nationalistic.

By the time Gao Yong emerged from the subway, he had become part of a group united by a common purpose: to protest against Japan. The immediate cause for this outpouring of anger was the Japanese government's purchase in September 2012 of disputed islands in the East China Sea from their private owners. The rocky outcrop—known as the Senkaku islands in Japan and the Diaoyu islands in China—is controlled by Japan, but simultaneously claimed by Japan, China, and Taiwan. The march was particularly charged because it took place on the Day of National Humiliation, which is the anniversary of the Japanese invasion of Northeast China on September 18, 1931. Every year, in Gao's hometown of Huludao, in Northeast China, at exactly 9:18 in the morning on that day, the wails of air-raid sirens pierce the air.

Gao Yong had been in Beijing buying used cars, which he intended to sell back home, when he heard about the anti-Japanese protests. He knew immediately he had to take part; he saw it as his duty as a Chinese citizen to stand up to Japan. As he put it, "Back when China was weak, it would say, 'If you want it, then take it.' But now China has become a great power. You can't just give in to others." We were talking over lunch in an upscale Chinese restaurant in a shopping mall. Smartly dressed in a Western suit, Gao Yong had the self-assurance of an older man, so I was surprised to find out that he was just 32 years old. Judging from the demographics at the marches, displays of nationalism are a young man's game. "Young people have more of a sense that they need to protect national sovereignty," he explained earnestly.

This anti-Japanese protest was Gao Yong's first demonstration, and he had tried to take in all the details: the volunteers handing out Chinese flags and bottles of mineral water to the demonstrators; the throngs crowding the boulevard bringing to his mind the Chinese idiom "people-mountain people-sea"; and the efficiency with which the marchers were organized. At first, he was corralled into a makeshift holding area where he was told to wait 20 minutes. An officious man was waving off clumps of protesters with the solemn authority of an Olympic starter. Finally, it was Gao's group's turn to march up one side of the main road, pausing briefly to shout abuse at the Japanese embassy, and then circle back down the other side of the street in a small, highly controlled loop of fury.

Gao Yong had enjoyed marching and screaming slogans like "End Japanese Imperialism" and "Declare War!" He had also sung the Chinese national anthem vigorously and shouted "Go China!" as he punched his clenched fist skyward. It was empowering to be part of an enormous and seething crowd of young people. Although he was only marching around and around the same short circuit, he felt invigorated. Before he knew it, three hours had passed, and he suddenly realized how tired his feet were.

This was actually the fourth day of these rallies in Beijing. I had been tracking their progress. The word on the street was that the first protesters were anti-riot cops who had melted away as civilians joined in. That was never proven. But the government had certainly facilitated and encouraged the protests by allowing a major thoroughfare to be closed for the better part of a week, gridlocking traffic throughout the capital, so that the demonstrators' voices—which echoed the government's position—could be heard. As the days passed, the marchers' organizational machine became more sophisticated; by the time Gao Yong joined in, the demonstrations had all the spontaneity of a North Korean military parade.

Not only were flags being distributed, so were posters of Chairman Mao, the Great Helmsman, which protesters waved aloft. Mainly in their 20s and 30s, the marchers included groups of tracksuit-clad students posing for photos while pairing telegenic smiles with ubiquitous V-for-victory fingers. I came across a group of construction workers who were delighted to have been bussed in from their building site to spend the day demonstrating instead of working. As I watched the spectacle, a middle-aged onlooker stopped alongside me. "I haven't been organized to demonstrate," he told me wistfully, eyes fixed on the bellowing crowds. "The government controls and organizes the demonstrations. You can't just go if you like. At the very least, there's organization among the universities. There are at least half a million college students in Beijing. If they all came at once, it'd be unimaginable."

Some marchers, like Gao Yong, had clearly arrived spontaneously. But my suspicions of official incitement were stoked when I interviewed a middle-aged man with a neat buzz-cut and a Chinese flag draped over his shoulders.

"Why are you here?" I asked him.

"I feel extremely proud to be able to play a tiny role in defending my motherland's sovereignty," he answered glibly. As we chatted, I commented on the big police presence on the streets.

He looked straight at me. "How do you know I'm not a policeman?"

"I don't," I replied, suddenly noting that he had the haircut, the bearing, and the slightly bossy air of a cop. "Are you a policeman?"

"Don't ask me that," he said, stiffening visibly, and looking around for an escape route. Suddenly, I noticed that we were surrounded by male protesters with identical short haircuts and trim physiques. The Internet was abuzz with such rumors; in one city, a man who had led protesters to overturn three cars was even outed as a policeman, though this news was quickly expunged from social media.

Should there be any doubt about who was in ultimate control, the entire ecosystem of the state security apparatus had been mobilized. Helicopters whirred overhead, swooping low over an avenue better known for its high-end shopping opportunities. Tiers of elite, helmeted riot police protected the Japanese embassy, glaring warily through a wall of plexiglass shields, while navy blue-clad paramilitary police bookended each cluster of marchers. Every 15 feet policemen in pale-blue summer uniforms were stationed, while sinister-looking black-clad youths milled around the entrance to the enclosure penning in the marchers. Even those on the lowest rungs of the security apparatus were out in force: hundreds of neighborhood volunteers, many of them elderly matrons, lined the streets. They were wearing red armbands and perched every few feet on folding stools, their tea jars tidily stowed by their feet, as they took the chance to get in a good stretch of uninterrupted knitting. The authorities may have felt such disproportionate manpower was necessary. Though the marches were contrived, the rage expressed by the marchers was very real.

This I discovered with a shock when I marched alongside a young college student named Zhu Zeyao. He blushed when I spoke to him and disclosed, haltingly, that he was studying auto engineering at university. I asked what he was hoping to do with his degree. "I want to learn to make tanks, in order to exterminate the Japanese," he answered, his nostrils flaring with anger.

Next to him was a strapping young man by the name of Mu Peidong, who described his job as involving Internet marketing strategy. Toting a homemade banner reading "Even if we have to kill every single Japanese person, we must recover the Diaoyu Islands," he led the marchers in their chants, alternately bellowing, "Declare War!" and "Never Forget National Humiliation!"

• • • •

That four-word phrase—"Never Forget National Humiliation" — lies at the center of the party's post-Tiananmen strategy of regime legitimization. By unleashing the PLA against its own people in 1989, the Communist leadership had accelerated an ideological crisis that had been brewing for years. "Socialism and Communism were no longer an ideology for the Chinese people," said Zheng Wang of the Wilson Center and the author of *Never Forget National Humiliation: Historic Memory in Chinese Politics and Foreign Relations.* "There was a sort of spiritual vacuum. Nationalism was the easiest tool to use."

In the immediate aftermath of June 4th, Deng Xiaoping himself concluded that the party's biggest failure had been a lack of ideological education. In his address to the martial law troops five days after the suppression, he said, "I have told foreign guests that during the last ten years our biggest mistake was made in the field of education, primarily in ideological and political education—not just of the students, but of the people in general. We didn't tell them enough about the need for hard struggle, about what China was like in the old days and what kind of country it was to become. That was a serious error on our part." These words kicked off one of the most wide-scale attempts at ideological reeducation in modern history.

In the wake of Deng's words, textbooks were rewritten to change the prism through which the past—and present—were viewed. Class struggle was out; national humiliation was in. China as victor was out; instead, China was cast as the victim of a century of foreign bullying and semi-colonization, from which only the Communist Party offered deliverance. The Century of National Humiliation had begun with the treaty that Britain imposed on the Qing Dynasty to end the First Opium War in 1842, and continued with China being carved up into different spheres of influence by foreign powers, peaking with the brutal Japanese occupation that began in 1931. It only ended with the Communist Party's "liberation" of China from this state of "semi-feudalism and semi-colonialism" in 1949. Thus the interests of the nation and the party formed one seamless mass; loving the nation became synonymous with loving the party, and criticism of the party came to be seen as treachery.

This focus served to outflank the students' claims that they had been driven by patriotism, as well as dovetailing with the party's interpretation of the 1989 protests as whipped up by hostile foreign forces intent on overthrowing the Communist Party and the Socialist system.

The "instigators of the riots" were accused of receiving financial help from these overseas hostile forces, which were also active in "spreading rumors, stirring up trouble and adding fuel to the turmoil" through the foreign press such as the Voice of America. In this context, Western economic sanctions after June 4th were seen as yet one more humiliation, which, in the eyes of Deng Xiaoping, was comparable in scope to the invasion of China by the eight-nation alliance of Western countries in response to the 1900 Boxer Rebellion. The subsequent collapse of the Soviet bloc provided further justification to China's Communist leaders for the necessity of suppressing the pro-democracy movement. In 2001, Li Peng, who had been premier in 1989, reportedly said that "the tide of liberalization" had reached dangerous levels. "If this trend had continued for three more years, something similar to the fall of the Berlin Wall would have happened to China and the Communist Party would have crumbled."

By 1994, the new patriotic education campaign had been rolled out nationwide and was greeted with enthusiasm by teachers and students alike. The old textbooks, emphasizing class struggle and the impending demise of parasitic capitalism, had been hard to teach, since students only had to look out the window to see capitalism blossoming unimpeded, contradicting everything they were learning at school. The new focus on national humiliation was easier to accept, as well as being relatively fresh; one American political scientist, William Callahan, checking the records at the National Library of China, could not find a single new book on national humiliation published domestically between 1947 and 1990.

The post-Tiananmen revision of the textbooks was so comprehensive that certain historical figures were transmogrified from villains into heroes. One example was a Qing Dynasty general named Zuo Zongtang—incidentally the inspiration for the "General Tso's Chicken" dish—who was formerly judged a class traitor for suppressing peasant rebellions in the 1860s. However, his success in defeating the Russian invasion of Xinjiang and defending China's territorial integrity now allowed him to be reclassified as a hero.

In China, the rewriting of history books goes back to the very first emperor, Qin Shihuang, who unified the country in 221 B.C. To consolidate control over political thought, he decreed the burning of all scholarly books, sparing only the chronicles penned by his own historians. Such a pattern whereby each dynasty rewrites history to its own ends persists to this day. Though the Communist Party remained in control after 1989, its complete rewriting of history shows how shaken it had been by the events that began in the square.

• • • •

Gao Yong's hometown of Huludao was occupied by the Japanese in 1932, one of more than 900 cities in China to suffer that fate. Today, it is a scrubby beach resort up the coast from its more upscale cousin Beidaihe, where the party leadership gathers for its annual summer enclave. The main beach in Huludao, named after an army hospital, is populated by swarms of Chinese holidaymakers, standing knee-deep in the soupy brown sea, holding umbrellas over their heads, and wearing rubber tubes around their midriffs. It is a holiday destination on the make; along the seafront, the bare bones of a half-dozen skyscrapers under construction emerge through the murky haze as sunbathers jostle for space along the small, grainy strip of sand littered with potato chip bags and candy wrappers.

Beyond the city limits is a promontory overlooking a container terminal and a large plot of reclaimed land. Like so much else in Huludao, it is under construction. It is a bleak site, not improved by a desolate concrete pavilion and a granite monument resembling a ship whose sculptor gave up on it midway in despair. According to the monument's inscription, 1,051,047 Japanese prisoners of war were repatriated from this very spot after the end of World War II. An inscription engraved on the back of the monument reads "We will absolutely not allow this historical tragedy to play out again, and we sincerely look forward to Sino-Japanese friendship being passed from one generation to the next." In today's China, such a sentiment now appears quaint.

During the Japanese occupation of the northeast, Gao's paternal grandfather was taken prisoner by the Japanese. According to family folklore, he was saved by his wife, an underground Communist Party worker with bound feet, who was judged so insignificant that she was never even given a proper name. It became the stuff of local legend, though nobody ever told Gao the details and, as a child, he never thought to ask. By the time he was 11, both grandparents had died, and the opportunity to hear the story firsthand was gone forever. As Gao talked to me about his family history, it became clear that any animus against Japan was not stoked by the half-forgotten past, but rather by more contemporary forces.

Gao Yong's view of the past is conflicted, reflecting the party's own efforts to highlight certain episodes and forget others. Regarding the suppression of the pro-democracy movement in 1989, he was quick to point out that he had been only seven years old at the time. "I have no thoughts about it," he told me firmly. "Even now, I don't have any impression of it. I just want to live a good life and earn some money. If you're always looking back, what's the point of that? There are so many problems, you can't solve them all."

Yet, for the party's patriotic education strategy to work, looking back is necessary, as long as the retrospection happens under strictly controlled circumstances. Certain periods of history should be forgotten—notably those when the wounds were self-inflicted through misguided internal policies, such as the Cultural Revolution and June 4th. But the memory of other episodes—when the pain was inflicted by external sources—should be kept alive to ensure that China's citizens remain grateful to their Communist leaders for delivering them from the depredations of the past.

With this, Gao Yong had unconsciously fallen into step. On his car-buying trips to Beijing, he liked to visit Yuan Ming Yuan, the old Summer Palace, a rococo pleasure park designed for China's Qing emperors replete with classical palaces sprouting ornate columns and Botticelli-like curlicued shells. It was razed to the ground by the British and French armies during the 1860 Second Opium War, after their envoys were killed by the Qing. The destruction has been left for posterity; to this day, the park is dotted with broken marble chunks and signs emphasizing the great crimes of the British and French. The sacking of the Old Summer Palace was, as Gao Yong himself put it, a "flesh wound" for China. Such humiliation, however, paved the way for the road to revival.

"The Road to Revival" is in fact the title of a massive permanent exhibition at the National Museum of China, which also functions as a shrine to the party's historical orthodoxy. Among the 980 photos on display is one of Deng Xiaoping congratulating the martial law troops post-Tiananmen—the single, elliptical reference to June 4th—but the exhibition's ambitions are far greater. It outlines its mission as charting "the rejuvenation of the country under the leadership of the Communist Party of China," beginning at the dawn of modern Chinese history as defined by the Communist Party: the First Opium War. The most valuable object on display is a remnant of the original flag hoisted on the first National Day, October 1st, 1949. Due to fabric shortages, it was made from strips of material sewn together by a tailor.

The first outing by China's new leadership committee after Xi Jinping's ascension to the top post in 2012 was a symbolic pilgrimage to the "Road to Revival." The seven men posed soberly for pictures, all head to toe in black as if at an undertakers' convention, while Xi unveiled the centerpiece of his ideology, announcing, "In my view, to realize the great renewal of the Chinese nation is the greatest Chinese Dream for the Chinese nation in modern history." Xi Jinping's "China Dream" marks a tipping point: The Communist Party's focus on political or social issues has given way to nationalism. The vagueness of the China dream makes it all-encompassing—covering improvements in the standard of living, building military strength and general national rejuvenation—but its beating heart is nationalistic.

• • • •

The China Dream first percolated into the Chinese consciousness in 2011 as the title of a bestselling book written by a senior colonel in the People's Liberation Army, Liu Mingfu, who also teaches at the National Defense University. Senior Colonel Liu is tall and handsome with a military man's ramrod posture and a bureaucrat's tendency to talk in lists, punctuated by finger-jabbing gestures. When *The China Dream* first came out, Senior Colonel Liu managed to get my assistant and me into his military compound in Beijing for an interview. Foreigners were not normally permitted into this army zone, so he asked us to slouch down low in the back of a black military sedan as it sped through the gate and into an enormous residential complex of basketball courts, squat brick blocks, and small shady parks, all entirely hidden from the main road.

When we got to his apartment, however, the senior colonel sat down behind a gigantic desk and, smiling stiffly, declared that as a serving army officer, he could not talk on the record to the foreign media. We entered into lengthy negotiations that threatened to break down several times until at last we hammered out a convoluted compromise that involved two Chinese journalists from a specialist defense publication sitting meekly across the table. The senior colonel announced that they would record his words with their own equipment, and then post the audio on their website. One of them leapt into action, switching on an ancient recording device, and then promptly fell asleep, his head lolling uncomfortably on his chest until the end of the interview. It didn't matter that the results made Colonel Liu sound as if he had been recorded at the bottom of the sea by phonograph. He was satisfied with this arrangement. Technically, by giving an interview to Chinese journalists, he could be absolved of the sin of talking to the foreign media.

When we met two years later, again in his apartment, Senior Colonel Liu's mood was far more expansive. He had retired from active service, so there was no need for complicated compromises. Better still, his book had garnered a mention in Henry Kissinger's

On China. He rushed off to fetch both the English and Chinese versions of Kissinger's tome, so we could admire his fame in full bilingual glory. Kissinger cited the book as premised on the assumption that the West was much weaker than previously thought, while at the same time emphasizing that China should build up its military as a deterrent, thus rejecting the concept of a "peaceful rise." That an unabashed nationalist like Senior Colonel Liu would attach such value to American recognition is not surprising in a society in which even President Xi Jinping's own daughter chose to attend Harvard over China's elite universities.

Senior Colonel Liu's views can be summed up succinctly: China should become the world's leading military power. He is confident that President Xi shares his dream. "My China dream and President Xi's China dream are in essence the same—to realize the great rejuvenation of the Chinese people," he told me, "but the language is different. I was a scholar from the National Defense University, and when I talked about China wanting to be the world's number one, the Americans got upset. If President Xi talked about becoming the world's number one, Americans would be unable to bear it."

This dream of China comes at a moment when Beijing's approach toward regional affairs has become increasingly assertive. China is embroiled in territorial disputes with neighbors, including Japan, the Philippines, Malaysia, Vietnam, Brunei, and Taiwan. Indeed, China now claims almost 90 percent of the South China Sea, using as its basis a U-shaped "nine-dash line" that first appeared on a map published by China's Nationalist government in 1947. The government is pressing forward with its territorial claims, even pursuing a programme of land reclamation to build islands on previously submerged reefs in the South China Sea. It is also sending ships to conduct drills as far as a thousand miles from the Chinese mainland, including one drill just 50 miles from Malaysia. In recent years, Beijing has also made greater use of an array of nonmilitary agencies—such as the China Marine Surveillance, the Maritime Safety Administration, the Fisheries Law Enforcement Command, and the State Oceanic Administration—to pursue its maritime claims.

Few corners of the world now seem beyond the reach of the Chinese. Beijing has sent its Jiaolong submarines to plumb the ocean depths, and a steady stream of Chinese space travelers orbits the earth. A permanent space station is planned by 2020, after which, according to current plans, a manned moon landing will follow. China's increasing presence in space just as the United States ends its own shuttle program delivers a powerful message. In 2008, after astronaut Zhai Zhigang completed China's first-ever space-walk while wearing a four million U.S. dollar Chinese-designed spacesuit, he told President Hu Jintao, "In the vastness of space, I felt proud of our motherland."

• • • •

In China, the passage of political seasons can be measured by the rise and fall of slogans. The roster of numerical mottoes includes the "Two Whatevers," the "Three Represents," the "Four Modernizations," and the "Five Principles of Peaceful Coexistence." These slogans tend to flit in and out of the public consciousness without leaving much of a trace. So it was with a jolt that I suddenly remembered that just five years before the China Dream, a slogan trumpeting a far more ambitious dream had been everywhere, and then was almost immediately and completely forgotten. This slogan picked from 210,000 possible entries for the 2008 Beijing Olympic motto was: "One World, One Dream."

But the vaunted universality of the dream was exposed as a mirage when human rights activists and Tibet supporters protested against the Olympic torch on its 85,000-mile, round-the-world "journey of harmony." The extent of the dream's bifurcation became clear when young Chinese living overseas—distraught at the tarnishing of the motherland's moment of glory—began to stage counter-demonstrations facing off against the protesters along the torch route. The crisis came to a head in Paris, where a Chinese Paralympian in a wheelchair was forced to use her upper body to shield the Olympic flame from screaming protesters trying to wrest it from her. These scenes of utter chaos were far from the dignified spectacle envisaged by the Beijing Olympic Committee. In response, Chinese nationalists turned their wrath onto the French supermarket chain Carrefour, staging protests outside the China-based branches and trying to launch a boycott of the stores.

For foreign journalists, 2008 was an unsettling period. The touchpaper of nationalistic fury could be ignited by a single word, an incorrect caption, or even simply by the implication of words left unsaid. At least 10 foreign reporters received death threats. Some had been on a government trip to Tibet and, after returning to Beijing, began receiving as many as 30 harassing phone calls an hour, even though their contact information was not in the public domain.

At that time, I was sharing an office in Shanghai with the BBC correspondent Quentin Sommerville. During a press conference televised live, he asked what measures the authorities would take to protect the Olympic flame on its journey through Tibet. For that, he received death threats from angry nationalists, who saw the question as a veiled insult. At first, we monitored the online fulminations that Quentin should "drown on his own saliva" without taking them seriously. Yet within hours, our office address had been posted on the Internet. Our Chinese coworkers were being vilified as traitors. The threats were no longer a laughing matter. We all worked from home for a few days; our Chinese colleagues' nerves persisted for far longer.

This was my introduction to the bully pulpit of nationalism and its power. The party's education program has succeeded in raising a nation of patriots, but one whose love of country is tipping over into state-backed nationalism. The twin poles of China's century of victimization and the Communist Party's act of deliverance have created public sentiment that veers schizophrenically between self-hatred and self-aggrandizement.

The Beijing Olympic opening ceremony proved to be a watershed. As the first fireworks raced their way round the rim of the Bird's Nest stadium and flashes of light illuminated 2,008 drummers pounding away in surreal synchronicity, the roar of the crowd was that of a nation finally finding its voice. Choreographed by film director Zhang Yimou, who spent 13 months training the performers, the spectacular opening ceremony reinforced patriotic sentiment as it charted China's four historic inventions—paper, gunpowder, printing, and the compass—and its reemergence as a world power. Of the nearly 14,000 performers, almost two-thirds were members of either the People's Liberation Army or the paramilitary forces, confirming Orwell's dictum that serious sport is "war without shooting."

As the Chinese gold medals began to roll in, the popular mood swung from righteous indignation to triumphalism. Cushioned by a post-Olympic glow, this sentiment continued to build as the unfolding global financial crisis reshuffled the world order to leave Beijing surpassing Japan to become the world's second-largest economy and the largest foreign creditor of the United States. Politically and economically, China is no longer the "sick man of Asia." And its youth is determined their country should be treated with the respect they believe it deserves.

• • • •

The lessons of patriotic education have inexorably seeped into every aspect of Chinese life. Walk down any street and you are likely to pass a street committee blackboard bearing uplifting patriotic sentiments. Flick through any school textbook, even a grammar book, and you will find expressions of national pride. Turn on the television, and Japanese soldiers are incessantly being routed in battle by brave Chinese warriors. Given strict governmental controls over content—ghost stories, time travel, adultery, and even shows featuring spy sagas have been variously banned by censors—anti-Japanese shows have filled the void, to the point where the regulator reined in chop-socky anti-Japanese action sequences for being "overly dramatic."

In 2004, 15 television shows approved by the regulator featured battles with the Japanese. By 2011 and 2012, that figure had increased to 177. The appetite for anti-Japanese entertainment has become so overwhelming that one-third of the productions filmed in China's biggest movie studio, Hengdian, involve battles against the Japanese. Some have even dubbed the film studio a "huge anti-Japanese revolutionary base."

Indeed, so mainstream has anti-Japanese sentiment become that one local newspaper devoted an article to outlining the tricks of the trade for extras playing Japanese soldiers, whom it called "devils."

The article drew on advice from Shi Zhongpeng, a Chinese extra who has become famous for his skill at portraying Japanese soldiers. It wrote, "As an experienced 'devil,' Shi summarizes what he's learned in one sentence: 'The more horrible you look, the better.' The casting teams specifically select people who are less attractive and somewhat vicious-looking to play 'devils.' During interviews, Shi hunches his back, squints his eyes and presents a fierce, wretched look to boost his chances of being chosen for the part." On his most productive day, Shi was slaughtered 31 times. Showing his grasp of political correctness, his stated dream is to play a Red Army soldier.

As part of its patriotic education effort, the Communist Party has rolled out star power in its attempts to mythologize its own creation myth. In the lead-up to its 60th anniversary in 2009, it produced two blockbuster movies, using hundreds of the country's most bankable stars, who donated cameo performances to this propaganda epic for a new age. It was no surprise when *The Founding of a Republic* smashed box office records, bringing in more than $65 million, helped along by audiences of students and government workers who were strong-armed into attendance by their institutions.

In line with current political dictates, class struggle is barely mentioned in the film. Instead, Chairman Mao is seen bemoaning his inability to buy a cigarette, which he attributes to a lamentable lack of capitalists. "If there aren't any businessmen, I can't even buy cigarettes," he says, "let alone talk about market prosperity. We have to invite them back." Of course, he never uttered those words. This film and its 2011 sequel *The Beginning of the Great Revival* are filled with scenes that never happened, including one moment when in 1919, the young Chairman Mao is depicted as appearing on the docks with his suitcases, about to board a boat for France with 16-year-old Deng Xiaoping, when he suddenly changes his mind. Such attempts to spin the country's history were much mocked online. Yet the constant rewriting of history has made untangling truth from fiction ever harder.

The patriotic education campaign has not only transformed history books and popular entertainment, it has also reshaped domestic tourism. In 1994, a Red Tourism policy began to subsidize "patriotic education bases." Two decades later, there are 10,000

Red Tourism destinations in China, Communist Disneylands that memorialize a manipulated version of the country's past. Their success can be measured in numbers. In 2011, more than a half billion visitors went to Red Tourist sites, accounting for one-fifth of all domestic tourism.

One town entirely transformed by Red Tourism is the mountain base of Yan'an, where the Communist Party ended the Long March in 1935. It was in the hillside caves of this dusty little place that Chairman Mao and his fellow revolutionaries cloistered themselves for the next dozen years, hammering out the party's ideology. When I first visited Yan'an as a student in 1991, it was a down-at-heel town whose main attraction was a few dank caves scooped out of the hillside. There were so few shopping opportunities that in one deeply embarrassing misunderstanding, we ended up being shooed out of a funeral shop after attempting to try on burial clothes meant for corpses.

Two decades later, the town has been rebranded the "Holy Land of China's Communist Revolution," somewhat of an oxymoron in a state that remains officially atheist. A cavernous Revolutionary Memorial Hall was built in 2009 at a cost of $80 million in which such relics as a lilac-colored metal soapdish once used by the Great Helmsman are lovingly displayed. A gigantic statue of Chairman Mao, arms akimbo, dominates a huge, empty square that has been leveled in front of the hall. On a recent visit, the Memorial Hall's lobby was filled with people dressed as Red Army soldiers in brand-new pale-blue cotton jackets and pedal-pushers. I had assumed they were government officials or perhaps staffers from a state-owned enterprise on a state-sponsored freebie. In fact, they turned out to be China's top Amway salespeople, who had earned themselves a Red Tourism holiday for their prowess in selling skincare products and protein powders. Lining up for the obligatory group photo, they enthusiastically shouted chants that I couldn't quite decipher. I assumed it was a Communist slogan until I was informed that this new Red Army was shouting out the name of that year's bestselling Amway product.

Tour buses clog every road as they shuttle some of the 20 million annual visitors from one revolutionary site to the next. Many of the tourists are government officials or party members on organized tours to better understand their patrimony. At night, they crowd into a state-of-the-art theater to enjoy some ideologically correct Broadway-style glitz in the form of a lavish—$5.5 million—production called *Nursery School of the Red Capital* about orphans whose parents had died fighting the Japanese. As for shopping opportunities, Mao-themed souvenirs, from Mao Zedong cigarettes to shiny golden busts of the Great Helmsman, are available on every street corner.

In the hills outside Yan'an, a battle against the Nationalists is recreated every single day for the tourists. For an extra couple of dollars, visitors can even don a costume and help defeat the Nationalists. It is a highly choreographed spectacle that includes lots of whizz-bang shooting, an antique tank, and, for the finale, a rusty aircraft zooming down a zipwire. The day I went, the wooden benches were packed with tourists who spontaneously erupted into loud applause when a Chairman Mao look-alike appeared on the scene to deliver one of his speeches. After the battle, I met Yang Xiaowu, a jovial distributor of grain alcohol, who had made the 150 mile trip from his home to visit Yan'an more than 10 times. This time, he had brought along his sales staff for a group bonding exercise. It was the right place to come, he told me, because Mao's classic essay "On Protracted War" was his business bible. He used it to help his team map out their strategy for marketing booze.

The transformation of Mao's stronghold symbolizes the ideological contortions that China's Communist party has twisted itself into over the past 65 years. In one meeting hall, a 1940 banner, unnoticed by the crowds, forlornly calls for the early adoption of democracy. Mao himself advocated multiparty democracy, though he abandoned this position after gaining power. Nowadays, Yan'an has become a giant theme park designed to milk nostalgia for an imagined past in order to instruct—and make money from—those too young to have suffered through it. Communism is being put into the service of consumerism.

By emphasizing the hardships that revolutionaries suffered to build today's China, Red Tourism is designed to foster gratitude toward the Communist Party. Although most of the visitors

I met seemed to be enjoying themselves—especially if they were on government-subsidized holidays from their jobs—there was discontent too, even at the heart of the Revolutionary Holy Land. At one of Chairman Mao's caves, an elderly man who was visiting with his village party committee was so enraged by government corruption that he couldn't contain himself, even in this shrine to Communism. "Now there are 80 million Communist Party members," he said. "I think half of them should be killed. If every official serving at county level or above was shot by a firing squad, I don't think any innocent blood would be shed."

Even at the National Museum's "Road to Revival" exhibition, open dissent to the party's view of history was scrawled throughout the guestbook. The museum's relentlessly positive representation of history devotes just one photograph and three lines of text to the decade-long Cultural Revolution, with similarly cryptic treatment of June 4th. For those who have lived through the party's mass campaigns, the lacunae are glaring. One outraged visitor had written, "The historical perspective of the Road to the Great Revival has problems!" Another commented, "At the exhibition, there is little about the darkness of the blood-and-tears history of the Great Leap Forward or the Cultural Revolution. After constructing our Road to Revival, the country needs to look squarely at its own history to avoid going down the same route."

• • • •

Such an assessment echoes one of the great fears of Cong Riyun, a scholar who teaches at the Chinese University of Politics and Law. We met in a small town about an hour and a half from Beijing at an anonymous coffee shop divided by booths. With his doughy face, neat comb-over, and black briefcase, Cong Riyun is the very picture of a mid-level Chinese bureaucrat, yet he is a respected academic who dares to differ from the official party line. The course he teaches has the unthreatening title "Western Civilization and History," yet its content is far edgier: It examines Chinese misunderstandings of Western history.

Cong's epiphany came in 2005, when he spent the year at Yale as a Fulbright scholar. There he witnessed the unintended consequences of China's patriotic education campaign playing out. He noticed that the discovery of other perspectives on their own history was not a mind-opening experience for newly arrived Chinese students; it had the opposite effect, simply reinforcing their own beliefs. The students tended to conclude that American professors had simply failed to understand Chinese history or, worse still, that the U.S. education system was peddling misinformation as part of a Western conspiracy to stop China's rise. So steeped are many of these students—China's elite—in patriotic education that they simply cannot accept any other version of their country's history. Often, they ended up arguing with their professors, causing class discussions to degenerate into bitter squabbles.

As increasing numbers of young Chinese venture overseas for an education, such experiences are becoming more common. In 2014, nearly 275,000 Chinese students studied at universities in the United States, accounting for almost a third of all foreign students in the country. In 2006, the Massachusetts Institute of Technology became embroiled in controversy when two professors received hate mail and death threats after angering Chinese students. Their offense was using a century-old Japanese woodblock print, depicting a scene from the Sino-Japanese War of 1894, in their multimedia course on "Visualizing Cultures." The print showed a Japanese soldier poised to behead a kneeling Chinese prisoner of war, his sword ready to swoop down in a deadly parabola. Rows of Chinese captives sit in the background, awaiting their own deaths; in the foreground, the pigtailed heads of other Chinese prisoners roll in pools of blood. The mere use of this picture was enough for the Chinese students to accuse the two professors, John Dower and Shigeru Miyagawa, of endorsing Japanese militarism and racism. In a statement, the Chinese Student and Scholar Association condemned "the emotional damage the inappropriate presentation had caused to thousands of Chinese people worldwide," and demanded that more context be given to the picture.

In fact, Dower's essay for the online course described how such woodblock prints were used to pump up Japan's newly emerging sense of nationalism, militarism, and imperialism. He called the print an "unusually frightful scene" that was "disdainful of Chinese," and he criticized its implicit racism. Yet the Chinese students had been so quick to anger that some had not bothered to read the essay, but simply posted the print online stripped of all explanation, thus committing the very offense about which they had complained. During a town hall meeting, the Chinese students called for an official apology, the permanent shutdown of the site, and the cancellation of related academic workshops. For some of the faculty, this episode threatened the core values of MIT's mission. Peter Perdue, who has taught Chinese history for a quarter-century first at MIT and then at Yale, was the most direct, telling the Chinese students in an open letter "that they had violated fundamental academic norms of civil discourse and respect. As future leaders of China, they had a responsibility to open their minds, in order to make China strong, and not to indulge in destructive narrow-minded self-righteous indignation." In the end, the website was taken down so more context could be added, and then re-launched. But such episodes offer a sobering glimpse of how a generation of new nationalists is asserting itself.

So what is at the root of such acts of blind nationalism? Professor Cong blames China's examination system, which requires conformity of education and thought. Each high school student's future is determined by the *gaokao* exam, which dictates whether the student can attend university and which one, putting teachers under pressure to stick to the curriculum to maximize their students' chance of exam success. In this way, the exam system ensures teachers' ideological purity and political correctness, as well as those of their students, who must stick to the acceptable answers to guarantee their own futures.

At university level, lecturers can take a more independent line, but doing so carries its own risks. Professor Cong learned this firsthand during the anti-Japanese protests of September 2012. Seeing the marchers carrying Chairman Mao's portrait, Cong thought it would be a good opportunity to discuss the Great Helmsman's actual record when it came to territorial disputes. Far from taking a tough line—as the young demonstrators believed—Mao actually ceded disputed Chinese territory to neighbors, including North Korea, Russia, Mongolia, and Vietnam. Cong paid the price for puncturing his students' illusions. During class, he had mentioned that in 1953 when Chairman Mao was in control, even the *People's Daily* had carried an article stating that the disputed islands in the East China Sea were part of the Ryukyu Island chain, thus implicitly acknowledging that they were Japanese territory. For this, the students informed on him to the university authorities. He was summoned for an explanation of his behavior. "They accused me of telling them that the Diaoyu Islands belong to Japan," Cong said, smiling ruefully.

Cong also worried about the psychological cost of constructing a national identity through the inculcation of hatred. "Before it was class hatred against landlords, capitalists and the Nationalist party," he told me. "Now we talk about Western imperialists, and how they invaded us, how bad they were, how savage and unreasonable." Cong feared such underlying messages were fostering an instinctive mistrust of the West at street level, which would ultimately add to the pressures on decision-makers.

His biggest fear is that patriotic education has created "a new generation of Red Guards and Boxers." This is a reference to the violent Cultural Revolution-era rebels—and before that, the Boxers, who at the turn of the 20th century were anti-foreign nationalists who murdered missionaries and their Chinese converts. Today's young, Cong believes, slip into a wired iteration of such youthful anger. "Firstly, they're ignorant, their brains are full of prejudice. Secondly, they're made violent by this education of hatred. Thirdly, they're xenophobic, not just toward foreigners but also they show their hatred towards domestic traitors."

• • • •

Back at the protests, as Gao Yong was swept along in the sea of people, he found himself yelling "Declare War!" and "Boycott Japanese goods!" at the top of his lungs. Neither were sentiments he actually supported, as he admitted to me over lunch, but he had become carried away by the novelty of protesting and the adrenaline of the crowd. In actual fact, he was firmly opposed to war with Japan, which he believed would be disastrous. As for a boycott of Japanese products, he believed that to be unnecessary, since market forces were making Chinese products increasingly attractive to domestic consumers.

Rather sheepishly, he admitted that in fact his own camera was Japanese, because Chinese cameras weren't quite as good yet. As for Japanese cars, he was happy to continue selling them, even though he personally judged German and American cars to be of better quality. His mood seemed to reflect wider sentiment; right after the demonstrations, Japanese car exports to China plummeted by 80 percent. But after a few months, as the furor died down, Japanese car exports began to pick up, since Chinese consumers—like Gao—are too pragmatic to allow politics to get in the way of business for long.

In general, Gao Yong was grateful for what he had. Though he had never gone to college, his China was a land of opportunity, a place where hard work was enough to realize his dream of becoming wealthy. Since leaving school, he had variously run a bathhouse, driven a taxi, and started a small barbeque restaurant before embarking on his used-car business. His parents' lives had been far more circumscribed, working until retirement in a semiconductor factory and a quartz glass factory respectively. Unlike them, he was in charge of his own life and felt no constraints, political or otherwise. Far from wanting more freedom, he actually felt that life in the United States might be too free, believing that there should be more gun control to curb mass shootings.

"Right now I'm content with my lot," he told me, as we used our iPhones to snap pictures of our artfully presented dishes of mushrooms and bean curd garnished with flowers. "I'm very appreciative of this society. I'm not an angry youth. I love my country."

Gao Yong had been taken aback by the raw anger at the marches. Outside the Liangmaqiao subway station, eggs donated by a patriotic pancake stall-owner were scooped up by demonstrators, who gleefully smashed them onto Japanese flags on the ground. Gao had been shocked to see the crowds pelting the Japanese embassy with eggs, tomatoes, and bottles of water, while Chinese riot police stood by and watched. Some of the police were even injured by these makeshift missiles falling short of the embassy gates.

Outside Beijing, some of the protests had degenerated into mob violence that even targeted Chinese perceived as traitors. In the central city of Xi'an, a Chinese driver was dragged from his car and beaten over the head with a heavy metal bicycle lock, even as he shouted, "I'm also a Diaoyu supporter! I'm also anti-Japanese!" His offense was driving a Japanese car, a Toyota Corolla. His head injury was so serious that even weeks later, he had still not regained the ability to speak properly. In Qingdao, a Toyota plant and a Panasonic factory were set on fire, while elsewhere, goods were looted from Japanese department stores and Japanese restaurants were attacked.

The Chinese state-run media criticized the violence but made a point of supporting the demonstrations, as well as lashing out at the Western demonization of patriotic education in China as brainwashing by drawing parallels with the United States. In an editorial, the *China Daily* stated, "Many Chinese have demonstrated their patriotism by responding appropriately to Japanese right-wing activists' provocations over the Diaoyu Islands dispute.... Patriotic education is at the core of a country's strategy to realize its goals."

One day after Gao Yong protested, however, the rallies were abruptly shut down. Within a few days, the whole spectacle seemed to have been some kind of collective hallucination. Had thousands really marched down these traffic-clogged streets while helicopters hovered overhead? The yellow smears marking the Japanese embassy's gateway were the only sign that something unusual had happened. The spasm of anti-Japanese anger had convulsed the big cities leaving almost no trace, though long afterward the reverberations were still rippling outward to smaller places. About six months after the protests, when we visited my husband's hometown in Yunnan, near the Vietnamese border, everyone was talking about war with Japan as if it were imminent. Graffiti featuring Chinese soldiers bayoneting Japanese were scrawled on dusty cars. My favorite snack stall was displaying a huge red banner reminding its customers to "Never Forget National Humiliation" as they crouched on plastic children's stools to eat spicy ducks' tongues and eel-and-mint noodles. A clothing store had even pasted a large Japanese flag on the ground with instructions for prospective shoppers to "Stamp the little Japanese to death!" as they stopped by to pick up a new shirt. The raw anger may have faded away in the major cities, but in the outlying areas, the anti-Japanese message was a unifying one.

"The Chinese memory of national humiliation is really the key to understanding China's foreign policy," says scholar Zheng Wang, who believes that the strident voice of the young nationalists, magnified by the Internet, has become a factor in foreign policy decisions. "This government is finding itself the victim of its own patriotic education campaign. It has very limited choices. Backing down becomes weakness or even a new humiliation. The government is the guardian of China's national face, so being tough and strong is the only choice."

After 1989, the Communist Party gambled on nationalism as a way to extend its mandate and offer distractions from demands for political reform. As the beneficiaries of that gamble come of age, they just might end up undermining the Communist Party's mandate.

Over lunch, Gao Yong struggled as he tried to put into words the mix of duty, love, and gratitude he feels toward China. "Patriotism is a feeling that is always in our hearts," he told me, though he acknowledged that the anti-Japanese protests had also provided a much-needed release. That was explicit in the police handling of the protests, allowing marchers to yell anti-Japanese slogans—no matter how incendiary—but forbidding them from shouting slogans against corruption. "This was a channel for people to vent," Gao Yong said. "These sentiments had built up among the ordinary people. If you don't allow them to express their sentiments, then the people could turn around and say the government is completely useless."

7 :: Official

When the unfamiliar black sedan drew up to collect his father, Bao Pu knew he would not see him again for a long time. His father, Bao Tong, was one of the most important officials in China: secretary to the Politburo Standing Committee, the five-man leadership group, as well as director of the Central Committee Office of Political Reform, and right-hand man to the Communist Party general secretary Zhao Ziyang. By this point, the high-level political struggle between Zhao Ziyang's reformist camp and the conservatives had already played out, and Zhao had lost. The date was May 28th, 1989; it had been more than a week since Zhao had disappeared from public view. When Bao Tong received a phone call summoning him to attend an emergency Politburo Standing Committee meeting, but ordering him not to use his own car and chauffeur, the whole family knew that he would not be returning.

As the car pulled up, Bao Tong turned to his wife, Jiang Zongcao. "I don't know when we will meet again," he said simply. Then he got into the black sedan, sandwiched on either side by officials who slipped in beside him, and the car drove away.

Bao Tong was driven into the leadership compound at *Zhongnanhai*, but not to the building where meetings of the Politburo Standing Committee usually took place. He was met by Song Ping, who was at that time head of the Communist Party

Organization Department, a powerful body in charge of personnel matters. After some preamble, Song Ping sighed deeply and asked,

"Are you safe or not?"

"What do you mean, am I safe?" Bao Tong replied, perplexed.

"Is it safe where you live?"

"My office is in Zhongnanhai, and I live in the ministerial residential complex in Muxidi. How can that not be safe?" Bao Tong said.

"Maybe it would be best if you went somewhere else," Song Ping suggested. "The students are planning to go after you."

"No way. The students know me. This is not a problem," said Bao Tong, pointing out that Song Ping himself also worked inside the Zhongnanhai leadership compound.

"You're a big target," Song Ping replied. "The students are paying attention to you. You must move elsewhere."

Shortly after that, the meeting was over. Song Ping saw Bao Tong out, gripping his hand in a bone-crushing handshake as he escorted him toward a different car, this time a police vehicle. Flanked by guards on either side, Bao Tong was driven away—for his own safety, he was told. The vehicle wound its way through Beijing, taking one detour after another to avoid the streets clogged with protesters, until Bao Tong was completely disoriented.

But from the start, he had known the final destination. The car glided through the suburbs toward the mountains on the outskirts of Beijing. When it finally pulled to a stop, Bao Tong got out and passed through two large metal doors and into a lobby, where three men were waiting for him.

"Is this Qincheng?" he asked, referring to the prison that holds the country's most important political prisoners.

"Yes," he was told by a man who identified himself as the warden.

"From now on, your name is 8901," a second man informed him. From that, Bao Tong deduced that he was the first prisoner to arrive at Qincheng that year. Others would follow, including student leader Zhang Ming.

Bao Tong was taken to a small cell furnished with a table, a stool, and a single bed consisting of a board balanced on two sawhorses. There was no door, just an open doorway with a desk placed in front of it, at which two guards stood 24 hours a day. A third sat at the table, noting Prisoner 8901's actions at one-minute intervals: 1:01: sitting. 1:02: sitting: 1:03: stood up.

After arriving at his cell, Bao Tong lay down on the bed. He was neither scared nor nervous, but rather felt a perverse lightness. His arrest had been inevitable. When it happened, the burden of constant anticipation was lifted from him. Everything that he had been waiting for had come to pass. His future was out of his own hands, and he could finally rest. With that, he fell asleep.

When he woke up, Bao Tong was given dinner—two vegetarian dishes and two pieces of fruit. This was a sign of his special status; other prisoners, even important ones, received a single piece of fruit. In the middle of that night, he was informed that he had been placed under investigation. Soon afterward, he began the age-old practice of petitioning for justice. He started by writing to the Politburo Standing Committee, the body for which he nominally still served as secretary. He argued that his detention was illegal given that no legal documentation had been produced, in violation of the party rules, the constitution, and the legal code. He concluded, "Today it has happened to me. Tomorrow it could happen to someone else. Today it happened to one person. Tomorrow it could happen to several people. Consequently I have a responsibility to report to you that this has happened. I await your response."

He never received an answer.

That evening, Bao Tong's wife received a phone call. She was told that her husband was being looked after for his own safety since the situation was so chaotic. She should not expect him home for a while. She knew he was in the hands of the Communist Party, but had no idea where he was being held and on what charges. More than two years would pass before the family would be informed of his whereabouts, then another year before the party was ready to put Bao Tong on trial. His vertiginous fall happened within the span of a few hours. He had started the day as one of the most important officials in the entire land and ended it as a prisoner with no rights, no future, not even a name.

• • • •

Sitting in the corner of a McDonald's restaurant beside a bank of red, yellow, and blue balloons, the diminutive old man was engrossed in stirring his coffee with a small, beige plastic spoon. His grey hair was clipped short, his eyes were misty with cataracts, and deep grooves etched his face with the worries of several lifetimes. Overlooking the Military Museum of the Chinese People's Revolution, which served as a staging area for troops on the night of the suppression, this McDonald's has become Bao Tong's favored meeting spot, for both its proximity to his apartment and its free coffee refills, in which he takes great delight. At first glance, Bao Tong resembled any other senior citizen eking out a life on modest funds, once even sheepishly admitting to leaving the house without his false teeth because they were so uncomfortable. Then, without skipping a beat, he mentioned that he had drawn inspiration from Roosevelt's New Deal when drafting the reformist proposals separating party and state for the 13th Party Congress in 1987, and his whole extraordinary history came roaring back into focus.

Bao Tong is the highest-ranking government official to serve time for the events of 1989. He has become a symbol of conscience. Since being released from jail in 1994, his status has remained ambiguous. He has been at large, though not free, dogged by a team of constant and silent tails. When a policewoman walked past us to preen herself in a nearby mirror, he glanced over. He shook his head, "No, not her. There is a woman, but it's not her." He nodded toward a thickset bulldog of a man barreling past, his white-and-black hooded jacket pulled over his head. "He's one of them."

Unlike most other dissidents who spend interviews glancing around nervously, he showed an airy lack of concern toward his team of watchers.

"They always come with me. They sit near me. They might record. I'm totally used to it. If they're not with me, I feel lost."

• • • •

Bao Tong joined the Communist Party as a 16-year-old schoolboy in Shanghai just six weeks before it took power in 1949. He grew up under Nationalist—or *Kuomintang*—rule when the Communist

Party was still an illegal organization and its very name conjured up associations of danger. He was five when he first heard the word "Communist," as his family talked in hushed tones about a neighbor, who had been taken away for his political affiliations and never returned. Less than a few hundred feet from Bao Tong's home was the building where the Chinese Communist Party held its first meeting in 1921. So great was the secrecy surrounding Communism that he did not discover this fact for years. That historic meeting place has become a small museum, nestled among fancy shops selling overpriced cashmere shawls and café lattes, while Bao's family home now houses a boutique specializing in luxury silk clothing with a Chinese twist. This upscale shopping precinct is called *Xintiandi* or "New Heaven and Earth."

Bao Tong was politicized early by an uncle who gave him a subscription to a political magazine, from which he learned about the concepts of democracy and freedom. By the age of 13, the Communist Party had already made a tentative attempt to recruit him. The Communists liked to enroll members while they were still ignorant and malleable, he told me with a twinkle in his eye. Bao Tong turned down the offer; he wanted to finish his schooling.

Three years later in 1949, he was approached for a second time only weeks before Shanghai fell into Communist hands. This time he agreed. His recruitment was the stuff of spy movies. He was ordered to go for a walk in a particular Shanghai park at seven in the morning carrying a copy of the *Takungpao* newspaper tucked under one arm. He should look out for a contact carrying his own *Takungpao* newspaper, who would ask him the time. Bao Tong was to reply, "I'm not wearing a watch, but I think it's around seven o'clock." This exchange went exactly according to plan, and by the end of the day, 16-year-old Bao Tong was in charge of an underground Communist Party cell at his high school.

Six weeks later, the takeover of Shanghai marked the end of his formal education and the start of his life as a party official. One of the first tasks entrusted to the teenaged Bao Tong was to confiscate houses belonging to people designated as war criminals, including former President Chiang Kai-shek, who had fled to Taiwan. These houses—33 in all—were to be secured, then handed over to the in-coming troops. For the next 40 years, Bao Tong was a party man.

• • • •

In the late 1980s, "reform" was the buzzword, and Bao Tong was at the very heart of the project. As director of the Office of Political Reform, his job was to try to redesign China's political architecture while keeping it within the framework of the Communist system. It was a task that Bao's then-secretary, Wu Guoguang, describes as "dancing with chains." The Office of Political Reform invited experts from around the world to give symposia on political change, and they examined the role of the party, the government, and the legislature in various political systems. Wu was still in his 20s at the time and was exhilarated by working with Bao Tong, whom he described as "very intelligent, very quick-thinking, very smart. What impressed me was that he was not really constrained by ideology."

The political reforms and the new sense of freedom ushered in a cultural renaissance that culminated in February, 1989, with China's first-ever avant-garde art exhibition to be held in an official site, the National Art Museum. This was temporarily shut down after one artist shot her own work with a handgun. Poignantly, the exhibition's theme was "No U-Turn," an expression of support for the political reforms. (In 2009, the 20th-anniversary commemorative exhibition was also shut down by police, showing how very little has changed.)

This period of political liberalization was mandated by the patriarch Deng Xiaoping, who had decreed, "Without political reform, economic reform cannot succeed." Deng's idea of reform—streamlining the administration—did not dovetail with Zhao's vision, which was to reduce the party's role in economic and social affairs. Thus, Bao Tong had to tread carefully to win support from Deng. In an interview with French journalist Michel Cormier, Bao Tong described Deng's unpredictability, "He went back and forth like a pendulum. Sometimes he favored the reforms, sometimes he asserted the Four Principles of Socialism. He was both a sincere supporter of the reforms and a determined defender of the things we had to reform." After the 1986–1987 student movement was curbed and reformist Hu Yaobang was removed from his post as party general secretary, the conservative camp gained ground, launching its campaign against bourgeois liberalization.

The liberal reformers and the conservative camp had differed sharply not only over economic strategy but also over the necessity for political reform. Once the students took to the streets in April 1989, tensions between the two camps reached a new pitch. When it came to the question of how to handle the students, Zhao favored a more conciliatory approach featuring dialogue; he had been on a state visit to North Korea when the inflammatory April 26th editorial was issued, and later on, he lobbied to revise the editorial in order to reduce tensions, a move that was unthinkable to many of the elders who feared it would damage the image of Deng Xiaoping.

Describing the mood at the highest levels of government, Bao Tong painted an atmosphere so weighted by factional mistrust that any discussion of the issues was impossible. By then, he had worked with Zhao Ziyang for nine years, and their rapport transcended words. According to Bao Tong, they never had a single conversation about what stance to take toward the student movement. "This wasn't something you would discuss," he said. "He was clear and I was clear. That was enough."

During those weeks—from the death of Hu Yaobang on April 15th until Bao Tong's imprisonment at the end of May—he was present at some of the most critical moments. The speeches that he drafted for Zhao Ziyang would play a key role in his boss's downfall; the party later pointed to the address Zhao gave—written by Bao Tong—on the anniversary of the May 4th Movement as a turning point. In Bao Tong's original draft, he had written, "There will be no turmoil in China," to which his boss had added the word "major." "There will be no major turmoil in China" was used against Zhao, who was accused of creating "two voices" within the leadership.

When Zhao Ziyang decided to write his resignation letter on May 17th, he turned to Bao Tong. Zhao had just returned home in a highly emotional state from a Politburo Standing Committee meeting at which he had voiced his opposition to martial law. "I told myself that no matter what, I refused to become the General Secretary who mobilized the military to crack down on students," Zhao wrote in his secret journal. At the time, there was just one other person in the room: Zhang Yueqi, the deputy head of the General Affairs Office. "The center has made a decision," Bao remembered Zhao telling them. "What the decision is I cannot tell you because I need to maintain the secret, but I cannot follow through with this decision. If I am not able to follow through with this, it would just delay it and get in the way, so I think I should resign." Bao responded by asking whether Zhao was quitting his post as the general secretary of the Communist Party or his post as first vice chairman of the Central Military Commission. Zhao replied that he would resign both positions. Bao Tong drafted a simple note, which Zhao submitted. The next day, he was persuaded to retract it.

It was then that Bao Tong began to prepare himself and his staff for the inevitable fallout. He had been informed by Zhao that Premier Li Peng had accused him of leaking state secrets, one of the most serious of all accusations. But Bao never considered leaving China; it was not an option he was willing to countenance, then or ever. That day, he consulted a lawyer and an expert on the party constitution within his department. "I said, 'You guys write out some of the issues regarding citizens' rights to freedom, the rights and duties of party members and how investigations should be handled, including what to do if someone uses extra-legal means or illegal means against you.'" They drew up a field guide specifying which articles in the constitution and party charter could be used to protect themselves. It was then photocopied and circulated to about a dozen staff members. "I told everyone that night—17th May—I said that someone will probably want to fire me. There might be an investigation. And if it comes to that, then people should not be anxious. Be strong."

Meanwhile, Zhao Ziyang had taken three days of sick leave. During those days, Bao Tong felt his fate closing in on him; all the ways out seemed to culminate in dead ends. He continued to go to work, just as he always had, yet the days that followed were terrifyingly out of the ordinary. He sat in his office, but there were no documents to sign. Nobody solicited his opinion on policy decisions.

There were few visitors. Bao Tong brooded angrily on the accusation that he had leaked state secrets; such charges were not made lightly. His office had become the eye in the dizzying vortex of a government in crisis.

Bao Tong began to prepare his family for the worst. He had been working round the clock, returning home once a week for dinner and to collect clean clothes. His son remembered one family meal at which Bao Tong spelled out what lay ahead. "He just showed us the party charter, he showed us the constitution, and he said, 'These things are probably not enough to protect me.'"

Still Bao Tong found it hard to believe that his boss and mentor—the leader of China's Communist Party—could end up as a political victim. It seemed impossible. Bao Tong visited Zhao at his courtyard home during his sick leave and found him looking pale and weak. Bao Tong was careful to police his own words, so their conversation was freighted with meanings that could not be expressed openly. "I said to him, 'You have a good rest, and in a couple of days—a month—you should go to play golf,'" Bao Tong remembered. "He laughed." Later on, Zhao Ziyang used his love of golf as an excuse to leave his courtyard home, where he was kept under house arrest for 15 years until his death in 2005.

The two never met again. They were forbidden to see each other. When Zhao Ziyang died, Bao Tong was prevented from leaving his apartment to attend the funeral. At one point during the ensuing scuffle, Bao's guards even shoved his wife to the ground, fracturing a bone in her lower back and putting her in the hospital for three months. His presence at such a high-profile gathering of old reformers and dissidents was seen as too risky.

Back in 1989, after June 4th, Beijing Mayor Chen Xitong gave a speech in which he accused Bao Tong of leaking the news of impending martial law. By then, Bao Tong was already in prison, though no formal charges had been made against him. When he went on trial in 1992, he was charged with leaking an unspecified "important state secret"; no details were given. Bao Tong himself has consistently denied the accusation, arguing that he had not known that martial law would be imposed. He was, nonetheless, found guilty of the crime, as well as of "counterrevolutionary propaganda and incitement." The show trial lasted just six hours, after which he was sentenced to seven years in prison, which he spent in solitary confinement.

• • • •

In Bao Pu's first memory, he is three years old. He is standing at a railway station with his father, sister, and grandparents, wild with excitement at the prospect of a train ride. What little Bao Pu did not realize was that their journey was one of internal exile. The year was 1970, and his father was one of the millions of victims of Chairman Mao's Cultural Revolution, having been labeled a "capitalist roader."

After hours of travel, the train stopped at a gloomy-looking station, and the family was driven to a house so dark the little boy thought it was a cave. He began crying, terrified of the black void of night in the countryside; electric light had not yet arrived in the Henan village where the family would spend the next four years while Bao Tong was "re-educated" on a tobacco farm. For his young son, it was a period of bucolic freedom, living with his grandparents, running around the village with the chickens and dogs. Bao Pu was too young to fully comprehend how political dictates had divided his family. His mother, who had been an underground Communist during Nationalist rule, trusted with the task of spying on her classmates, was also sent for re-education. She was assigned to Jiangxi province, far from the rest of her family.

Bao Tong had been working in the Organization Department since 1954. His immediate superior was Deng Xiaoping. Bao had been trained by his mentor, An Ziwen, to become a kind of human computer, able to memorize the résumés of 3,000 party members, and then summon up each of their details in an instant. Such feats of memory may account for his vivid recollections of 1989, though his son says his memory is not as sharp as it once was.

At the tobacco farm, Bao Tong's duties included cooking for 300 people, all of whom had been sent for re-education. He was not permitted to live with his family, whom he saw only once a week, between six and eight o'clock on Sunday nights. Each weekly visit was spent walking back and forth to the well to draw enough water to fill three big vats so that his elderly parents and young children would have enough water for drinking, cooking, and washing until his next visit. As he carried the buckets of water back and forth, young Bao Pu would skip alongside him, making the most of his only chance to see his father.

This was the era of brutal sessions against those accused of opposing Chairman Mao; they were subjected to intense public humiliation and sometimes even driven to suicide. Bao Tong noticed that those who denied their crimes or tried to defend themselves were given a far harder time, so he tried not to give his accusers too much ammunition. "If they asked me whether I'd done something, I'd just admit it. I wouldn't deny it. 'Did you say this?' 'Yes, I said it.' 'Did you write this essay?' 'Yes I wrote it.' 'Did you oppose such-and-such?' 'I opposed it.' Where's the fun in struggling against that?" This early experience of struggle combined with Bao Tong's absolute certainty in his own moral position may have given him the mental fortitude to cope with his own post-Tiananmen life.

• • • •

From the first moment the students began to mourn Hu Yaobang in April 1989, Bao Tong had a strong sense of foreboding. "He knew right from the beginning few days this was going to be a tragic event," Bao Pu told me, as he downed a coffee with an extra double-shot of espresso at a Hong Kong café. In his mid-40s, Bao Pu has a clean-cut appearance with floppy bangs and an American accent that are the legacy of his 10 years in the U.S., studying computer engineering, followed by public administration, at Princeton.

By 1989, Bao Tong had 35 years of experience of dealing with Deng Xiaoping, the ultimate political survivor who had been purged three times by Chairman Mao and three times had clawed his way back to positions of power. Bao knew that, having been responsible for Hu Yaobang's downfall, Deng would view the students' calls for a reappraisal of Hu's legacy as a challenge to his own power. Bao also realized that his boss's sympathetic attitude toward the students would likely be interpreted as an act of disloyalty toward Deng.

Bao Tong warned Bao Pu, then a 22-year-old college senior, not to get involved. Two years earlier, Bao Pu had taken part in the student movement. This time, he was explicitly told that—given his father's position—his participation could have an adverse effect on wider political forces. The idealistic young Bao Pu did not heed the warnings. His curiosity and excitement drew him to Tiananmen Square every day. "Everybody was there," he remembered, "it was like a big party." In retrospect, he believes that his father understood the nature of the regime better than anyone else.

Understanding the nature of the regime has become Bao Pu's career too. He runs New Century Press, a Hong Kong publishing house that has become a major irritant to Beijing. Bao Pu describes his mission as filling in the "blank spots" in Chinese history. It is a business created and sustained by the Chinese government's censorship, but driven in no small part by his father's circumscribed existence, which throws his own mission into sharp relief. "How to use freedom is up to yourself," he told me. "Some people want to make money, that's their freedom. I'm going to use freedom to its fullest extent." To this end, he has published dozens of books that cannot be published in China, including a thriller featuring the assassination of the Chinese president, the memoirs of an early unsuccessful challenger to Chairman Mao, and, most galling of all for Beijing, insider accounts of more recent elite political struggles.

In Bao Pu's view, history is not in the grand sweep of things but in the granular details. To that end, he has published a number of memoirs, retracing the run-up to June 4th, 1989, with an almost archaeological approach, peeling back layer after layer of events through the eyes of different high-level participants. As these memoirs appear, the effect is prismatic, splintering the narrative into a series of alternatives, each of which sheds a different complexion over the whole.

"History is always dangerous," Bao Pu told me. He has become adept at gauging the level of danger each of his books is perceived to pose to the Communist Party by measuring the harassment he undergoes ahead of publication. Although he is based in Hong Kong, whose freedoms were guaranteed under the "One Country, Two Systems" formula, his experiences show just how thin that promise has been stretched since 1997. When I asked him how many books had attracted mainland pressure, he tried to count them on his fingers but eventually gave up.

Bao Pu's biggest scoop was published free from mainland intimidation, since he managed to keep it under wraps until the moment of its release in 2009. This was the posthumous publication of the diaries of Zhao Ziyang, based on tapes the former party general secretary had recorded secretly during his years under house arrest. Not even Zhao's own family had been aware that he had been recording over audiotapes of music and his grandchildren's nursery rhymes, and then passing some of the tapes to trusted friends for safekeeping. After Zhao's death in 2005, one of the friends passed a message to a family member asking them to search the house. Not long after, they found a stash of cassettes. Bao Pu then persuaded them to let him compile the material into this beyond-the-grave account of the secret struggles within the leadership. The book included Zhao's own feisty letter to the Central Committee in which he described his house arrest as a "crude trampling of the socialist legal system" and a violation of the party charter.

Bao Pu's list of publications reveals the extent to which the ghosts of Tiananmen haunt those responsible for the suppression. Though the official party view on June 4th has never wavered, those who supported martial law are now keen to distance themselves from that decision. One recent example is former Beijing Mayor Chen Xitong, whose alarmist reports to Deng Xiaoping about the dangers posed by the students are widely thought to have pushed him toward martial law. But in 2012, in a book published by Bao Pu, Chen tried to abnegate responsibility, arguing that Deng was not someone so easily manipulated, "How could Deng possibly have been deceived? To say he was is to underestimate Deng."

In his attempts to sidle away from responsibility, Chen cast himself as a closet liberal and called the crackdown "a regrettable tragedy that could have been avoided and should have been avoided." Chen was later jailed for 16 years for corruption. Some believe he had been the victim of a power struggle. In the conversations that make up the book, he chooses to portray himself as a puppet of the regime in the spring of 1989, apparently viewing this as less damaging than having been a decision-maker. For example, he insisted that he had played no role in preparing a long report that justified the government's repression. "I was not present when the report was discussed. They asked me to read it, and I read it, without changing a single bit of punctuation."

Even the man sometimes called the "Butcher of Beijing," Premier Li Peng, has done his best to avoid responsibility. In his secret Tiananmen diary, which Bao Pu attempted to publish in 2010, Li Peng tries to shift the onus of the decision firmly onto Deng Xiaoping, whom he quotes as saying, "Martial law will eventually pacify. We should as much as possible minimize injuries, but we should prepare to spill some blood." Li Peng also claims that the PLA opened fire only in self-defense after "armed rioters...first opened fire at the military, burning military vehicles and brutally beating, burning and killing the warriors."

Bao Pu's attempt to publish Li Peng's memoirs brought the full ire of the Chinese state down upon him. In the run-up to the release of the book, a team of senior Chinese officials flew to Hong Kong to try to persuade him to drop the project. Back in Beijing, police called his father daily, asking him to exert his influence over his son. At one stage, members of the Hong Kong mafia even got in on the act, warning Bao Pu that he was treading on dangerous ground. Just days before publication, Bao Pu pulled the plug. At the time, he told newspapers that information about the copyright of the material had left him with little choice. But when we spoke, he said that his main reason for canceling was the fact that the diary had already been leaked online. Since then, he has come to regret not publishing the diary, because its release without textual analysis or context meant that it was widely overlooked. "Read it very, very carefully," he urged me. "It's very crucial." For his father Bao Tong, a handful of lines in Li Peng's diary entirely changed his understanding of what had happened a quarter-century ago. "Only after I read those couple of lines did I know what was going on," he told me. "Then I was afraid."

• • • •

Bao Tong's home is a spotless sixth-floor apartment inside a utilitarian gray residential block splashed with garish yellow and green details. Inside the lobby, a desk had been set up. An officer took my name and checked my press credentials before allowing me to enter. Bao Tong's apartment itself was bright and modern, entirely devoid of the overstuffed armchairs and antimacassars so beloved by his generation of bureaucrats. Instead, orange-dotted throws brightened the couches, while on the desk, two large computer monitors sat side-by-side. Above the television hung a glossy portrait of three generations of the family, all beaming, as if from a college alumni magazine. The only immediate clue to his past was a photograph of Zhao Ziyang propped high on a bookshelf; it is one of the few pictures taken while he was under house arrest. He is dressed in a casual denim shirt, arms akimbo, a wide smile on his face, his hair snow white. The photo sits next to a ticking clock.

Despite his age, Bao Tong's wardrobe is surprisingly up-to-date, favoring Nike T-shirts and Crocs. Back in 1989, even his clothing choices were remarked upon by one of the revolutionary elders arguing for his arrest. According to the *Tiananmen Papers*, Li Xiannian accused Bao Tong of "pure bourgeois stuff. He's over fifty but follows fashions like a youngster. He wears gaudy jackets and blue jeans inside *Zhongnanhai*—what kind of Party official is that? His head is full of bourgeois liberalization." When I mentioned this to Bao Tong, he chuckled and commented that such a response only illustrated Li Xiannian's shallowness.

I was curious as to why he had been so shaken by Li Peng's diary, and so I began to read it. I was struck by two passages in which there are clear hints that Deng Xiaoping had been looking for a way to remove Zhao Ziyang even before the student movement gained momentum. In the diary, Deng's bridge partner Ding Guan'gen— incidentally the brother-in-law of the Tiananmen Mother Zhang Xianling—related to Li Peng conversations that Deng had held with another elder, Li Xiannian, a year earlier about "some problems" concerning Zhao Ziyang. "At that time Comrade Xiaoping could see clearly that Zhao was pushing liberalization, and sooner or later he must be made to step down. But because the impact would have been too great, and he could not find an appropriate candidate at the time, he was not yet ready to make the decision. This January,

Comrade Xiaoping was talking, and he said, 'The norm will not change,' meaning that he did not yet have the idea of moving Zhao Ziyang." The second passage repeats a similar conversation held on a separate occasion.

For Bao Tong, these passages were evidence that Zhao Ziyang had been a marked man before 1989. "This had nothing to do with the students," Bao told me. He believes that Deng used the students as a tool to oust his designated successor. "He had to find a reason. The more the students pushed, the more of a reason Deng Xiaoping had. If the students all went home, then Deng Xiaoping wouldn't have had a reason." According to Bao's theory, the gradual escalation of tensions between the Communist leadership and the students may not have been due to mishandling by a divided party, but part of a deliberate strategy. Bao Tong believes that the timing of events supported this reading. "When Deng Xiaoping sent in the army, it was not when the students were at their greatest numbers," he pointed out. "Only when most of the students had gone home did he send in the army."

As for the sentence that had inspired such fear, it was one that few would notice. On April 23rd, Li Peng wrote about his fears that the country could slip back into turmoil similar to the Cultural Revolution. "I had no resolution about how to handle the chaos before us. At this time, Comrade Shangkun suggested I take the initiative to seek instructions from Comrade Xiaoping, and he would go with me." That single sentence doesn't reveal whether or not the pair actually visited Deng Xiaoping that day. But if the meeting did happen, it has been removed from Deng's official schedule of appointments. Bao Tong began to wonder whether a meeting might have happened that day, during which Deng gave orders to Li Peng about how to deal with the student movement. The significance of such a secret meeting is that the entire chain of decision-making would then have bypassed the party's institutions, undermining the legitimacy of the process.

Does it even matter? Soon the party's institutions were ignored and Deng's elderly supporters were brought into play to stack the decision-making process. What happened during those seven weeks was that the old patriarch Deng Xiaoping engineered a coup,

during which he circumnavigated the institutions of state in order
to oust the party leader he himself had chosen. But the major difference would be in terms of legacy. Bao Tong believes history has been
too kind, remembering Deng as the architect of Chinese reform; he
believes Deng's role in June 4th points to a more complicated truth.
"What's really important is that Chinese people need to know that
he was a dictator."

• • • •

On June 4th, 1989, as the sun rose on the war zone that was central Beijing, Bao Tong was in his prison cell, unaware that anything
had happened. His suspicions started to take shape, however, when
his copy of the *People's Daily* never arrived, and they solidified over
the next two days as the news blackout continued. Finally, on June
7th, he was given a newspaper, which he read with growing horror.
"When I saw it, I thought that Deng Xiaoping had shot dead the
Communist Party," he told me.

From Bao Tong's perspective, what happened on the night of June
4th is the defining act of modern-day China, from which stem all
its major ills, including the rampant corruption, the crippling lack
of trust in the government, the widespread morality crisis, and the
ascendancy of the security apparatus. The government's decision to
turn arms on its own people sent out a clear message that violence
was an acceptable tool. As Bao Tong put it, "If that was now possible
at the highest levels of government, then why not at the lower levels?
There was one big Tiananmen. But how many little Tiananmens
have there been? How many little Tiananmens are there every day?"

Unlike in the past, these "little Tiananmens" now play out in real
time, often shown live online, as disgruntled victims need only a
smart phone to send proof ricocheting around the Internet. In 2012,
activists even invoked Tank Man, after photos went viral of the pul-
verized body of a villager who had been resisting the construction
of a new road. According to one eyewitness report, he had been
lying in front of a steamroller, shouting, "Dare to run me over!" In
the pictures, one of the villager's hands can be seen stuck between
two of the steamroller's front tires, while his brain matter lies in

front of the vehicle. In a side shot, his feet, clad in thin cotton shoes are visible beneath the vehicle. A crescendo of equally lurid cases, underscored by stories of outrageous official rapacity, has created a fin-de-siècle atmosphere on *weibo*.

Despite improvements in the standard of living, unrest has risen exponentially due to mounting discontent over land seizures, government corruption, and ethnic issues. "Mass incidents," as large protests are euphemistically known, have skyrocketed from 10,000 in 1994 to 180,000 in 2010, the last year for which there are reliable figures. In the majority of cases, the threat of force is employed more often than violence itself. However, in recent years, reports of deadly violence being used to disperse protests have become more common, especially as the country's center struggles to deal with increasing ethnic discontent in Uighur areas in the northwest of the country, and among Tibetans, whose desperation has crystallized into more than one hundred suicidal self-immolations in the ultimate protest against Chinese control.

Back in 1989, the violent suppression of the protests initially led to a collapse in economic growth, as Western governments imposed sanctions on China. Frustrated by continued wrangling inside the party over the pace of economic reform, in 1992, Deng Xiaoping again ignored his own party's institutions and launched a Southern Tour to kick-start three decades of high-speed economic growth. Today, many young Chinese see the country's prosperity as a post-facto justification for the crackdown. In fact, disposable incomes have increased by a multiple of 17 since 1989. The benefits have not been equally distributed, however, with urban incomes at least three times higher than rural ones.

Before 1989, an income gap had existed, but rural incomes were growing faster than urban ones. After, the pattern was reversed, and the gap widened into a chasm. Between 1978 and 1988, rural incomes grew by more than 10 percent a year—exceeding GDP growth—but between 1989 and 2002, that figure slowed to just 4 percent growth a year—or less than half of GDP growth.

If the party had hoped to buy stability in the cities, it also succeeded in entrenching inequality in the countryside, turning China's farmers into second-class citizens. Curbing Zhao Ziyang's political reforms also hit the countryside harder, as the reforms had gone furthest there. Gates Hill, an anthropologist studying private enterprises in Sichuan in the late 1980s, noted that the post-Tiananmen repression was not just political but also resulted in a slew of new taxes while officials sought to regain control of the economy. She wrote, "The political crackdown after Tiananmen was followed by a low-key but strikingly efficient economic repression aimed at disrupting the accumulation of private capital and the lowering of consumption."

For Bao Tong, undertaking economic reforms without the accompanying political reforms was dangerous. The subsequent dismantling of state-owned enterprises without proper supervision has created a princeling kleptocracy, far exceeding the nepotism and profiteering that drove some of the 1989 protests. "This was called 'progress,'" Bao Tong told me, his words heavy with sarcasm. "It sounded so good. In reality, it was simply taking things from the people—the state-owned enterprises—and giving them to the officials. And the officials became millionaires."

Thanks to a series of painstaking journalistic investigations, the hidden value of revolutionary ancestry has been quantified. A Bloomberg News investigation found that relatives of the current President Xi Jinping had investments in companies with total assets worth $376 million, though it did not find any specific wrongdoing by the president or his wife. In a follow-up, the Bloomberg team turned its focus on the wealth of the descendants of China's revolutionary leaders—the progeny of the "Eight Immortals." It discovered that in 2011 just three individuals—General Wang Zhen's son Wang Jun; Deng Xiaoping's son-in-law He Ping; and Chen Yuan, the son of Chen Yun—headed state-owned companies with assets of $1.6 trillion, an amount equivalent to more than 20 percent of China's annual economic output. As far back as 1990, one of the Immortals, General Wang Zhen, was reported to be so disillusioned with his two sons' scramble for wealth that he referred to them as "turtle eggs," popular slang for bastards, and told a visitor to his hospital bed, "I don't acknowledge them as my sons."

Even more explosive was the Pulitzer Prize-winning *New York Times* investigation into the wealth amassed by family members of

China's former Premier Wen Jiabao. This report, which led to the *New York Times* being blocked inside China, traced corporate and regulatory records, concluding that Wen's relatives have controlled assets worth at least $2.7 billion. Even Wen Jiabao's nonagenarian mother, once a humble schoolteacher, was worth $120 million five years ago. His younger brother has a company that was given government contracts worth more than $30 million to handle wastewater treatment and medical waste disposal, while his wife has built her own fortune managing state diamond companies that were later privatized.

One of the enigmas surrounding Wen Jiabao had been his appearance, his face a pale mask of dissimulation, at the side of Zhao Ziyang, as Zhao made his final public appearance visiting the students in Tiananmen Square in 1989. Ever the ultimate balancer, Wen, who was then the director of the General Office of the Party, managed not simply to survive this political crisis, but to continue climbing through the ranks of the party to become the premier, sparking hopes that he would reveal himself as a closet reformer. Throughout his term, he paid lip service to the need for reform, but there were few concrete gains. Bao Tong believes that those such as Wen, who once shared his ideals, ended up selling their souls in the economic free-for-all. "The reformists are in this for the spoils of reform," he pronounced, noting that in the current system, corruption is almost expected.

"If I were an official, I'd definitely be corrupt," Bao Tong once told me. "People would say, 'How about your son becoming the chairman of the board in a state-owned company?' If I refused, they would say, 'If my son can become one, why can't your son?' If I still said he wouldn't do it, then they wouldn't see me as being in the same boat. So they would push me out of the boat."

With the glee of a child calling attention to the emperor's lack of clothes, Bao Tong pointed out the discrepancy between hereditary privilege deriving from revolutionary bloodlines and the Communist Party's original ideal of equality. "The father is an official, the child should be an official," Bao Tong said. "What kind of revolution is that? What's that got to do with Marx and the proletariat? This is Chinese-style socialism. It's false socialism. It's more feudal than feudalism. It's about staying in power. Its guiding principle is, I have to stay in power, I need to be in power, I need to be corrupt. That's the Chinese system."

These are the kind of trenchant views that Bao Tong expresses in the commentaries he still writes for Radio Free Asia. That he is still allowed to publish such criticism shows that dissenting views are tolerated, so long as they are not seen to incite action. It also underlines the party's dilemma of how to handle such a high-profile dissident. Bao once told me offhandedly that one advantage in being jailed as an octogenarian would be to expose the party's real face to the outside world. His fearlessness is born of conviction, but also of guilt, knowing that he had been complicit in some of the party's earlier crimes.

The one time his composure wavered during our conversations was when we talked about the Great Famine of 1958 to 1961, during which an estimated 36 million people starved to death. Bao Tong admitted that he had known people were starving to death, though he hadn't known the true extent of the numbers. Regardless, he had believed wholeheartedly in Chairman Mao and had continued to do so despite the famine. He was labeled a 'rightist' in 1965. On December 28, 1966, as his wife was giving birth to their son, Bao Tong was in a 'struggle session' after which he spent six years doing hard labor.

Now, he bitterly regretted having shouted, "Long Live Chairman Mao!" during the Cultural Revolution, though he emphasized that his mind had not really been liberated from the party's ideological shackles until the moment he was expelled from it.

In many ways, Bao Tong remains frozen at a particular point in time. "In over 20 years, he considers this as an ongoing political struggle that he's never given up," said Bao Pu. "And he's lived in this one fight from that day to today." With his roster of gadfly publications designed to erode the party's control of information, Bao Pu too seemed to be fighting the same fight, albeit punching from a different corner. But to Bao Pu, the difference between himself and his father can be summed up in one crucial word: hope. The old revolutionary still believes he can change China, while his son professes to have lost all hope that political reform can happen in the current system.

How has an elderly, half-blind, ex-Communist, ex-prisoner, living such a severely circumscribed existence under the watchful eyes of the state, managed to remain hopeful? His answer invoked the stubborn belief in the power of the masses to enact change. "I think every single person in China has the ability to change China. I don't think any one person's efforts are a waste of their sweat and blood. I think we are like 1.3 billion ants. The strength of any ant combined with the others has the ability to push China forward or backward or into stagnation."

• • • •

The last time I saw Bao Tong was at our old meeting place in McDonald's on a stifling July morning. When I walked in, he was already standing at the counter, looking frailer than ever, his twig-like legs protruding from beneath beige shorts. He had already ordered for both of us. "I didn't know whether you wanted hot or cold, so I got one of each," he explained with a smile, gesturing to his tray which contained two coffees and two ice-cream sundaes. Our usual spot at the back was occupied by a homeless person whose plastic bags of possessions were spread across the floor, so we opted for a corner table.

Bao Tong looked very old indeed, as if the years had caught up with him all of a sudden. Just a couple of days earlier, he'd heard that his son's visa had been rejected for the third time that year. No reason was given.

"How are you?" I asked, out of genuine concern.

"Very tired," he replied, with none of his usual vigor.

His legs had no strength in them, and he could no longer keep his spirits up. He thought it was the hot weather. When he got up in the morning, all he wanted to do was go straight back to bed again. He was too tired to write commentaries, and he could no longer see the point. Everybody knew what he thought anyway. His voice had gone whisper-quiet. I wondered what had happened to take the fight out of him.

The tables around us were filled with children whose parents were taking advantage of the summer holidays to cram in some extra lessons. For the price of a soft drink, McDonald's doubled as a perfectly adequate classroom, with air conditioning into the bargain. In the silence as he sat back in his chair, the arpeggios of a child doing Korean language drills at the next table rose and fell in the background.

Then Bao Tong seemed to rally.

"You definitely know what I will write about next," he said, with a small smile.

I had no idea. "What?" I asked.

"About disappointment. Everything that I have seen has made me disappointed."

He went quiet again, and I regretted rousing this tired, old man from his bed to walk over to a noisy fast-food restaurant on such a blisteringly hot day. I mentioned that a prominent lawyer, Xu Zhiyong, had been detained on a trumped-up charge of "gathering a crowd to disturb social order." His real crime had been calling for officials to declare their assets, which seemed to be in line with the government's stated aim of fighting corruption by catching "tigers" as well as "flies." Yet he had been arrested, along with other anticorruption activists, on charges of inciting subversion of state power. "The leaders' courage is diminishing," Bao Tong said very quietly. "They're scared of the sky falling. These detentions are not a sign of strength, but of weakness."

While the official anticorruption campaign had already landed a few scalps, including that of the rail minister who had acquired 18 mistresses and 374 apartments, Bao Tong believed it was doomed to fail without the necessary political reforms. "Even if you kill 1,000 flies and 10,000 tigers, so long as the system remains unchanged, then the system will give birth to another 10 million flies and a million tigers. It is called systemic corruption."

Not only had calls for asset disclosure become dangerous, merely the suggestion that the Communist Party should respect the country's constitution had also become a suspect activity. Articles had been appearing in party publications suggesting that the concept of constitutional governance was only suitable for bourgeois capitalism and constituted a covert call for the overthrow of Socialism. The perceived threat of Western ideals was being taken so seriously that an April 2013 document nicknamed the "Seven Unmentionables" was being circulated to party members. Among the seven taboo subjects are "universal values," civil society, judicial independence, and criticism of the Communist Party's historical mistakes. Even activists trying to attend training sessions on the United Nations' human rights mechanisms in Geneva were being prevented from leaving the country, and one had disappeared after being detained at the airport.

As we talked about these recent developments, Bao Tong's voice rose, and he seemed to gather strength. Slowly, as he marshaled his outrage, he began to resemble his old self, pursing his lips carefully just before a particularly salient point, his shoulders gently quaking with laughter. There was a light in his eyes, a glint that wasn't just from his cataracts. There was a gentle grace to this elderly man who had lived several different lives, in and out of power, at the heart of government and in a prison cell, and who was now living this strange half-life, not fully free, though not incarcerated either.

What was happening today, he said, was all cosmetic. "Have you ever seen a dead person? After they have been made up, they look amazing. Better than a live person."

China's much-touted aircraft carriers, its high-speed railways, the satellites it shot into space—these were all cosmetic measures designed to try to keep China's economic growth rate aloft. The government's own statistics didn't really matter, he said bitterly, since they were all falsified anyway. What mattered was pacifying the populace to ensure that they maintained confidence in their leaders, so that they would continue spending money and not causing trouble. The cynical strategy was one of massive Potemkin projects designed to disguise the rot within.

"Every year, they have an expo, or something like it: a garden exhibition or an Olympics. They'll set off some fireworks, or a satellite, or a flying saucer. Everyone will see them. Oh! Up it goes! And so does the GDP!"

That also fed into what Bao Tong defined as the "second prong in the government strategy": nationalism that had begun to tip over into militarism. Pick an island, any island, to fixate upon but don't actually start a war, since you won't win anyway. But use the perception that imperialists are trying to prevent China from being number one to build nationalism, which serves to increase cohesion and distract the masses from more pressing social issues. China's growing international might was progress of one kind, but for Bao Tong, it conjured up the short-lived reign of strongman empires characterized by cruelty and control.

"During the time of [China's first Emperor] Qin Shihuang, the country was great and during the time of Genghis Khan, the country was great, but how good was it for the people? The country can be doing well, but the people can be doing badly."

The lunchtime crowd was beginning to flood into McDonald's, and I could see that Bao Tong was keen to smoke his pre-lunch cigarette as he walked home, trailed by his ever-present watchers. As I took my leave, he asked the Korean teacher nearby to take a picture of us together, posing awkwardly among the tables of schoolchildren. Then I ended our conversations as I had started so many months earlier, by asking him whether he still thought he would see the events of June 4th reassessed within his lifetime. "I hope so," he answered. "But I don't think that God can consider every single person's wishes, since there are too many wishes, and God can't deal with them all."

I was surprised by his reply. "Do you even believe in God?" I asked. "I believe in myself," he said, his filmy eyes looking steadily into mine. "I believe that I have a conscience. My conscience is God."

8 :: Chengdu

Chairman Mao still oversees Tianfu Square in the city of Chengdu in Southwestern China, his gigantic white marble hand outstretched either in imperious greeting or, as the locals joke, like someone betting five Yuan in mahjong. The site over which the hundred-foot-tall Chairman Mao statue keeps watch once housed an Imperial Palace that was razed by Red Guards in the Cultural Revolution. Back then, the all-seeing chairman dominated the city. Today, as BMWs and Audis cruise casually past his feet, the Great Helmsman increasingly resembles an ineffective traffic policeman. Follow his line of sight and he's peering toward a Louis Vuitton boutique facing a newly opened Gucci shop. In the evening, crowds of Chinese tourists gather in the square to snap photos of the fountains spurting sinuous helixes of water into the air, their arcs synchronized with screeching music.

Chengdu's Mao bore silent witness to one of the huge untold stories of 1989. Far from the viewfinders of foreign cameras, tens . of thousands also marched through these streets, camping around the chairman's feet and launching their own, smaller hunger strike. When Tiananmen Square was forcibly cleared of its students, so too was Chengdu's Tianfu Square, though the latter was largely a peaceful operation. What happened next, however, has, until now, never been fully told. I have tried to piece together the events that unfolded in Chengdu, assembling shards of memories, declassified U.S. diplomatic cables, diaries, hastily written reports of the time, contemporaneous photographs, and Chinese government-approved accounts published in the immediate aftermath. I have spoken to locals who were caught up in the events, as well as tracked down many of the foreigners in Chengdu at the time—professionals, travelers, English teachers, students—who bore witness to an atrocity.

My search for information has taken me to a 400-year-old Swiss chalet perched high above Alpine meadows, where I talked to a retired American diplomat against a backdrop of sonorous cowbells. It has taken me to Ann Arbor, Michigan, to consult a young graduate student who had painstakingly dug up local government archives for his research on the student movement in Chengdu. Through e-mail, *weibo*, and Skype, I began to make contact with those who had been there, while attempting to navigate the gaping chasm between what I was hearing and the state-approved version of events. And it has taken me to Chengdu itself.

• • • •

At night, the entire city of Chengdu simmers in the aromas wafting from the snack stalls lining the roads: the mouth-watering, eye-stinging pungency of hot red chili peppers and Sichuan peppercorns, small brown buds that make your lips tingle and your tongue lose sensation. This is the smell of Sichuan: *mala*, both chili-hot and numbing. And in temperament, the Sichuanese, following suit, are quick to anger and fiercely rebellious against the central authorities.

After the death of Hu Yaobang, events in Chengdu mirrored what was happening in the capital, although there was a time lag. The first memorial gathering in Tianfu Square happened two days after his death, and it took five days for a large-scale demonstration to coalesce. By April 21st and 22nd, there were huge marches, and some arrests, but the class boycott and hunger strike did not start until May 15th, several days after the Beijing students had begun to refuse food. By then, the Chengdu colleges had come alive with protest, especially at night, when a chorus of chants snaked around campuses, as lines of students ran through the grounds shouting slogans, singing the "Internationale," and gathering in front of faculty apartments.

But their demands were different from those of the Beijing students. "One of the main things that sticks in my mind was that it was never a protest in favor of democracy," said Paul Goldin, then an American student studying Chinese at Sichuan University and now a professor of Chinese thought at the University of Pennsylvania. From his vantage point, the students' aim was to make the system more pure from the inside out, in an attempt to hold the Communist Party to its word rather than to overthrow it. "It was supposed to be a protest against corruption," he said, and it stayed that way until almost the end. "Very, very late, after everybody had found out about the [Chinese version of the] Statue of Liberty that had been built in Beijing, at that point, people started using words like freedom and democracy."

That view was shared by Jan de Wilde, who was then U.S. consul general in Chengdu. He said of the protesters, "I don't think they had the foggiest idea what freedom and democracy actually meant in China or anywhere else. They were still very much [operating] in the framework of a one-party state." The party officials whom he met were sympathetic to the students, partly due to the local popularity of the reformist party leader Zhao Ziyang, who had been Sichuan's Communist Party secretary when he pioneered his groundbreaking economic reforms.

In Chengdu, the movement's turning point came in the early hours of May 16th, when more than a thousand policemen scuffled with about two hundred students, beating them with sticks and belts to try to clear the square. For Judy Wyman Kelly, an American doctoral student researching social conflict in modern Chinese history, this act served to galvanize the movement, even winning it support from university authorities, who had previously locked school gates to prevent students from taking part in demonstrations. Wyman Kelly had originally been skeptical of the students, believing their base of support was too narrow, but she noted how the police brutality against the students led to an outpouring of public sympathy. In a letter home, she wrote, "All of these students are on strike, and professors are out walking with them in support. Even workers, newspapers and party units are supporting them. I've never seen such popular mobilization, either here or in the U.S.

Nearly everyone seems to support the students, and by the same token, nearly everyone seems to have zero faith in their top leaders."

As the protests mounted, the mood was one of growing optimism and hope in the ability of the masses to bring about change. Even the official account in a section on the unrest in the 1990 *Chengdu Yearbook* comments on the shift in sentiment, noting that several hundred thousand people took to the streets immediately after the police action, with as many as 1,700 students taking part in the hunger strike.

Chengdu became a focal point for marchers, who flocked in from the surrounding regions with delegations coming from as far west as the Tibetan prefecture of Aba to take part in the protests. Students poured out their hopes and aspirations in the posters they plastered on the walls, which bore slogans such as, "If we cannot live freely, we should die struggling!" Protesting became so commonplace that in certain circles, the standard greeting, "Have you eaten yet?" was sometimes half-jokingly replaced by, "Have you demonstrated yet?"

Sichuan's Communist Party secretary in 1989, Yang Rudai, was a protégé of Zhao Ziyang, twice promoted by him. Yang never rose any higher after the unrest, and as late as 2010, he revealed his true sympathies by breaking the taboo on mentioning Zhao in the mainland press. He wrote an article praising Zhao's agricultural reforms that was published in *Yanhuang Chunqiu* or the *Annals of the Yellow Emperor,* one of the country's most outspoken journals. During the protests, the Sichuan government even took the symbolic step of relaying the students' demands in a telegram to the State Council and the Central Committee, a move that hinted at sympathy with them. Officials held talks with the students and visited the hunger strikers on May 18th, with Deputy Party Secretary Gu Jinchi telling them, "We clearly understand your hunger strike in support of the Beijing students and your patriotic zeal of fighting corruption, promoting democracy and the legal system, and deepening the reforms."

After martial law was imposed in Beijing, the Chengdu movement began to peter out. The hunger strike was called off, and local residents lost interest in the handful of students who continued to hold a sit-in around the base of the Mao statue. By early June, so

few protesters remained that a crackdown seemed increasingly unnecessary. The possibility of trouble seemed so unlikely that the
U.S. consul general Jan De Wilde almost left Chengdu to go on a
yak-trekking trip, canceling only at the very last minute.

On the morning of June 4th, after Beijing's Tiananmen Square
had been cleared, police received orders to expel the protesters
from Chengdu's Tianfu Square. In fact, only around 300 students
remained, and most left voluntarily. According to official accounts,
the remaining 51 students were removed in a peaceful operation
that took just half an hour. But within hours, news of the killings
in Beijing had crackled through the shaky static of the BBC World
Service and the Voice of America, and thousands of enraged citizens returned to the streets of Chengdu.

This was an act of sheer solidarity and outright bravery; protesters were taking to the streets in the full knowledge that troops had
opened fire on unarmed civilians in Beijing. Thousands marched
down the main thoroughfare in Chengdu, carrying mourning
wreathes and signs saying "We Are Not Afraid of Death," "June 4th
massacre, 7,000 dead and injured!" and "Down with the Government
of Dictators!" When the first wave of marchers reached the front-
line of the People's Armed Police (PAP), the paramilitary wing
of the police, the situation quickly became tense. Jostling turned
into shoving, and police began beating the protesters with batons.
This escalated quickly into full-blown fighting, with the protesters
attacking the security forces with shoes, bricks, ripped-up pieces of
sidewalk, and anything else they could grab.

At the universities, the first sign of trouble came as students staggered back through the gates, heads bound with crimson-stained
towels, blood dripping down their faces. One American citizen,
Dennis Rea, who was teaching at Chengdu University of Science
and Technology, was determined to bear witness, so together with
two Western friends, including American Kim Nygaard, he set off
on his bicycle to head into the fray.

They passed protesters clutching stones, bottles, and chisels. The
closer they got to the Mao statue, the more chaotic the situation,
with the acrid reek of tear gas billowing up the street amid the boom
of concussive grenades. Thousands of onlookers were clogging the

roads, but every few minutes, a new blast would send them stampeding backward in panic. The three foreigners pressed on until they feared for their own safety.

"At a certain point, you could go no further, unless you really wanted to get involved and get your head split," Rea told me. Then they stumbled onto a small clinic treating the injured. A channel had opened up in the sea of protesters, with a human chain linking hands to hold back the crowds to allow casualties to be ferried from the battlefront, as Rea remembered: "We saw them come in on people's shoulders, draped over bicycles and carts, and we saw a lot of blood."

For 20 minutes, Rea watched a constant stream of injured people being shuttled to receive medical care. Nygaard was carrying a camera and was invited inside the hospital. Her pictures capture the panicked urgency of that day, as grimacing medical staff hoist a casualty from a van; the injured man is still lying on a park bench, his legs smeared with garish blood. Inside the clinic, wounded people sit on benches, their heads swathed in white bandages, arresting visual proof of the security forces' chosen strategy of beating protesters on the head; the most poignant photograph shows a tearful man clutching his bloody head, his eyes wide with fear, shock, and utter disbelief, with the collar and shoulder of his white shirt stained scarlet from his head wound. As the women walked around the hospital, they saw rows of injured people lying on the floor, who begged them, "Tell the world! Tell the world!"

The people of Chengdu were not intimidated by the state-backed violence. On the contrary, it incensed them, raising the pitch of their fury. In his memoir *Live at the Forbidden City*, Dennis Rea describes seeing a mob discover a barely disguised policeman. "The infuriated crowd sniffed him out at once and fell on him like a flock of buzzards, brutally stomping the life out of him right before our eyes. My mind reeled at this harsh dispensation of vigilante justice, which graphically underscored the depth of people's antipathy toward the police." Nonetheless, Rea never felt in direct danger from the crowds, who greeted him with loud cheers. What horrified Rea was the sheer number of casualties he saw, including one unfortunate fruit vendor whose head was split open simply for parking his cart in the wrong place at the wrong time. By the afternoon of June 4th, police had begun throwing tear gas at the crowds. One Chinese citizen who got caught up in the fighting near the square told me he heard gunshots being fired into the crowd from a police station on South People's Road near the square.

One breakthrough in my research was a 27-page report that arrived one day on my doorstep. Written by hand in crabbed Chinese characters, it was titled "An Investigation into the June 4th Chengdu Massacre." This extraordinary document was written by an elderly Communist Party member who entrusted it to a friend to smuggle out of the country; that friend, who requested their identity be kept confidential, passed it on to me. The Communist Party member had been so horrified by the beatings he had seen on the streets that he secretly visited hospitals to collect firsthand accounts of police brutality. He carefully describes 35 victims, mostly by name. The report mentions at least one student who had died in the hospital, and six people who had been wounded by gunshots.

Most of the casualties had been badly beaten, such as one student surnamed Pan who was suffering cerebral concussion, full body edema, and multiple cartilage injuries. From his hospital bed, Pan described with great difficulty how he had been injured by police, "When they got ahold of me, I was already lying on the ground. They forcefully stomped on my arms, and kicked me until my arms became very swollen and wounded. Then they pulled me several dozens of meters and handed me over to the police in the rear line. They gave me another round of cruel beatings. Then, they pulled me to the lawn on one side and kicked my abdomen and hit me on my face with their fists until I lost consciousness." When he came to, he was beaten with electric prods until he heard a police doctor saying, "His pupils are already enlarged. I'm afraid he will die if you continue with these beatings."

The author describes another student named Liu Yishen whose "teeth were knocked out completely and his lips turned inside out due to swelling. His features were totally distorted and he was in a deep coma." He also describes the random police violence against bystanders, for example, two brothers returning home from a public toilet who were beaten unconscious. The author concludes, "The bloody incident of June 4th happened, deeply shaking people's consciences. How many people wept and angrily shouted and bled that day? How many people in Beijing, in Chengdu, in the whole of China lost their sons and daughters, fathers and mothers, wives and husbands, brothers and sisters that day? Heaven has eyes and earth has a soul."

Chengdu's geography is such that the street battles—and subsequent injuries—were seen by many thousands of residents. The government did not attempt to cover up what had happened; instead, it tried to flood the information space by hastily releasing its authoritative account of events, *The Whole Story of the Chengdu Riots*, just a month later with an initial print run of 700,000 copies. According to this paperback book, the fighting left eight dead in Chengdu, including two students. The book reports that 1,800 people sought medical treatment, including 1,100 policemen, though the majority had only light wounds, with 353 people admitted to the hospital for treatment, among them 231 policemen, 69 students, and 53 others. But a U.S. State Department cable released by Wikileaks indicates that the real toll was probably higher. This cites medical personnel confirming seven deaths at one hospital alone, and a Sichuan university official as disclosing that nine students had been confirmed dead, while many more were still missing. American consular officials told the *New York Times* that at least 100 seriously wounded people had been carried out of the square. Later, some U.S. diplomatic cables referred to 300 deaths, though that figure may have been reached in error by conflating the numbers of dead and injured.

By nightfall on June 4th, angry mobs were setting fire to anything belonging to the state, including buses and police vehicles. The crowds threw stones, tiles, and gasoline bottles at a police station near the square where detained protesters had been beaten, and eventually set it on fire. The flames spread to the People's Market—a state-owned market that took up an entire city block—but not before it was looted. Just after midnight, a mobile fire command post and three fire engines were deployed, but they were waylaid by the crowds, which set them on fire too, according to the official account. By early morning, the market had been reduced to ashes, as had a nearby cinema.

The blaze at the People's Market was puzzling to Paul Goldin, who told me, "I was in fairly regular contact with a lot of students, and none of them had ever said anything about burning down the marketplace. It seemed incongruous and not in keeping with what they were planning and what they had in mind to do." The story circulating was that the government had used provocateurs, perhaps even criminals released from jail to set the fires, in order to both discredit the student movement and provide justification for a crackdown in one fell swoop. Other rumors spread that stallholders had known about the plan ahead of time and had managed to remove their stock. Strangely, photographic evidence of this exists in the government's own propaganda. *The Whole Story of the Chengdu Riots* features one photograph showing a line of policemen helping shop owners transport boxes of stock down the steps of a building, accompanied by the caption, "People's armed police warriors assisting shop [owners] to move their stock to avoid it being burned by ruffians." In the photograph, it appears a perfectly orderly scene, with no sign of unrest, and no indication of an approaching blaze, such as smoke or flames. It is not clear if this is the People's Market.

Even former U.S. Consul General Jan de Wilde, who is now retired, had heard the rumor about the fires being started deliberately. He is a debonair man with a background in Chinese language and history, and when we met at his Swiss chalet, he made clear that his memories of Chengdu are sketchy, mainly focusing on his consular duties, such as sheltering American citizens and organizing their repatriation. But he remembered how many people seemed to believe the fire was a case of deliberate arson.

"Was it believable?" I asked him.

"I wouldn't discount it, no," he said carefully. "I'm prepared to believe almost anything about that: that it was arson; that it was set by protesters; that it was set by the government. I simply don't know."

The Sichuan Daily Editorial Board estimated the damage to the market at 100 million yuan even though the market, described by Goldin as "an awful old relic," was widely believed to have been slated for destruction. In any case, the market's fiery end was a propaganda coup for the authorities, who leaned heavily on the criminal damage as a rationale for suppressing the student movement. *The*

Whole Story of the Chengdu Riots shows how the state immediately constructed a new narrative discrediting the students' motives. Using language that demonized the demonstrators as "hooligans" or "ruffians," the account says, "The criminal behavior of the ruffians exposes their real face. The turning point was when they set fire to the People's Market. Then public opinion in the Chengdu streets changed from one-sided [sympathy] to doubts about the ruffians' behavior. 'Hey! They said they wanted freedom and democracy, so what's that got to do with burning down houses and stealing things!'"

• • • •

On the morning of June 5th, Chengdu residents awoke to an extraordinary scene. The streets, dotted with charred, smoldering buses, were eerily quiet. State property had been singled out for attack, with every pane of glass smashed in the government buildings, while the private businesses alongside them were left completely untouched. There was no police presence at all. Even the traffic lights had stopped functioning, symbolizing the complete and sudden withdrawal of the government from public life. As the sun rose, the streets filled up, first with curiosity seekers snapping photos of the wreckage, then, as the day wore on, with yet more protesters.

The government appeared to have lost control entirely. Security forces were completely outnumbered and forced to retreat to the municipal government compound for their own safety, according to a declassified U.S. cable. Every time the armed forces tried to emerge, they quickly withdrew in the face of overwhelming numbers, though they occasionally lobbed smoke bombs at the crowds.

By the evening of June 5th, People's Road—which led to the Mao statue—was once again swarming with protesters. At around 9 p.m., Kim Nygaard was among the crowds, swapping battle stories with other European visitors, when they heard blasts that she believed were gunfire. "People started screaming and running, and the whole mass of people on that avenue started running back down the avenue, away from the Mao statue, and of course we started running," she remembered. They ran back to their hotel—the

Jinjiang—where the U.S. consulate was also based, but shortly afterward, the hotel guards closed the gates, shutting out the mass of people seeking sanctuary inside. Nygaard was distraught, fearing that those outside would be killed by the advancing security forces. She begged the guards to let more people in, but they refused and ordered her back to her room. She was monitoring the situation from a hallway window when she realized that the crowd's mood was shifting from panic to aggression. In an instant, the mob began ramming the hotel gate. She heard glass shattering in the lobby beneath her. Suddenly, she was struck with fear that the hotel would be burned to the ground, so she decided to seek refuge with the U.S. Consul General Jan de Wilde, whose residence was at the back of the hotel.

In his quarters, she found about 15 Westerners, barricading the doors with furniture and filling the bathtubs with water. Amid a cacophony of noise outside, the trapped foreigners crawled on their bellies to the balcony to see what was happening outside. Inside, in a surreal touch, Kurt Weill's music from *The Threepenny Opera* was blaring, leaving Nygaard feeling as though she were in an Oliver Stone movie. She heard de Wilde telling the embassy in Beijing that the Chengdu consulate was under siege. That phone call, in which de Wilde said, "There is no sign of police anywhere," is noted in a declassified State Department cable. The U.S. diplomats also reported that many workers had gone on strike, and that the death toll from riots was continuing to mount.

For de Wilde, the act of sheltering fellow foreigners created echoes from Chinese history, bringing to mind the siege of Beijing's Legation Quarter in 1900, when insurgents from an anti-foreign, anti-Christian movement called the Boxers trapped 900 foreigners and more than 2,000 Chinese Christians in Beijing's Legation Quarter for 55 days. He told me, "I had visions of the siege of the Legation Quarter, and eating donkey meat and drinking champagne—except we had neither. Maybe a few bottles of champagne." In the end, he sheltered the other foreigners for just a few hours before judging that it was safe for them to return to their own rooms.

In fact, neither the foreigners nor the U.S. consulate were the targets of those attacking the hotel. In a cable the next day, de Wilde reported rumors predicting more attacks that night, saying, "Once again, the attacks seem to have nothing to do with the presence of the consulate or resentment against foreigners but are more linked with the hotels (sic) stock of imported cigarettes, beer and liquor." The second night of attacks never materialized. But other foreigners believed the crippling inflation and economic woes faced by many young Chinese informed the choice of target; after all, the smart state-owned hotels where officials entertained their cronies stood as a symbol of the corruption and growing inequality that had been at the root of the protests, both in Beijing and in Chengdu.

Meanwhile, on the other side of the hotel, order was being restored in a brutal fashion after the arrival of the security forces, who rounded up dozens of protesters in the hotel courtyard. One Western visitor, who requested that her name be withheld due to continuing dealings with China, described in e-mails what she had seen from a fifth-floor balcony. She watched about 25 people kneeling in the courtyard, their heads bent toward the ground and their hands tied behind their backs. They were pushed face first to the ground, and then the guards walked around them for more than an hour. Finally, an order was given. At this point, "men with black trousers and white shirts went around and smashed the heads to the ground with iron rods." Physically sickened by this brutality, the witness vomited in the bathroom. Several days later, after fleeing China, she told a Scandinavian newspaper, "They murdered them one by one while the ones remaining pleaded for their lives."

Those sheltered in de Wilde's quarters had no idea what was happening on the other side of the hotel. But after de Wilde announced that the authorities had regained control, some caught glimpses of what was happening as they returned to their rooms. They included one young Australian, Jean Brick, who had been studying Chinese in Shanghai, but who had arrived in Chengdu that day, determined to find out what was happening there. As she walked to the hotel from the train station earlier in the day, she was told by angry locals that between 40 and 70 people had been beaten to death the day before, a figure that included policemen killed by the irate crowds.

After returning to her hotel room from de Wilde's quarters, Brick watched the treatment of the detainees, who were being held in a small guard house by the gate. She described what happened in testimony given to Amnesty International, "One by one, protesters were dragged out of the guard house. Soldiers formed a ring round them, linking arms. Several soldiers in the center of the ring then beat the protesters, using clubs. After the beating, the protesters were carried or dragged back inside. It was not possible to ascertain whether protesters were alive or dead." Even a quarter of a century later, when she remembers those scenes, they play out in black and white, with all color leached away. "I was quite traumatized," she told me. "It became like a black and white film in my mind, drained of color. That made it slightly easier to cope with."

She remembers watching policemen hiding in the bushes and behind the plane trees beside the road, then leaping out to seize unwitting passers-by, who were then beaten and returned to the guard house. In the early hours of the morning, she watched as the security forces dragged the bodies of those they had beaten out of the guard house. "None were able to walk, and all were unconscious," Brick told Amnesty International. "I do not know how many people were arrested and beaten as I was not watching continuously and I was also in despair."

When Kim Nygaard returned to her room from the consul's quarters, she saw a strange sight out of the window. Under the yellow lights, sandbags were stacked in the hotel courtyard. She was wondering what these were for, when she spotted one of the sandbags moving. With a chill of horror, she realized the sandbags were in fact people lying on the ground, their hands behind their backs. Rooted to the spot, she watched the security forces wiring one detainee's arms behind his back. "I remember so well, because I was thinking, 'Oh my god, they're breaking their arms when they're doing that!' This was obviously to totally incapacitate these people," she told me. "It's actually very painful to remember now. It was very, very distressing. You knew that something terrible was happening and you were witnessing it. All that I could think was that I must stay and bear witness." Eventually she was forced to return to her room by a Chinese security guard standing behind her.

But first she watched as two trucks pulled in, and the security forces began to load up the bodies. "They threw them into the truck, they threw them like garbage," Nygaard said. "I don't remember anyone screaming. There was no noise, just the bodies piling on top of each other. There were definitely lifeless bodies. I imagined if anyone were still alive they would not survive in the pile. It was horrifying."

Four other witnesses described exactly the same scene. Jean Brick said the bodies were slung into the trucks "as if they were slabs of meat." The Western tourist on the fifth floor wrote to me, "I was so shocked... by the way they threw the people, like sacks of potatoes, into the trucks. I'm not sure that all died by the beating, but many of them for sure. When [your] brain mass is out over the paving, I don't think you can survive." Another witness repeatedly used the word "carcasses" to describe the bodies in the truck, though he was careful to say that he did not see anything to indicate that the detainees were dead. The final witness was point-blank in his assessment, saying, "People who were treated like that would not survive." Their estimates of the number of bodies they saw thrown into the trucks varies between 25 and 100.

As to the identities of those beaten, there were few hints except their clothing. Some wore the students' white headbands. Others were dressed like workers in white shirts and navy trousers. In the early hours of the morning after the trucks had left, Jean Brick went down to the front gate, where she saw 30 to 40 abandoned plastic flip-flops commonly worn by workers, farmers, and unemployed people.

The American diplomats were aware of the detentions. One of their cables recounts the situation in terms similar to those of the eyewitnesses; it says 200 helmeted People's Armed Police (PAP) and 50 to 70 plainclothes police were deployed to the Jinjiang hotel. Within an hour they had restored order to the hotel compound, and to the Minshan Hotel across the street, by arresting "approximately thirty looters caught outside or on the grounds. Hotel security forces identified their individual roles in the looting. The datainees [sic] were forced to squat bent forward for over an hour, before haling [sic] their hands tied behind their backs and thrown lengthwide [sic] the ground, often face first. They were later thrown onto PAP trucks, and taken away." The violence was omitted from the cables, likely because the embassy lacked secure communications.

Seeking confirmation, I turned to the official Chinese sources. Inside *The Whole Story of the Chengdu Riots*, there is a mention of the detentions. The book reports that by the time the armed police arrived at the hotel, "ruffians" had already smashed some huge flower vases in the lobby, as well as the expensive light fixtures, glass doors, and glass windows of the shop in the reception area. A noticeboard and the carpet were ablaze. The account describes how "after a battle lasting half an hour, they detained seventy ruffians on the scene." Both the timeline and the figure of 70 detainees was also repeated in a People's Armed Police assessment of the security response published in June 1990. This document describes how more than 300 PAP troops surrounded and detained the 'ruffians' before transferring them to police custody. It does not mention what subsequently happened to the detainees. The report ascribes counter-revolutionary motives to those detained, describing their decision to attach the hotels as part of a plot that would lead to the overthrow of the Communist Party. It writes, 'The rioters saw that many security forces were guarding the municipal government and the Municipal People's Congress, and these troops were frequently launching attacks, so they did not dare to act rashly in the square. Therefore, the rioters threatened they would "attack the Minshan [Hotel], burn the Jinjiang [Hotel], expand their influence, overturn the Communist Party." As for official brutality, this is mentioned in approving tones in the *Sichuan Daily*, which reported that "at 5 o'clock in the morning of June 6th, a group of ruffians was caught at the site of the crime, including one ruffian who resisted crazily with an iron rod. He was attacked and wounded by our paramilitary police at the scene, which hit hard at the ruffians' arrogance." According to another official account, the foreigners staying at the hotel were so pleased to see the restoration of order by the security forces, they cried "hot tears" of gratitude.

Several foreigners who had taken shelter in the U.S. consulate did not see the violence, but were told about it the next day. One was Austrian anthropology professor Karl Hutterer who, after leaving China, wrote a letter to the *New York Times* that was printed under the title "Chengdu had its own Tiananmen Massacre." He noted that controlling the demonstrators was not the government's main aim, since "even after having fallen to the ground, victims continued to be beaten and were stomped on by troops; hospitals were ordered not to accept wounded students (at least in one hospital some employees were arrested for defying the order), and on the second night of the attack the police prevented ambulances from functioning." Hutterer believed the security forces' action was designed to annihilate the student movement. He also shed doubt upon the spontaneity of the attack on the hotel, noting that several hours earlier, hotel staff had warned some of the foreigners staying there of an impending attack. In his letter, Hutterer condemned the "cautiously critical" stance of the U.S. officials as insufficient.

Estimates of the number of dead vary widely; American diplomats believed that between 10 and 30 people had died in the Chengdu unrest, with up to 300 people injured. Hutterer estimated that 300 people had died, a figure repeated in the Amnesty International report. The report also charged that officials had ordered the secret execution of dissidents and imprisoned about 10,000 people nationwide in connection with the protests. China rejected all the accusations as "entirely ungrounded and unreasonable." Although the authorities had taken measures to prepare to suppress the Chengdu protests, they were still poorly equipped to deal with the task. The People's Armed Police Report describes a lack of ideological preparation, as well as shortfalls of manpower and equipment. "For three days and three nights, the paramilitary police did not sleep properly," the report says, "Because so many were gathered together and repeatedly being deployed, they could only nap in the offices and stairwells, in the corridors and on the grass. Often they had only just lain down to rest when they would be sent out again." The assessment disclosed that 25 canisters of tear gas were used against protestors in the square, initially to clear the crowds in order to save the lives of five paramilitary policemen, who were being badly beaten. It was the first time the division had used tear gas in an urban setting. A total of 4,000 members of the People's Armed Police were deployed to restore order in Chengdu, according to the report, including reinforcements brought in from nearby cities including Leshan and Mianyang. It also describes, but does not elaborate upon, 'active cooperation with the army,' mentioning that an army detachment 'changed clothes, entered the city and was stationed there.

In the days following the rioting, government retaliation in Chengdu was swift and severe. The internal PAP report said that 488 'criminals' were arrested in Chengdu. The first executions, of two peasants found guilty of setting fire to vehicles, happened within six weeks. At least three others were executed for "unbridled beating, smashing, looting, and burning," while one person was put to death for overturning a jeep and setting fire to it. Three separate life sentences were given for arson, looting, and disturbing the peace. But public enmity toward the police, who put down the protests together with the PAP, was so intense that some policemen stopped wearing their uniforms in public for a time.

• • • •

So who were these people who were dispatched so summarily in the hotel courtyard? In search of an answer, I went to Chengdu, which is now a thriving metropolis of 14 million people. In fact, it styles itself as the "New Chengdu" in gigantic billboards depicting its mascot, a giant panda wearing a Western business suit. The New Chengdu was taking shimmering shape beneath a welter of cranes barely visible through the murky haze. Its lavish developments include the "Little Bird's Nest," a complex resembling Beijing's famous Olympic stadium. The Little Bird's Nest was originally designed for use as the Chengdu government headquarters until its ostentation made it a political liability. Work was just finishing on the world's largest building, the New Century Global Center, which boasts a 14-screen IMAX cinema, fake nautical breezes, and an artificial beach that can accommodate 6,000 people.

The Jinjiang Hotel had also remodeled itself for a new age. It was unrecognizable from the grimy, sullen-looking place I had first patronized in the early '90s, having been reinvented as a luxury hotel with a gleaming marble lobby and homegrown designer boutiques with exorbitant price tags. The parking lot inside the hotel, now covered by a glass roof, had become a swanky breakfast bar where wealthy guests nibbled on croissants, while the courtyard where the beatings had taken place was filled with black Audis and Mercedes-Benzes.

In Chengdu, I happened to meet a woman who has spent a quarter of a century trying to get a straight answer about the events that played out during the violent tumult of 1989. She was a tiny, elderly woman, who shuffled into the room wearing pink plastic sandals, her wild grey hair escaping from a wire headband. Tang Deying was an old-school peasant, visibly out of place in Chengdu's new incarnation. When she spoke, her sharp, gravel-edged words tumbled out amid whiffs of pungent, garlicky breath in a local dialect so indecipherable that I needed an interpreter to repeat her words in standard Mandarin. As we talked, it became clear that she was a double victim, both of the 1989 violence and the fast-paced modernization reshaping her city. She is now a landless farmer, whose fields were requisitioned and house demolished to make way for the New Chengdu. But the defiant jut of her chin and her flinty eyes showed her to be a woman not to be underestimated.

Her struggle began on June 6th, 1989, when her 17-year-old son Zhou Guocong disappeared while riding home on his bike. She never saw him alive again. She was told he had broken curfew and been taken into police detention. Several months later, another detainee told her that the police had beaten her son to death the day after his detention.

That was the beginning of Tang Deying's attempts to seek restitution and accountability. Her efforts were deflected by officials, who provided various unsatisfactory explanations for her son's death: He couldn't take the interrogation, so he sat down and died; he was beaten to death by other detainees; he died from his illness. For 11 years, Tang Deying refused to accept these stories. Then one day, in a sudden and inexplicable admission of responsibility, police handed over a photograph of her son's corpse. It is a grainy picture of a young man's head and shoulders. He is lying on a concrete floor, improbably wearing a spotless white shirt. Blood has congealed around his nostrils and on one side of his mouth. There is a large bruise across the bridge of his nose. His face appears swollen and uneven, though one side is obscured by a shadow. One of his eyes is slightly open. On seeing it, his mother fainted. In death, her son was still watching her.

For years, Tang Deying's daily routine has been a pilgrimage of hope over experience, as she trudges from the police station to the courts, seeking justice for a murder committed a quarter-century ago. This septuagenarian has visited Beijing five times to lodge official complaints. Each time, she has been sent back. She has been detained by police, beaten, twice locked in an iron cage, and, for two years, had a police car stationed outside her home. Tang Deying has even become a one-person employment opportunity. At politically sensitive times of the calendar—such as the anniversary of the crackdown—watching her provides work for 20 people, who operate in shifts. They are mostly retired soldiers or "young hooligans," she says, paid salaries of around 1,000 yuan per month [$162] plus three meals a day. Her attitude to her watchers is typically direct; she calls them "sons-of-bitches," berates them for taking "dirty money," and tries to lose them whenever possible.

But she has made history as the first beneficiary of a government payout in connection with a 1989 death. In 2006, she accepted a payment of 70,000 yuan [about $8,700], though it was labeled a "hardship allowance," thus sidestepping recognition of any official culpability in her son's death. When Tang Deying took the money, it was made clear to her that she was expected to stop petitioning. She simply refused to play the game. "They haven't admitted their responsibility," she told me, her mouth set firmly. "I need the compensation that is due to me according to the law, and I want to see those responsible punished."

Tang's earthy cackle, her fruity language, and her lack of education do not disguise a deeply moral person. Her peasant mantra is "Facts are facts. Right is right. Wrong is wrong." Such a simple statement has put her at odds with the authorities for a quarter-century.

I was curious to ask Tang Deying whether she had heard of any other deaths. There were others, she told me, especially university students whose bodies had never been found, but she had only ever been in direct contact with one other family. So was it possible that other people had been beaten to death in the same way as her son?

Without missing a beat, this feisty old warrior looked me straight in the eye and answered, "Even if I knew, I wouldn't say."

• • • •

Could dozens of people have disappeared in Chengdu without anyone appearing to notice? Few outside Chengdu even knew that anything had happened there. The huge demonstrations, the rioting, the pitched battles, and the police brutality were all eclipsed by the enormity of events in the capital. Rumors were rife that something bad had happened in Chengdu, but by the time the Western journalists arrived to follow up, many of the foreign witnesses to the brutality in the Jinjiang Hotel had already been repatriated, while any local witnesses were likely too scared to talk.

A British camera crew from ITN had trouble getting any information at all. When they tried to interview students at Sichuan University, the crew was arrested and deported for traveling on tourist visas rather than having journalists' visas. They had arrived one day before their arrest, so had managed to film some footage of the riot's aftermath; one of the journalists, Vernon Mann, remembers seeing burned-out cars and bullet holes in one wall. They had been staying at the Jinjiang Hotel; Mann said he had seen no sign of anything amiss, though he found the local staff were aloof to the point of rudeness. He told me, "None of the Chinese in the hotel were talking to us at all, basically. They were being pretty offensive to be honest." As they later discovered, contact between Western journalists and local Chinese had become fraught, even dangerous. After Mann and his crew were deported, their local translator was arrested and spent several months in jail. After he was released, the British crew sent him some money. When he went to retrieve it, he was promptly thrown back into jail again.

Even in Chengdu's thriving dissident community, there is a complete information vacuum surrounding the brutal beatings in the Jinjiang Hotel. "If it had happened, I would have known about it," Chengdu rights activist Huang Qi told me when we met. He runs a website charting rights abuses. He was not, however, in the city in 1989. Another participant in the Chengdu movement who fled into exile told me that he had never heard of any deaths in the hotel. But the location of the violence inside the gates of the Jinjiang Hotel meant that few would have seen it, apart from foreigners and hotel staff who were likely to be too terrified to mention it.

There is, nonetheless, one government institution that has clearly not forgotten the events of 1989, and that is the local judiciary. Judicial authorities in Sichuan have recently tried a number of cases linked to 1989. One example was the 2010 case of activist Tan Zuoren, who was detained following his investigations into the deaths of children whose shoddily built schools collapsed during the 2008 Sichuan earthquake. Yet according to leaked U.S. cables, his indictment did not mention this. Instead, the charge of inciting subversion of state power was wholly focused on his activities commemorating those who died in 1989. At the heart of the indictment was an essay he had written describing what he had seen in Beijing, entitled "Bearing Witness to the Ultimate Beauty; the Diary of an Eyewitness in the Square." The prosecution argued this was a "distorted account" constituting libel. The indictment also referred to a drive for voluntary blood donations that Tan had launched in Tianfu Square on June 4th, 2008, and an e-mail he had sent suggesting a "Global Chinese blood drive" to mark the 20th anniversary. The indictment said that Tan had "fabricated things out of whole cloth, distorted news, and spread speech that is injurious to state power and the socialist system in order to damage the image of state power and the socialist system in the eyes of the people." The crime was clear, it read, the evidence certain and abundant. Tan Zuoren was sentenced to five years in prison.

• • • •

Over the past quarter-century, the events of those seven hot summer weeks across China have become telescoped into one single word: Tiananmen. That shorthand has narrowed the geographic scope of events to the capital, relegating the massive protest movements in dozens of other cities to silence. But Beijing's demonstrations were not the only ones, nor were they the only ones to be suppressed. What happened in 1989 was a nationwide movement, and to allow this to be forgotten is to minimize its scale. The protests in Chengdu were not merely student marches, but part of a genuinely popular movement with support from across the spectrum. The pitched battles and temporary loss of control of the streets in Chengdu show the depth of the nationwide crisis facing the central government. According to the *Tiananmen Papers*, demonstrations against the brutality of the June 4th killings in Beijing broke out in 63 cities across China with thousands marching in cities including Harbin, Changchun, Shenyang, Jinan, and Hangzhou, in addition to Chengdu.

What happened in Chengdu has not only been forgotten; it has never been fully told. The people of Chengdu were not cowed by the killings in Beijing, but rather incensed by them. However, lacking an independent media to amplify their voices, their short-lived scream of fury became a cry into thin air, drowned out by the ensuing violence meted out by both the state and the protesters themselves. Although Chengdu was the site of some of the most shocking brutality, the witnesses had no one to tell. There was no charismatic protest leader, no Wu'er Kaixi, and while some of those involved did eventually flee into exile, nobody had ever heard of them. The Western witnesses were so traumatized by what they had seen that most were initially purely focused on trying to get out of China as quickly as possible. Safely back in their homelands, many of them gave interviews to the media and contacted rights groups, as Jean Brick, Kim Nygaard, and Karl Hutterer had done, but there was so little interest in events outside Beijing that they eventually gave up trying to raise awareness.

The Western media was also complicit in controlling the narrative in convenient ways; what happened outside Beijing was largely overlooked, due to the lack of information and the difficulty of confirming exactly what had happened. Acts of violence carried out by ordinary Chinese against policemen—and soldiers in Beijing—were often downplayed. After all, these did not fit easily into the West's favored narrative of freedom-seeking students versus a repressive state. "I felt like a lone voice in the wilderness," said Dennis Rea, whose memoir about living in Chengdu includes descriptions of the 1989 protests and of the violent murder of a policeman. "I thought hard about whether or not it was appropriate to include that story in there. I thought that in the end it would be irresponsible of me to write a musical memoir while that was going on, and not relate the account."

My attempt to piece together what happened in Chengdu cannot be anything but incomplete; too much time has passed, too many unknowns remain. The accounts of the protagonists are missing, especially those thousands who had dared to call for change and were then muzzled by violence. One factor ensuring their silence was the official verdict—emphasized in all the government propaganda— that Chengdu's own student movement was serious "political turmoil" on a par with what had happened in Beijing. The insistence on the wrongdoing of the "rioters" stigmatized all who had been present, discouraging Chinese witnesses from reporting what they had seen. At the same time, the focus on the criminality of a small number of "hooligans" gave those who had joined the marches cover to distance themselves from the subsequent rioting, while providing them with a reason to support the government's crackdown.

Despite the passage of the years, the accounts by the foreign eye-witnesses of the brutality in the Jinjiang Hotel courtyard are remarkably consistent. The fact that people who had never met each other corroborate one another's stories, despite having no idea that others saw the same acts of violence, is telling. Time after time, I heard the same tone of shock when interviewees discovered that there had been other witnesses. "What other people saw it?" one man asked me, before admitting that he was convinced he had been the only one.

For Kim Nygaard, hearing that her story had been corroborated by other witnesses was an overwhelming emotional experience. In an e-mail to me, she wrote, "I lived for years disturbed by the fact that we had witnessed a crime and that it seemed no one else knew about it or cared enough or would risk enough to make sure it was told." After being evacuated, she alerted Amnesty International and shared her story and photos with an Italian newspaper. She returned to Chengdu about a month after being evacuated and had desperately tried to find out more details. The atmosphere on the campus was thick with rumors of missing students, but no one dared to speak to her. When I first e-mailed her, she replied, "I have always wondered how long it would take for the truth to come out."

The whole truth may never come out. But what happened in Chengdu was very nearly the perfect case study in first rewriting history, then excising it altogether. The local government in Chengdu was untrammelled by the factors constraining the authorities in Beijing: after all, in Chengdu, there was no foreign footage of crimes committed by the state; the victims were silenced either by force or fear; most of the foreign witnesses removed themselves from the scene almost immediately; and there were few lasting physical reminders, such as the tank treads dappling the access roads to Beijing's Tiananmen Square (though even those too were speedily removed.) In Chengdu, the events largely existed in memory alone, but the party knew all too well that memories are mutable, even the memories of tens of thousands of people.

For a quarter of a century, the 'Technique of Forgetting History' has worked spectacularly well in Chengdu. Those who tried to remember publicly, like Tan Zuoren, were silenced by prison. The only thread left dangling was the government's initial attempts to control the narrative by flooding the market with its own accounts of events. Once issued, all that propaganda could not be retracted. That thread, now grasped, unfurls into a very different narrative when viewed in conjunction with those elements that could not be controlled by the Chinese government, such as the eyewitness accounts from foreigners and the diplomatic cables from the U.S. consulate.

Despite all this, we will likely never know how many survivors there were from those 70 or so people who were brutally beaten in that hotel courtyard.

What remains very clear is that, in addition to the deaths in Beijing, people died in Chengdu too, and in numbers greater than the government acknowledges. Exactly how many is not clear: In Chengdu, the government said there were eight deaths; U.S. diplomats put the figure between 10 and 30; those watching from their hotel windows believed that dozens, up to a hundred by some accounts, were beaten to death before their eyes. This is just one of the many untold stories of 1989. Here the Chinese government's attempt to rewrite and erase history has been frighteningly successful. In a country the size of China, how many other forgotten victims might there be?

Afterword

Does what happened in Tiananmen Square a quarter of a century ago still matter? One answer may lie in words written by China's greatest modern author, Lu Xun, after an earlier instance of government-backed killing in 1926, when armed police in Tiananmen Square opened fire on demonstrators protesting against warlord Zhang Zuolin's acceptance of Japanese demands. The killing left 47 people dead and hundreds injured. Lu Xun was moved to write, "This is not the conclusion of an incident, but a new beginning. Lies written in ink can never disguise facts written in blood. All blood debts must be repaid in blood: the longer the delay, the greater the interest." The words "All blood debts must be repaid in blood" were inked onto the sheets carried by the students in Chengdu through the streets after the killings in Beijing. The same sentiment was voiced another way by exiled student leader Shen Tong, who compared the Chinese leadership's attitude toward the killings to a man falling from a skyscraper, shouting, "I'm ok! I'm ok!" until the very moment he hits the ground.

But the legacy of 1989 has not just been dark. The decisions that Deng Xiaoping made in the immediate aftermath of June 4th shaped China as a world power, driving its extraordinary economic transformation and strident nationalism. Within a single generation, the state had largely retreated from its management of people's day-to-day lives, no longer wielding the power to assign jobs or withhold permission for marriage or travel. Everyone got richer, much richer, as incomes rose exponentially. People shifted focus, devoting their energies to buying apartments, setting up companies, and navigating the myriad of new opportunities offered by the economic liberalization that was changing the world around them. All this happened not despite Tiananmen, but because of it.

The violent suppression of the 1989 movement was not an anomaly. Its precedents were the May 4th Movement in 1919, the Tiananmen killings that Lu Xun wrote about in 1926, followed by the repression of mourning protests after the death of Zhou Enlai in 1976, and the failed student movement of 1986–1987. Thus Chinese history loops endlessly in on itself in a Möbius strip of crushed aspirations, cycling from one generation to the next, propelled by the propensity to embrace amnesia.

The Communist Party has rewritten its history, but it has not forgotten what it did in 1989, nor is at peace with it. That much is clear from the mounting list of those punished for acts of remembrance, from the sentencing of Chengdu rights activist Tan Zuoren for incitement to subversion, to dissident Zhu Yufu, who in 2012 was given a seven-year prison term for writing a poem that included the words,

> It's time, Chinese people!
> The square belongs to everyone.
> Your feet are your own.
> It's time to use your feet and head to the square to make your
>   choice.

The party's paranoia is such that these words—never published but simply sent to a friend via Skype—were judged an incitement to subvert state power. The passage of the years has not blunted the party's sensitivity to memorials. If anything, the fact that some still refuse to forget underlines the party's vulnerability. Knowing the power of China's peasant rebellions to unseat dynasties, and the range of grievances percolating through the masses, the fear of unrest has quickened over the years. Stability has become the party's watchword, its obsession, its raison d' être.

So compelling is the overarching imperative to quash dissent that local governments have no compunction about using all the tools at their disposal. I saw an example of this firsthand when I visited Chengdu in the spring of 2013. When I arrived, every single person I met—from taxi drivers to urban professionals to petitioners—was talking about an upcoming protest with the intensity of high schoolers awaiting their first prom. The demonstration was to show opposition to a $6 billion petrochemical plant in Pengzhou, about 18 miles from Chengdu, due to fears about pollution and safety given its proximity to a seismologically active fault line. The date of the planned march was doubly freighted: Saturday, May 4th, 2013, which echoed both the 1919 student movement and the fifth anniversary of a protest "stroll" against the very same plant.

The authorities began by moving against the obvious targets, first finding a scapegoat: a woman who was detained and then appeared on local television apologizing for a widely circulated social media post that had wrongly claimed that the march had government approval. Then at least half a dozen rights activists were sent on "forced holidays." Others were detained in their homes, while still more were invited to "drink tea," a euphemism used to mean they were interrogated by state security. Printing shops were offered rewards if they turned in customers photocopying flyers about the march.

The next round of preventative measures went further still. Government workers were summoned to meetings at which they were warned they would be sacked if they took part in the march. Overnight, the entire city was leafleted with posters tacked up in apartment foyers and slipped under doors. The language on the leaflets echoed that of 1989, ordering Chengdu residents "to stand firm, not believe rumors, and not participate [in protests] in order to prevent people with ulterior motives from seizing this opportunity to create turmoil." The leaflets had the unintended effect of bringing the Pengzhou plant to the attention of those who had never heard of it, creating an even greater groundswell of suppressed discontent.

So far, such measures were in line with tried and tested stability maintenance strategies. But then the local government stepped into new territory: It decided to reschedule the weekend. With no warning, it announced that, for one week only and in Chengdu alone, Saturday and Sunday would be workdays, and the weekend would be postponed until Monday and Tuesday. As Saturday, May 4th dawned, government workers once again straggled into their offices, while schoolchildren reluctantly went back to school for emergency pre-exam revision. On the university campuses, it was preternaturally quiet. The students were busy attending extra classes scheduled to take up the entire day. The word was that some universities were even providing lunchboxes to ensure that no one left campus at midday. In case any student felt the sudden urge to go out, busloads of policemen stationed at the campus gates served as a deterrent.

Yet even these Orwellian precautions were deemed insufficient. The evening before the scheduled day of protest, a "virtual combat exercise" was suddenly announced for the next day. On Saturday, May 4th, security forces blanketed the entire city. Tianfu Square was entirely sealed off, with policemen stationed every 20 feet around its periphery. At the site of the planned protest, the Jiuyanqiao covered bridge, policemen were patrolling in pairs while plainclothes police strutted around, gabbling ostentatiously into their walkie-talkies, and firemen sat in their trucks. At a nearby teahouse, several dozen anti-riot police dozed at tables in full gear, plastic handcuffs dangling from their bulletproof vests. Under these circumstances, no one dared protest.

Around the corner, I saw a tearful woman being questioned by police; she had unwittingly made the mistake of wearing a cheap white facemask, commonly used on days with heavy smog or by people with colds. But because the protesters had suggested using facemasks as a wordless protest against pollution, the simple act of donning a mask had been enough to cast suspicion on her.

Such a citywide show of force demonstrates how far the authorities will go to head off unrest. Today, environmental issues are becoming the biggest cause of social unrest, outpacing political demands or land disputes. With air that is often hazardous to human health, water that is largely undrinkable, and a range of toxins in foodstuffs too numerous to even track, environmental concerns unite Chinese across the divides of rich and poor, rural and urban. In recent years, the cities of Xiamen, Dalian, Ningbo, and

Kunming have seen large protests against major industrial projects because of concerns about pollution. In Chengdu, however, no such demonstration of people power has been permitted, perhaps due to the unspoken memory of the 1989 riots.

In any case, the stability maintenance apparatus was so ruthlessly effective that by the time I had returned from Chengdu to my home in Beijing, I had already begun to doubt what I had seen. Could a provincial government really just move the weekend without anyone remarking on it? The very idea seemed like a totalitarian throwback. I went online, but there was nothing at all about it on the English-language Internet. Then I turned to *weibo*, China's version of Twitter. There, to my relief, was confirmation: photos of warning notices pinned up in elevators, shots of police vans lining the roadside, and dozens of disgruntled, sardonic commentators angered at having their lives turned upside down. The suppression of any real displays of dissatisfaction had led to an explosion of virtual discontent. One person wrote, "You can block [the march at] Jiuyanqiao, but you can't block the accumulation of protests inside Chengdu people's hearts!" Another asked, "Who are your combat enemies? The Chengdu people?"

The Communist Party will take extreme measures to avoid unrest, using a hammer to crush a flea. However, the methods it uses slowly chip away at the government's mandate. Paying off protesters—like Tang Deying, whose son was beaten to death by Chengdu police—puts a price on stability. In her case, it did not work, yet it did create a market for instability, as well as those who benefit from it, including the "hooligans" paid to watch her. In the short run, such stability preservation buys the Communist Party time; in the long term, that time is only borrowed.

Could a mass movement like Tiananmen happen again? Yes, it could. Rapacious land seizures, widespread official corruption, and choking environmental problems are creating pockets of discontent among people who feel that they have little left to lose. As long as these remain localized, the likelihood of a mass movement is diluted. But these dots on the map are expanding in size and frequency, while the instability on China's margins—the "little Tiananmens" that Bao Tong refers to—picks up pace as the dictates of stability maintenance merge with nationalism to force ethnic minorities into visible shows of loyalty. In one incident in 2013, four Tibetans were shot dead and 50 injured in clashes that erupted after they refused to fly the Chinese flag over their homes. In October 2013, in another sign of escalating instability, authorities blamed Uighur separatists for a "terrorist attack" on Tiananmen Square itself. Five people were killed when a jeep burst into flames close to the portrait of Chairman Mao hanging in Tiananmen; foreign press reports said that national leaders had been nearby at the time.

To nip unrest in the bud, the authorities have installed some 20 to 30 million closed-circuit video cameras across the country to create a nationwide surveillance system dubbed "Skynet." The state may have withdrawn from dictating people's lives, but it has boosted its ability to monitor its own citizens. China's budget exposes its fears: Beijing's spending priorities favor internal security over its defense, suggesting that it views the major threats to Communist rule as coming from within, rather than without.

The "forgetting" that has engulfed China is not just enforced from above; the people themselves have colluded in this amnesia and embraced it. Forgetting is a survival mechanism, almost second nature. China's people have learned to avert their eyes and minds from anything unpleasant, allowing their brains to be imprinted with false memories—or allowing the real memories to be erased—for the sake of convenience. Parents shield their children from the past for it contains knowledge that could jeopardize their bright futures. There is no benefit to remembering, so why bother?

China's Communist Party constantly alludes to the nation's 5,000 years of history while omitting its more recent acts of shame. In a country that has done more to alleviate poverty than any other country in the history of the world, does it really matter? The answer is that it does. It matters because the national identity of this new world power is based on lies. When those lies are taught in schools, passed unchallenged from one generation to the next, and truth-telling is punished, a moral vacuum gapes ever larger, the debt grows greater, and the cost paid is the dearest of all: a loss of humanity.

Epilogue

The 79 days of street protests were summed up by words of whimsy disguising a threat. Emblazoned on a yellow cloth banner flapping from a pedestrian footbridge were the words, "You may say I'm a dreamer but I'm not the only one." Despite the banner's pacifist sentiment, the threat was implicit in the sheer mass of dreamers protest-waving smartphones whose bright screens converged into a shimmering river of light. A quarter-century after Tiananmen, another student-led movement had emerged on Chinese soil.

These young protestors were in Hong Kong, the former British colony that returned to Chinese sovereignty in 1997 with a promise that its rights and freedoms would remain unchanged for 50 years. Unlike the Beijing protestors of 1989, they had no grandiose demands for freedom and democracy. Instead, their unspoken agenda was to protect their way of life including the rights they already enjoyed, such as the right to protest, while demanding specific electoral reforms. The protests started on September 22, 2014 with a week-long class boycott, which had been planned at a meeting beside a replica of the Goddess of Democracy who had loomed over Tiananmen Square in 1989. Thus the symbol of one democracy movement oversaw the birth of another, also doomed to fail from the moment it was conceived.

The protestors occupying roads in Admiralty, near the Hong Kong government headquarers were focused on pressuring the authorities to rescind a decision allowing a committee stacked with

Beijing loyalists to vet candidates for post of Chief Executive, the territory's most senior official, in 2017. "We want genuine universal suffrage!" echoed through the streets, the words on the enormous yellow banners draped from some of Hong Kong's most recognizable landmarks such as its iconic Lion Rock. The promise of universal suffrage in 2017 had been dangled in front of Hong Kong people for years, but a ruling by the Standing Committee of China's National People's Congress in August 2014 whisked it away. As in 1989, the protestors' political demands were underpinned by growing economic discontent. The territory's economy is dominated by cartels, monopolies, and oligopolies seen to benefit the island's China-friendly tycoons at the expense of its ordinary people.

The life cycle of the street movement could be charted through the layers of colorful Post-It notes feathered on a concrete staircase called Lennon Wall, in tribute to the original in Prague which has been daubed with youthful expressions of anti-establishment anger since the 1980s. In Hong Kong, the earliest Post-It notes written at the end of September—buried beneath layers of newer ones—were statements of conviction and determination such as "Fighting for Democracy!" and "We Only Fight for Democracy. Nothing Else."

The next phase—anger and disbelief—came when police used tear gas and pepper spray to try to disperse demonstrators six days after the start of the protests, sparking such Post-It reactions as, "Police I hate you" and "No Violence. We love Hong Kong." The next layer of Post-It notes hinted at widening generational schisms and domestic tension: "Dad, Mum, and those who are against us: I hope you will be with us and support us one day. We want true democracy only" and "Mama. Today there's no need to worry about me." As the occupation stretched unexpectedly into its third month in December and began to lose public support, the tone of the notes became exhortatory: "Don't give up!" "Please, be strong!" and "To continue is to succeed. History will remember this day."

Pasted on the very top as the students packed up to leave in mid-December were the final messages of the movement: "We leave in order to return" and, most popular of all, "We'll be back." One white Post-It bore a single word: "Imagine."

Few in Hong Kong could ever have imagined they would rise up in such great numbers to transform the heart of the city into a chimerical encampment. I met Teressia Hui on December 10th, the last night of the occupation, when the mood was one of melancholic nostalgia. A 40-something business consultant, she came straight to the site every day after work and perched on the highway on a tiny stool, distributing free bookmarks. To her, the tent city was a microcosm of a better world. "We coordinate among ourselves even though we don't know each other," she said. "You need to move a tent, you just shout, 'Anybody can help?' And everybody will help you. This is like a utopia. This is a perfect planet. Everybody's dreamland."

This mass civil disobedience campaign represented the most serious challenge to China's political control since the last student-led movement was crushed a quarter-century earlier in Beijing. But Hong Kong's protestors were equipped with much their 1989 forebears lacked, including a world-class education free of Communist dogma, fluent English, and the tools of communication that allowed them to network, organize, and broadcast in real time. Yet for all that had changed, one overriding factor had not: the unwillingness of the Chinese Communist Party to brook any challenge or back down in the face of popular demands.

The week-long class boycott began on September 22 2014, organized by two student groups, both of which would play a key role. The Hong Kong Federation of Students (HKFS) mobilized university students for the initial strike. On the last day, their numbers were swelled by secondary students brought out by a second group called Scholarism. The latter was led by a bowl-headed, bespectacled 17-year-old named Joshua Wong, whose picture appeared on the cover of Time magazine as 'The Face of Protest'. At the beginning of the Occupy movement, Wong was too young to drive, drink alcohol, or even vote, yet he was already a protest veteran. At 15, he had spearheaded a 2012 protest and hunger strike that forced the Hong Kong government to withdraw plans to introduce 'moral and national education' into the school curriculum. To Wong, electoral reform was a generational issue. At the school boycott, he whipped up the teenagers with a rousing speech. "Now the red light is on for

Hong Kong's democratic future, and students, who could pay the highest price, are on strike. Just where are the grown-ups?"

Of all the Hong Kong student leaders, Wong was the one who traced the most direct lineage back to their 1989 forebears. In one interview he drew parallels between himself and Wang Dan, the Tiananmen-era student leader, by describing their encounter, "He doesn't really talk about the Tiananmen Square protests. We discussed potato chips. I get it—I feel bored talking about electoral reform. Poor thing! He's been talking about June Fourth for more than 20 years! But I really respect him." By September 23, the second day of the class boycott, the students had moved to Admiralty, near Central business district. They had left behind the bronze Goddess, whose short history reflected her complicated place in the territory's political culture, both worshipped and feared. In her four years of life, she had been confiscated by police from a shopping center forecourt, released to serve as the centerpiece at a massive commemorative vigil, and temporarily banned by university authorities who finally reversed their position after storms of protest. But this movement would spawn its own symbols, such as Umbrella Man—a twelve-foot-tall figure pieced together from small wooden blocks, brandishing an open yellow umbrella—a home-grown icon of a protest whose rallying calls included a chant of "Hong Kong People! Hong Kong People!"

One touchstone of Hong Kong's distinct identity from the rest of China is the ability to remember and publicly commemorate the 1989 killings with an annual candle-lit vigil. The right to memory is fiercely guarded, and attendance figures at the rally serve as a yardstick of the territory's fractious relationship with Beijing.

"The worry of whether June Fourth would happen in Hong Kong affected quite a lot of our decisions," admitted Benny Tai, a mild-mannered constitutional law professor who co-founded the third main organization driving the protests: a civil disobedience campaign with the hippie-era name of Occupy Central with Love and Peace. Like so many of his generation, Tai had watched the 1989 killings on television, frantic with worry about Hong Kong's impending return to Chinese sovereignty. Another co-founder, Reverend Chu Yiu-ming, had organized a million-person-march in

Hong Kong in May 1989, as well as setting up Operation Yellowbird to smuggle hundreds of dissidents out of China after the crackdown.

That generation's psychological baggage was not shared by the Hong Kong students, many of whom had not yet been born when the tanks rolled into Beijing. To them, the risk of a 1989-style crackdown in Hong Kong seemed vanishingly small. Less constrained by memories of the past, they were less fearful and more radical than their older counterparts.

Yet there was one moment when the protestors—old and young alike—feared that Hong Kong was teetering on the verge of repeating the past. The original aim of Occupy Central had been to mobilize ten thousand people to block roads in Hong Kong's Central business district for a couple of days beginning on October 1. But the movement was prematurely bounced into action on September 26, when the students tried to occupy a fenced-off public plaza called Civic Square. Dozens were arrested, including Joshua Wong and the two top HKFS student representatives, Alex Chow and Lester Shum. After police dragged the students away, crowds ballooned on the streets, galvanized by fears that Hong Kong's freedom to protest was under threat. Then on September 28, the police moved in, clad in full riot gear with gas-masks, bearing rubber-bullet rifles and hoisting signs that read "Warning Tear Smoke" and, more ominously, "Disperse or We Fire."

"The shadow from June Fourth was very, very massive," said Nathan Law, a 22-year-old HKFS representative, referring to that particular moment. His colleagues had been arrested, so he was responsible for deciding whether the students should remain. He called for a retreat. In the event, police fired 87 canisters of tear gas into the crowd, causing roars of panic and anger, as those on the front lines shielded themselves with their flimsy umbrellas. And so the Umbrella Movement was born.

One of the first victims of the tear gas was 76-year-old Martin Lee, the founding chairman of the Democratic party. He had come out in the early hours of the morning with his friend, the billionaire tycoon and staunch democracy advocate Jimmy Lai. As the riot police moved into position, the pair decided to try to defuse the crowd's anger, reminding protestors of the principles of love and

peace underpinning the campaign. Lee had climbed onto a concrete divider in the middle of the road, and was beginning to speak
when the police fired tear gas. The first canister struck Jimmy Lai,
who was not injured. "I heard, 'Boom!'" Lee recalled. Then he was
tear-gassed. Lee had to be helped, coughing and spluttering, to the
side of the road. "It never entered into my head that there would be
a Tiananmen Square," Lee remembered. "But teargas, I expected.
And maybe water cannon, that sort of thing. I said, 'If they send in
tanks, I would get myself a bicycle and will confront them with my
bicycle to see what they would do to me."

Meanwhile, rumors were buzzing through social networks that
Chinese anti-riot police were massing on the border and People's
Liberation Army trucks were driving through the streets of Hong
Kong. Far from dispersing the crowds, the tear gas gave the movement the broad base of support it had lacked. Over time, clusters
of tents began to spring up in Admiralty, forming streets that
later took on names like Umbrella Square and Freedom Quarter.
A "study hall" took shape, allowing students to combine occupation with homework. Carpenters built stairs to help people cross the
highway dividers. First-aid tents appeared, stocked with donated
supplies, which were distributed by volunteers using online spread-
sheets to assess need. Protestors even set up trash recycling stations.
New communities were forming on the street and online, facilitated by mobile messaging services. By the end of September, the
Occupation had begun to take root. And, following the failure of
the tear gas, the government decided to wait it out.

In the run-up to the student boycott, China's state-run media had
already begun echoing Tiananmen-era rhetoric. The Beijing-backed
Wen Wei Po newspaper accused Joshua Wong of being manipulated
by a hidden 'black hand'. Their report accused him of having met
US consular officials and accepted covert donations from American
organizations. Wong flatly denied all the accusations. Later Hong
Kong's chief executive blamed the protests on 'foreign forces' which
he refused to identify. In response Wong replied that any external
influences were "limited to my Korean cellphone, my American
computer and my Japanese Gundam [anime figurines]."

At the flag-raising ceremony for China's National Day, October 1st, members of Scholarism turned their backs. That day the People's Daily newspaper ran a front page editorial in a clear echo of the April 26th editorial from 1989. The language was not as harsh—there was no mention of 'turmoil'—but the article warned of 'unimaginable' consequences from this 'illegal gathering' which it accused of disrupting social order and harming the economy. Echoing the rhetoric of 1989, it blamed an extremely small number of people for stirring up conflict. The similarities in language alarmed the student leaders, who read it both as a coded warning and as an attempt to demonize the Hong Kong protestors for the mainland audience.

At times the Hong Kong students drew upon the actions of their Beijing forebears as object lessons in how not to behave. Unlike the far-reaching demands of 1989, the Hong Kong protestors focused on specific, local issues. When the Hong Kong government agreed to hold a live televised dialogue with five HKFS representatives, the students decided their negotiations should be conducted in a very different way from 1989. Referring to Wu'er Kaixi's appearance in pajamas, Nathan Law said, "We tried to be very humble because we think he was quite arrogant." To that end, they spent days marshalling their arguments in consultation with lawyers and academics.

The talks were held around a horse-shoe shaped table on October 21st. The students, wearing matching black T-shirts with "Freedom now!" in yellow across the chest, looked impossibly young. There was no hectoring or fainting. The government's top representative was not Chief Executive Leung Chun-ying, but the less polarizing figure of Chief Secretary Carrie Lam. The students argued with lawyerly precision but few could forget that the last such televised debate about democracy had been back in 1989.

The Hong Kong students mainly avoided the internal power-plays that dominated the movement in Beijing, though there were tensions between HKFS and Scholarism. The largest point of discord emerged towards the end of the occupation, when Joshua Wong and a small number of supporters announced a unilateral hunger-strike on December 1st. "We didn't expect it," admitted Nathan Law from HKFS. Within days, Wong's sharp features had become alarmingly gaunt and he was being pushed around in a wheelchair. He stopped the strike after 108 hours, citing medical advice.

For many of the younger protestors, Tiananmen in 1989 was ancient history, as distant as the Qing dynasty. One day, walking around the occupied zone in Admiralty, I was struck to see the numbers 4689—which in Chinese could refer to the date of June Fourth 1989—stenciled on the side of a yellow tent, above cartoons of protestors bearing umbrellas and sunflowers. It seemed visual proof that 1989 had not been forgotten. The tent had been named by a 22-year-old student, Rex Au, who was sitting outside, his face bathed in the pale glow of his computer screen. Had he been thinking about Tiananmen when he named the tent, I asked? "Oh, this is an accident," he answered, giggling.

He explained that 4689 was rooted in a complicated wordplay beloved of the protestors who used Cantonese as an assertion of their own linguistic and cultural heritage, distinct from the Mandarin of the mainland. The numbers 689 were a derogatory nickname for Chief Executive, Leung Chun-ying, a wealthy property surveyor nicknamed "Wolf," who had won merely 689 votes from a 1,200-strong Selection Committee, despite the fact that it was stacked with Beijing loyalists. So 689 both identified him and drew attention to his lack of legitimacy. The number 4 is a homonym, which in Cantonese sounds the same as 'die' or 'death'. Read in Cantonese, 4689 sent the message "Death to Leung Chun-ying!" Rex admitted that he had never even noticed that the numbers could be read as June 4, 1989. He'd only realized the connection when a passerby explained it. To him, the Tiananmen movement had no bearing whatsoever. "I don't think it was an inspiration," he concluded bluntly.

Occupy Central ended not with the tanks, but with bailiffs wielding court injunctions filed by private transport companies. As the final morning dawned, a kind of anti-riot chic gripped the camp. The hottest accessories were plastic helmets, anti-tear gas goggles and high-visibility vests sported by protestors, medical volunteers and journalists alike. Ultimately these proved unnecessary. Once under way, the clearance of the site was painstakingly slow, with government workers methodically dismantling barricades jerrybuilt from bamboo poles and metal railings. After a lunch break, police reclaimed the site, slowly kettling the several hundred remaining occupiers. The last holdouts sat on the highway, waiting to be carried away. The overriding sentiment was fatigue and boredom. The two other protest sites, in Mongkok and Causeway Bay, were also cleared in separate actions.

By the end of the clearances, 955 people had been arrested. The list of those booked in Admiralty resembled a Who's Who of Hong Kong's democratic politics, including Cantopop star Denise Ho, the billionaire tycoon Jimmy Lai, and Martin Lee, who was arrested, shouting "Give me democracy or give me death!" Nine HKFS members were arrested, including Alex Chow and Nathan Law, as well as a number of legislators.

One weary-looking man who shouted, "Down with the Communist Party!" as he was forcibly removed turned out to be Wang Dengyao, a 55-year-old retired steel worker from Beijing, who said he had taken part in the 1989 protests. Having read about Occupy Central online, he had made his way to Hong Kong. "They've done better than in 1989," he told me. "As a whole, they've raised citizens' awareness to a higher level. June 4th didn't manage that."

Yet the Hong Kong protestors left without any government concessions after losing much of their support from the wider public, who bemoaned the disruption to their everyday lives. However, as a consciousness-raising exercise, the Umbrella movement had been a roaring success, politicizing and radicalizing large swathes of the population, especially the young. Their willingness to embrace civil disobedience on a massive scale highlighted the marginalization of the traditional political parties from an electorate that no longer felt represented by their representatives. The gerrymandering of the electoral system had been designed to ensure pro-democratic forces were always in a minority, but ultimately exposed the impotence of the entire political process.

"The rules have changed and the game has changed," summed up Alex Chow. Like many of the student leaders, he had been arrested three times, but was unconditionally released. These student leaders were preoccupied by other matters, such as whether their phones were being monitored and their emails hacked. Some had become persona non grata in China, having been denied entry to the mainland.

Though the administration had won a short-term victory, its actions during Occupy Central had badly shaken public trust in Hong Kong's civil service, its judiciary, and the police force once known as "Asia's Finest." There were fears that the vaunted political neutrality of Hong Kong's institutions had been compromised, undermining the post-handover mantra of "One Country, Two Systems." These worries intensified after Chinese officials suddenly claimed that the treaty governing Hong Kong's return to Chinese rule, the Joint Declaration, became void after the change of sovereignty. The view from Beijing was uncompromising. A gleeful China Daily editorial, marking the end of the protests, crowed, "The political adventure, supported by outside forces that have been scheming to counter the rise of China, went against the overall interests of Hong Kong society and the nation—as well as the will of Hong Kong residents."

The first official mainland response after the end of the Occupy protests was instructive. Zhang Rongshun, vice-chairman of the legislative affairs commission of the National People's Congress, spoke of the urgent need to build a sense of national identity among Hong Kong people, who needed 're-enlightenment' about the principle of 'One Country, Two Systems'. It was a direct echo of Deng Xiaoping's post-Tiananmen comments on the need for education.

Meanwhile, fear of a contagion effect from the Umbrella movement sweeping across the border had set off a whole new wave of repression. More than a hundred mainland supporters of the Hong Kong protests were detained. The reasons listed by one overseas human rights group constitute a catalogue of paranoia: for posting a message of solidarity on the internet; for attempts to go to Hong Kong to show solidarity with the Occupy Central participants; for posting a picture of himself online with a shaved head, holding an umbrella, and sticking up his middle finger.

The blowback also extended to a ban on authors who supported Occupy Central and a blacklist of celebrity backers, rumored to run to 47 names. In an editorial, the state-run Global Times newspaper tried to rationalize this ban "'Burning books and burying Confucian scholars alive' will not be repeated today, but zones of sensitivity exist."

Online censorship spiked to a record level on September 28 when Hong Kong police fired tear gas at protestors. That day, censors deleted 1.5 percent of all posts on *weibo*, China's version of Twitter, a rate five times higher than normal. It was a deletion rate twice as high as on June Fourth, normally the busiest day of the year for China's censors.

By the time the protests in Hong Kong broke out, China's authorities had already been in the midst of the most intense period of repression for years. The pre-anniversary crackdown had begun early, with one outspoken dissident, Hu Jia, placed under house arrest in February 2014. By the anniversary, 152 people had been detained or placed under house arrest, according to one overseas rights group. Those swept up included gay rights activists, Buddhists, petitioners, and even an unfortunate factory worker who made a peace sign while taking a selfie at Tiananmen.

In the past, private acts of memorial had been permitted. But that no longer seemed the case. On May 3rd, 15 people—including Tiananmen Mother Zhang Xianling profiled in chapter 5—met in a private Beijing apartment, and took a group picture in front of a banner saying "June Fourth Commemoration Symposium." Within days, five had been detained for 'causing a public disturbance,' while the others were questioned and released.

Another person detained in the sweep was Chen Guang, the soldier-turned-artist from chapter 1 of this book. At the end of April, he had invited a handful of friends—including foreign journalists—to an art installation. As the guests sat in the pitch black, a four-year-old girl dressed in white shone a flashlight, illuminating walls painted with dates beginning with 1989 and ending with 2014. When the lights came on, Chen whitewashed the walls. "The history is like a blank," he told spectators, "It has been wiped out." For that act, he was detained for more than five weeks.

Another artist who marked the anniversary was Chinese-born Guo Jian, an Australian national who had witnessed the 1989 killings. He used an earlier work—a bleak diorama picturing the square as a war zone, with earth-movers churning up its surface and attack helicopters bombing it—which he covered with three hundred and fifty pounds of pork mince to create a rotten, stinking Tiananmen. The day after the Financial Times printed photos of the meat-covered diorama, he was detained in his pajamas and held for 15 days. After the anniversary, he was deported for "visa issues." In an unwitting piece of performance art, Chinese police smashed the tiny replica of Tiananmen into rubble to complete the cycle of violence he had envisaged.

As the anniversary approached, international news channels broadcasting in China flickered to black whenever Tiananmen was mentioned. Magazines and newspapers had pages ripped out. Foreign journalists were warned not to visit the square, or they would suffer "unspecified" consequences. One French television crew was detained while showing passers-by the photo of Tank Man. They were interrogated for six hours, accused of "disturbing public order." A repetition of the offense, they were told, would cost their visas.

The message was unmistakable: June Fourth was forbidden territory, more so in 2014 than ever before. The passage of time has not lessened the Chinese government's sensitivity towards the events of 1989. On the contrary, it has increased it. As George Orwell wrote in *1984*, "Who controls the past controls the future; who controls the present controls the past." Tiananmen was the past, Occupy Central is the present, and to control its future, China's Communist Party was doing its best to make both disappear.

The night before Occupy Central was to be cleared, a gaggle of volunteers began to dismantle Lennon Wall, painstakingly peeling off the Post-It notes and placing them in big plastic bags for archival purposes. One quiet young man had been assigned the job of collecting any legible notes on the ground. Wearing a single plastic glove, he was conscientiously picking up slips of paper and reading each one to judge its legibility. The most memorable read "Fuck the Students!" Each Post-It note was carefully packed away, all those hopes and dreams tamped down into bags to be placed in storage for the foreseeable future. By dawn, the wall had been stripped back to its original bare grey expanse. One single message was left, spelled out in defiant orange, blue, pink and green Post-Its: We Are Dreamers.

Inside the Occupied zone, it was almost as if the freedom to dream had released the collective imagination from the bounds of everyday life. This communal suspension of reality created a Wonderland where normal identities were transgressed, and stockbrokers by day became silk-screen printers by night. Art had been democratized, and everybody was creating something.

Artist Kacey Wong—who had made a sideline of protest art— was delighted. In 2012, Wong had turned up at a protest against patriotic education with his head encased in a washing-machine-style box labeled "Brain Washing Machine." At Occupy, he was perched behind a table where he was blind-drawing sketches of the Occupiers without looking down at his hands. Sometimes, he even drew the sketches inside a box. To him, this explosion of art was a rational response. "This is a war on culture," he said, as the wobbly black line of his pen meandered across the page. "If you lose, you have to change your language. That's why everybody came out: to support our culture, our way of life."

Across the border in China proper, a very different sort of art was in vogue with old-school propaganda posters having a renaissance. One of the most ubiquitous pictured an apple-cheeked girl clad in a red dress, her black hair in bunches, and her chin poised on her hands. The words read, "The Chinese Dream Is My Dream." This prescriptive pedagogical message stood a world apart from the scrappy anarchism of Lennon Wall, where dreams of every stripe and color rubbed up against each other.

With the killings in Tiananmen Square, any dreams of democracy on the mainland were crushed by tanks and guns. Given the rewriting of party history, even memory—that most personal of spaces—had become politicized, and now there was a state-mandated Chinese Dream. But in Hong Kong, a new generation dared to dream its own rebellious dreams of democratic change, dreams that stood counter to the China Dream, highlighting the nationalistic xenophobia at its core that only allowed one iteration of what it meant to be Chinese.

"Dreams of the young and the wild are so pure and messy, but I'm not afraid of being laughed at for having too many dreams," wrote the spokesman for that generation, Joshua Wong, in his hunger strike declaration. "I'm afraid of hearing the sounds of broken dreams when we grow up. I'm more afraid of not having dreams."

But to the rulers in Beijing, the freedom to dream of—and openly demand—a different future is a threat to Chinese control. Through Chinese eyes, Hong Kong's 'One Country, Two Systems' formula risks allowing the 'two systems' to threaten the 'one country', and the inevitable result has been a tightening of control. In the post-Occupy period, renewed calls to reintroduce patriotic education have accompanied political intervention in higher education and an erosion in press freedom, while police have begun stricter enforcement of public order laws. As in 1989, the Umbrella movement's immediate impact has been the opposite of what it intended, but its potency is magnified by the history of student protest in China.

Nine days after Occupy Central was cleared and Lennon Wall dismantled, it spontaneously reappeared. It was a Saturday evening, and a 32-year-old film critic named Francisco Lo arrived at the site with markers and sticky pads. He wrote, "We are here to stay" in English on a yellow Post-It note, then illustrated it with a little umbrella. Then he stuck it on the wall. Beside it, he wrote, "Told you we would be back" on a blue sticky note. More and more notes went up, as he was joined by passers-by, including 28-year-old English teacher, Gary Law. From their spot at the base of Lennon Wall, the pair decided to start a mobile messaging group to coordinate. Then they started a Facebook page whose tagline was, "The government can remove our Post-It notes but not our desire for democracy." By the end of that night, the wall was once again covered by a colorful patchwork of Post-It notes. The next morning, it was stripped clean by apologetic government cleaners.

The next night, Law appeared with twenty packs of Post-It notes, and the third iteration of the wall was under way. People began tweeting pictures of Lennon Wall v2.1 and more people kept turning up to post, snap and tweet. Law and Lo knew that by morning the wall would be bare again, but they planned to keep it alive virtually on Facebook by posting photos of the notes. On Lennon Wall v2.1's third night, a 14-year-old girl was arrested for vandalism for chalking two flowers on the wall. After that, policemen were stationed at the foot of Lennon wall. The only messages permitted read "Post No Bills."

ACKNOWLEDGMENTS

My biggest debt is to those who shared their stories with me. Without them, this book would not exist. Dozens of people gave generously of their time and expertise, sharing their stories, photographs, papers, diaries, and research. Many of them must remain anonymous. Although their names are not recorded here, their contributions will not be forgotten.

This book would never have happened without the intervention of Jeff Wasserstrom, and to this day I'm not sure whether to thank him or blame him. In any case, his enthusiastic support has been instrumental in bringing this book to fruition. I am indebted to my editor, Tim Bent at Oxford University Press, for his steady nerves, boundless patience and graceful editing. Keely Latcham, Alyssa O'Connell and Stacey Victor both helped shape this book, and I thank them for their careful attention to detail. I have also benefited immeasurably from the tireless assistance of Nancy Hearst at Harvard's Fairbank Collection, whose deep knowledge of the period has been invaluable. I would also like to thank Howard Yoon for his friendship and wise counsel.

I am especially indebted to Linsen Li, whose research on Chengdu was an important resource to which I returned time and again. I would also like to thank Dennis Rea for his generosity in sharing his detailed memories of that period, which he described in his memoir *Live from the Forbidden City*. I was lucky to receive advice and support from Stacy Mosher, Roderick MacFarquhar, Rowena He, Magnus Fiskesjö, Mary Gallagher, Nico Howson, Yaxue Cao-Ritter, Jon Watts, Chris Hogg, Adam Minter and

Anu Kuhltalahti. My deepest thanks go to Gregor Benton, Rachel Harvey, Scott Tong, Elinor Duffy, and Ariana Lindquist, who read early drafts of the book and offered thoughtful suggestions. Judy Wyman Kelly's willingness to act as a sounding board came at the moment when I most needed it, and her cogent analysis informed and markedly improved the last chapter.

This project could not have happened without staunch support from my bosses at NPR, especially Margaret Low Smith and Madhulika Sikka. Edith Chapin made it all possible, by working her magic to clear my schedule, while Anthony Kuhn and Frank Langfitt stepped in to cover for me while I was away. I have been privileged to work at NPR, and for that I am grateful to Loren Jenkins. A thousand thanks to my longtime editor, the legendary Ted Clark, and to Bob Duncan, who has saved me on more occasions than I can possibly remember.

A special mention is due to Charles Eisendrath, the director of the Knight-Wallace Fellowship at the University of Michigan, who offered me a safe harbor when I most needed it. Birgit Rieck and the team at Wallace House solved a host of problems, both major and minor, while Fu Liangyu's sterling services helped unlock the secrets of the Chinese collection in the University of Michigan library. Spending a year on fellowship has been an uncommon gift, and I am lucky to have shared it—along with endless caipirinhas— with my fellow Fellows, who have become my Michigan family, with special thanks to Jamie Wellford, Ilja Herb, Adam Glanzman, and Leila Navidi for their toil.

I'd like to raise a glass of rosé to Kathleen E. McLaughlin who kept my secrets and offered unstinting moral support. Finally, it is difficult to find the right words to thank my family, who have suffered alongside me through this book. My parents, Patricia and Poh Chye Lim, were my first readers, and a source of strength on the countless occasions when I wavered. The world's best sisters, Emma and Jo Lim, read for me, cooked for me, helped look after my kids as I wrote and listened to me complain endlessly. My own children, Daniel and Eve, cheered me on to the finishing line, despite having their lives turned upside down so that I could write this book. And finally, thanks and love to Feng, without whom this book could never have been written.

NOTES

INTRODUCTION

page 4. *The translation of the original Manchu name*: Cassel, P. K., "The Gate of Heavenly Pacification," June 18, 2008 at http://thechinabeat.blogspot.com/2008/06/gate-of-heavenly-pacification.html (accessed December 26, 2013).

page 5. *Two hundred million people have witnessed*: "Chinese Mark National Day," Oct 1, 2012, at http://www.cctv.com/english/special/news/20091010/103357.html (accessed December 26, 2013).

page 5. *an estimated 36 million people*: There are wide variations in the estimations. Official statistics estimate 15 million people died, but scholars put the figure much higher. Chen Yizi estimated 30 million died in the Great Famine, while Frank Dikötter put the figure at 45 million and Yang Jisheng estimated 36 million perished from starvation, while another 40 million failed to be born.

page 5. *history could not possibly be forgotten*: Fang Lizhi, "The Chinese Amnesia," *New York Review of Books*, tr. Perry Link, Sept. 27, 1990, at http://www.nybooks.com/articles/archives/1990/sep/27/the-chinese-amnesia/ (accessed February 2, 2014).

page 6. *but one in which we all participated*: Cui Weiping, "Why do We Need To Talk About June 4th?," *China Digital Times* at http://chinadigitaltimes.net/2009.05/cui-weiping-why-do-we-need-to-talk-about-june-4th/ (accessed December 26, 2013.)

CHAPTER 1

page 7. *The students had finally straggled out of the square after seven weeks*: Brook, 196.

page 7. *The preliminary Chinese account put it at 241*: Zhang, 436.

page 7. *the Swiss ambassador who had visited Beijing's hospitals*: Brook, 155.

page 8. *A U.S. diplomatic cable from June 22, 1989 concluded*: U.S. Embassy (Beijing), "What Happened on the Night of June 3," at http://www2.gwu.

edu/~nsarchiv/NSAEBB/NSAEBB16/docs/doc32.pdf (accessed December 26, 2014).

page 13. *At least seven PLA divisions*: Brook, 52.

page 13. *Their orders were to converge on the capital*: Ibid., 50.

page 13. *According to the Confucian philosopher Mencius*: *Mencius: A Bilingual Edition*, translated by D. C. Lau, Chinese University Press, 2003, xlii.

page 14. *did not appear to have resulted in an economically viable artistic destination*: "The First Cultural and Creative Industry Service Center Built in Songhuang, Tongzhou District, Beijing," *Beijing Daily*, April 29, 2009, at http://www.bopac.gov.cn/english/Investment/dynamic/2c998460304749720 13049b 813e5000b.html (accessed December 26, 2013); Farrar, Lara and Mitch Moxley, "The Rise of China's Songzhuang Art Village," April 15, 2010, at http://travel.cnn.com/explorations/none/chinas-song-zhuang-art-village-744184 (accessed December 26, 2013.)

page 16. *According to an official account, Liu's unit had been surrounded*: Brook, 130.

page 16. *Afterwards, his body was disemboweled by a savage rioter*: Beijing Turmoil Editorial Committee, 61.

page 16. *On the streets, a widely circulated alternative version of events*: Brook, 130; Wong, 255.

page 16–17. *In fact, the photos of him hanging from a bus*: Berry, 301.

page 22. *Yang met Xu twice*: Yang, 361–362.

page 23. *Xu looks less like a major general*: Ibid., 362.

page 23. *it was revealed that 21 officers*: Munro, 815; Schell, 123.

page 24. *His daughter later told his biographer*: Vogel, 626, 836.

page 24. *Deng's speech set in place*: Oksenberg, Sullivan and Lampert, 377.

page 24. *As soon as a trend emerges*: Ibid., 381.

page 25. *when American interviewer Barbara Walters asked*: Butterfield, Fox, "TV Weekend; China's Leader Calls Massacre 'Nothing' " *New York Times*, May 18, 1990 at http://www.nytimes.com/1990/05/18/arts/tv-weekend-china-s-leader-calls-massacre-nothing.html (accessed December 26, 2013).

page 25. *when American interviewer Barbara Walters asked*: Miles, 381.

page 25. *Foreign Ministry Spokesman Hong Lei emphasized*: Ford, Peter, "Tiananmen Still Taboo in China After All These Years," *Christian Science Monitor*, June 4, 2013, at http://www.csmonitor.com/World/Global-News/2013/0604/Tiananmen-still-taboo-in-China-after-all-these-years-video (accessed December 26, 2013.)

page 25. *Deng Xiaoping praised the martial law troops*: Oksenberg, Sullivan and Lampert, 378.

page 26. *the senior colonel tells the troops*: General Political Department, 463–465.

page 27. *accounting for one-fifth of all property under construction*: Huang and Ge, 169.

CHAPTER 2

page 33. *At that time, three thousand patriotic students*: Miles, 17; Schell, 21.

page 33. *Its impact was perhaps best summed up*: Mao Zedong, *"Towards a Golden Age." Xiangjiang pinglun*, July 1919, http://www.marxists.org/reference/archive/mao/selected-works/volume-6/mswv6_03.htm (accessed December 26, 2013).

page 34. *Western journalists encountered half a dozen checkpoints*: Wong, 241.

page 34. *one group was said to have changed presidents*: Chai, 158.

page 35. *As the students passed Xinhuamen*: Schell, 63.

page 35. *fervid inner-court power struggles*: Lubman, Sarah, "The Myth of Tiananmen Square," *The Washington Post*, July 30, 1989, C5.

page 37. *We cannot guarantee the safety of violators*: Zhang Liang, 378.

page 38. *One of the sites of the worst killings was Muxidi*: "List of Tiananmen Victims, No 120: Yin Jing, Male, Age 36" at http://www.alliance.org.hk/English/Tiananmen_files/victimlist4.html (accessed December 26, 2013).

page 39. *The earliest of those death sentences*: Chinese Human Rights Defenders, "The Legacy of Tiananmen: 20 Years of Activism, Oppression and Hope," June 1, 2009 at http://www.wmd.org/documents/0609dn13.pdf (accessed January 1, 2014), 46.

page 39. *Some of the longest sentences*: Munro, Robin and Mickey Spiegel (eds.), "Detained in China and Tibet: A Directory of Political and Religious Prisoners", Human Rights Watch, Jan 1, 1994, 101.

page 40. *Known to the outside world as Lingyuan Motor Vehicle Industrial Corporation*: Asia Watch, 15, China: Political Prisoners Abused in Liaoning Province as Official Whitewash of Labor Reform System Continues. http://www.hrw.org/reports/pdfs/c/china/china929.pdf (accessed December 26, 2013).

page 40. *It also held so many Tiananmen activists*: Ibid., 2.

page 41. *They were tortured continuously*: Ibid., 8.

page 42. *This hunger strike was declared*: Ibid., 9.

page 42. *The police commander told him*: Ibid., 10.

page 42. *Conditions were so bad in Lingyuan*: Miles, 32.

page 42. *The exiled poet Liao Yiwu has published*: Liao, *For a Song and a Hundred Songs*, 82.

page 43. *These areas were covered with adhesive bandages*: Ibid., 87.

page 45. *nine exiled student leaders wrote an open letter*: "Tiananmen's 'Most Wanted' Call for Retrial for Zhang Ming," June 2, 2004 at http://www.hrichina.org/content/1876 (accessed December 26, 2013).

page 48. *Ma has a religious fervor for small businesses*: Shiying Liu and Avery, Martha, Alibaba: *The Inside Story Behind Jack Ma and the Creation of the World's Biggest Online Marketplace* (New York: Collins Business, 2009), 50.

page 48. *Ma himself has acknowledged the good fortune of his timing*: "Talk Show: Charlie Rose-Jack Ma," September 29, 2010, at http://lchzfg.blog.163. com/blog/static/16248671320108291145918/ accessed December 26, 2013. Also on youtube: https://www.youtube.com/watch?v=rUwmakdaye4 at 12.02, (accessed December 26, 2013).

page 48. *a person in charge must make these kinds of decisions*: Transcript of Chinese interview with SCMP available at http://www.nanzao.com/sc/features/9204/ma-yun-fang-tan-lu-yi-cheng-gong-zhe-zhi-neng-zou-zi-ji-de-lu (accessed December 26, 2013).

page 49. *at least four million party members*: Miles, 27.

page 50. *You will be awarded power, fame and money*: Yan Lianke, "On State-Sponsored Amnesia," New York Times, April 1, 2013 at http://www.nytimes.com/2013/04/02/opinion/on-chinas-state-sponsored-amnesia. html?pagewanted=all (accessed December 26, 2013).

page 51. *For the CEO of a big company*: Pomfret, John, "Four Pathways from Tiananmen Square," *Washington Post*, June 5, 1999 A1, accessed at http://www.washingtonpost.com/wpsrv/inatl/daily/june99/tiananmen5.htm   (on December 26, 2013).

page 51. *By 2008, however, he was denying*: Larmer, Brook, "Building Wonderland," *New York Times*, April 6, 2008, accessed at http://www.nytimes.com/2008/04/06/realestate/keymagazine/406china-t.html?pagewanted=print&_r=0 (accessed on December 26, 2013).

page 51. *Her outfit included a Chanel necklace*: Goldkorn, Jeremy, "Should Chinese Political Delegates Wear $2000 Suits," *Danwei*, March 6, 2012 at http://www.danwei.com/should-chinese-political-delegates-wear-2000-su its/ (accessed December 26, 2013).

page 51. *One bold newspaper analyzed the professions*: Wu Jie, "Xiajie Quanguo Renda Daibiao Jiceng Daibaio Bili Jiang Da Fudu Zengji" (The NPC Will Greatly Increase the Proportion of Grass-roots Representatives), March 19, 2012 at http://www.infzm.com/content/72122 (accessed December 26, 2013).

page 52. *At last count, one-sixth of the members*: Silk, Richard, "Report: Seat in China's Parliament Pays Dividends for CEOs," *Wall Street Journal*, June 20, 2013 at   http://blogs.wsj.com/chinarealtime/2013/06/20/seat-in-chinas-parliament-p ays-dividends-for-ceos/ (accessed December 26, 2013).

page 55. *As I pondered his continuing fast*: Schell, 80.

CHAPTER 3

page 65. *An estimated sixty thousand students*: Suettinger, Robert, *Beyond Tiananmen: The Politics of U.S.-China Relations*, Washington D.C.: Brookings Institution Press, 2003, 30.

page 65. *Overnight, his father had aged*: Wu'er Kaixi, 199.

page 67. *Chinese rock and roll influenced students' ideas*: Baranavitch, Nimrod, *China's New Voices: Popular Music, Ethnicity, Gender and Politics, 1978–1997*, Berkeley: University of California Press, 2003, 35.

page 67. *Hou said that rock music*: Hou Dejian in "The Gate of Heavenly Peace: Transcript" at http://www.tsquare.tv/film/transcript.html (accessed December 26, 2013).

page 68. *Wong reported the yoghurt story*: Wong, 235.

page 68. *Pomfret described the scene as*: Pomfret, 153.

page 69. *Just as I said in the past, the greatest obstacle*: Oksenberg, Sullivan, and Lampert, 356.

page 69. *After the crackdown, Pomfret was expelled*: Abrams, Jim "Chinese Order Expulsion of Two U.S. Correspondents with PM-China," *Associated Press*, June 14, 1989, at http://www.apnewsarchive.com/1989/Chinese-Order-Expulsion-of-Two-U-S-Correspondents-With-PM-China/id-901c19a60ba1c538f875ef1128211846 (accessed on December 26, 2013).

page 69. *We will defend Tiananmen Square*: Spence, Jonathan, "Children of the Dragon, Collier Books, Macmillan Publishing Company, New York, 1990" at http://www.tsquare.tv/links/spence.html (accessed January 1, 2014).

page 69. *We are willing to lose our young lives*: Schell, 137.

page 70. *I will never forget that I left Tiananmen Square holding on to a dead body*: Ibid., 211.

page 70. *Operation Yellowbird took its name*: Sonny Shiu-Hing Lo, *The Politics of Cross-Border Crime in Greater China: Case Studies of Mainland China, Hong Kong and Macao*, Armonk, NY: M. E. Sharpe, 2009, 87.

page 70. *In the immediate aftermath of the crackdown*: Wu'er Kaixi, Chai Ling, Feng Congde, Liang Qingtun, Wang Chaohua, Zhang Boli, and Li Lu escaped from China, though it took Zhang Boli two years on the run before he left the country. The other fourteen students were captured or handed themselves in, and almost all of them served jail time. Mosher, Stacy, "Tiananamen's Most Wanted – Where are They Now?" China Rights Forum, No.2, 2004 at http://www.hrichina.org/sites/default/files/PDFs/CRF.2.2004/b6_Tiananmens Most6.2004.pdf (accessed January 1, 2014).

page 70. *brought some 400 dissidents out of China*: Lee, Samson and Natalie Wong, "Praise for Brit Agents Who Helped Students," *The Standard*, July 12, 2011 at http://www.thestandard.com.hk/news_detail.asp?pp_cat=30&art_id=113000&sid=32996305&con_type=1&d_str=20110712&sear_year=2011 (accessed on December 26, 2013).

page 70. *Hong Kong's democracy activists relied on*: Sonny Shiu-Hing Lo, 88.

page 70. *The gangsters who operated the smuggling routes*: More details were disclosed in the memoirs of Hong Kong's Democratic Party politician Szeto Wah.

page 71. *I think I see the problems of the Han better*: Pomfret, John, "Minority Student Leader Defiant in the Midst of Chinese Demonstrations," *Associated*

Press, April 29, 1989 at http://news.google.com/newspapers?nid=1917&dat=19890429&id=1nghAAAAIBAJ&sjid=EIkFAAAAIBAJ&pg=2305,7221712 (accessed December 26, 2013).

page 72. *When foreign journalists were bused*: Branigan, Tania, "Woman's Lone Protest Calms Tempers as Uighurs Confront Chinese Police," *The Guardian*, July 7, 2009 at http://www.theguardian.com/world/2009/jul/07/uighur-protest-urumqi-china (accessed January 1, 2014).

page 72. *Indeed, Internet communication between the province*: "Xinjiang Online, Controls Remain," Radio Free Asia, May 19, 2010 at http://www.rfa.org/english/news/uyghur/internet-05192010113601.html, (accessed December 26, 2013).

page 72. *It marked a dangerous deterioration*: Wu'er Kaixi, "A Declaration of Oppression," *The Guardian*, July 8, 2009, at http://www.theguardian.com/commentisfree/2009/jul/08/china-protest-uighur-deaths (accessed December 26, 2013).

page 75. *As rulers, you should not deprive us*: "Wang Dan and Others Appeal for Permission to Visit China," Human Rights in China, April 6, 2012 at http://www.hrichina.org/en/content/5948 (accessed December 26, 2013).

page 75. *The Western world has shown less support*: "Overseas Dissidents Scramble for West's Attention," *Global Times*, November 27, 2013 at http://www.globaltimes.cn/content/827937.shtml (accessed December 26, 2013).

page 80. *In 2012, she announced that her Christian faith*: Chai Ling, " 'I Forgive Them': On the 23rd Anniversary of the Tiananmen Square Massacre of 1989," June 4, 2012 at http://www.huffingtonpost.com/chai-ling/tiananmen-china_b_1565235.html (accessed December 26, 3013).

page 81. *But how can I explain any of this*: Chai Ling in "The Gate of Heavenly Peace: Transcript," at http://www.tsquare.tv/film/transcript.php (accessed December 26, 2013).

page 81. *Even if we had abandoned the square before June 4*: Chai, 276.

page 81. *The victims were presented as villains*: Ibid., 263.

page 82. *Wu'er Kaixi offered an off-the-cuff summary*: Wu'er Kaixi in "The Gate of Heavenly Peace: Transcript," at http://www.tsquare.tv/film/transcript.html (accessed December 26, 2013).

page 82. *Yet the political causes that the students wrote about*: Oksenberg, Sullivan, and Lampert, 258.

CHAPTER 4

page 85. *One unconfirmed report said*: Schell, 163.

page 88. *the crudeness of the government propaganda*: Ibid., 177.

page 87. *one survey carried out in 1990 by the Hangzhou Electronic Research Institute*: Ibid., 242.

page 89. *the number of colleges and universities has doubled*: Bradsher, Keith, "Next Made-in-China Boom: College Graduates," *New York Times*, January 16, 2013 at http://www.nytimes.com/2013/01/17/business/chinas-ambitious-g oal-for-boom-in-college-graduates.html?pagewanted=2&pagewanted= all (accessed December 8, 2013).

page 90. *merely 35 percent of recent graduates*: Jin Zhu, "More job training urged for graduates," *China Daily*, May 30, 2013 at http://www.chinadaily. com.cn/china/2013-05/30/content_16545493.htm (accessed December 27, 2013).

page 92. *Indeed, China accounts for three-quarters of the global decline*: "How Did the Global Poverty Rate Halve in 20 Years?" *The Economist*, June 2, 2013, at http://www.economist.com/blogs/economist-explains/2013/06/ economist-explains-0 (accessed December 9, 2013).

page 93. *the textbooks used by history majors devote a paltry few pages*: Bonnin, Michel, "The Chinese Communist Party and 4 June 1989: Or How to Get Out of It and Get Away with It," in Beja, 41.

page 93. *The passages follow an explanation of the larger context*: Zhang Qizhi, 366.

page 93. *Zhao Ziyang, had neglected the struggle*: He Qin, 358.

page 94. *editorial that appeared in the People's Daily*: "It Is Necessary to Take a Clear-cut Stand Against Disturbances," Renmin ribao editorial, April 26, 1989 at http://www.tsquare.tv/chronology/April26ed.html (accessed December 26, 2013).

page 94. *The situation at higher educational establishments in Beijing*: Zhang Qizhi, 367; He Qin, 360.

page 94. *Protests opposing the editorial*: Zhang Liang, 81.

page 94. *On the behavior of the military*: Zhang Qizhi, 368.

page 94. *As the soldiers were in a situation that was no longer tolerable*: Ibid., 368.

page 97. *the ground rules are still unchanged*: "Paper Reprimanded for Tiananmen Photograph," at www.cablegatesearch.net/cable.php?id=08BEIJING2915 (accessed December 9, 2013).

page 97. *One other major discussion of June 4th*: "Tiananmen Massacre A Myth," *China Daily*, July 14, 2011 at http://www.chinadaily.com.cn/ opinion/2011-07/14/content_12898720.htm (accessed December 26,2013).

page 99. *that China has entered an age of cynicism*: Liu, 47.

page 100. *memo was even circulated warning taxi drivers*: McDonald, Mark, "As Party Congress Nears, Beijing Fears Subversive Ping-Pong Balls," November 1, 2012 at http://rendezvous.blogs.nytimes.com/2012/11/01/as-transition-n ears-beijing-cracks-down-on-ping-pong-balls/ (accessed on December 27, 2013).

page 102. *And it is far from the gerontocracy*: "China's Communist party membership exceeds 85 million," Xinhua, July 1, 2013 at http://english.cpc.people. com.cn/206972/206974/8305636.html (accessed on December 27, 2013.)

CHAPTER 5

page 109. *Zhang Xianling wrote in "In Order to Record the Historical Truth"*: Zhang Xianling, "Weile Jilu Lishi de Zhenshi" (In Order to Record the Historical Truth), May 26, 2004 at http://www.64memo.com/b5/16310.htm (accessed on December 26, 2013).

page 109. *How could I know that he would never see another sunrise?*: Another essay she wrote that appeared on the Tiananmen Mothers' website includes many details of her struggle over the years. Zhang Xianling, "Wo Yu Tiananmen Muqin Yiqi Kangzheng He Molian" (My Struggle and Steeling Myself Together with the Tiananmen Mothers) http://www.tiananmenmother. org/tiananmenmother/20%20years/m090515001.htm (accessed December 8, 2013).

page 111. *From that day onward, all my illusions*: Ibid.

page 113. *But she was appalled that her son had lain dying on the street*: Ibid.

page 114. *But that process of discovery changed her*: Ibid.

page 115. *In an irony that the Communist Party is unlikely to appreciate*: Goldman, 68.

page 116. *When he was asked if the government would release a list*: Wong, 298.

page 116. *Since then, the Mothers have tracked down 202 victims*: Details of victims appear on the Tiananmen Mothers' website: http://www.tiananmenmother.org/index_files/Page480.htm (accessed December 8, 2013).

page 119. *he made it clear that in the future, protests should be nipped in the bud*: Oksenburg, Sullivan and Lampert, 381.

page 119. *starting in 2011, China has spent more on domestic stability*: Buckley, Chris, "China Internal Security Spending Jumps Past Army Budget," *Reuters*, March 5, 2011 at http://www.reuters.com/article/2011/03/05/us-china-unrest-idUSTRE7222RA20110305 (accessed on December 27, 2013).

page 121. *such as the landmark Charter '08*: "Charter '08," at http://www.hrichina.org/content/238 (accessed December 8, 2013).

page 123. *After the killings, he was even said to be in high spirits*: Barme, "Confession, Redemption, and Death," Part VIII.

page 123. *He subsequently spent 18 months in Qincheng Prison*: Liu, xvii.

page 123. *After all, Liu Xiaobo's hunger strike*: Chen, 36,

page 124. *in the foreword of a poem for Jiang Jielian*: Ibid., 13.

page 124. *When we look at those 'Tiananmen Mothers'*: Ibid., 12.

page 124. *Liu also turned his pitiless glare*: Ibid., 10.

page 124. *especially when viewed against the quiet dignity of the Tiananmen Mothers*: Ibid., 10.

page 126. *Prospects were looking dim*: "China Releases Tiananmen Relatives," *The Age*, April 3, 2004 at http://www.theage.com.au/articles/2004/04/03/1080941714228.html (accessed December 27, 2013).

page 128. *The group issued a stunned statement*: "73-Year-Old Member of Tiananmen Mothers Commits Suicide," Human Rights Watch, May 27, 2012 at http://www.hrichina.org/content/6074 (accessed December 8, 2013).

page 129. *In their open letter marking the 24th anniversary*: "Hope Fades as Despair Draws Near," Human Rights Watch, May 31, 2013, at http://www.hrichina.org/content/6709 (accessed December 8, 2013).

page 132. *In fact, due to the driving rain*: Wong, Kelvin, Stephanie Tong, and Rachel Evans, "Tiananmen Protesters Mark Crackdown in Annual Hong Kong Vigil," *Bloomberg News*, June 4, 2013 at http://www.businessweek.com/news2013-06-03/hong-kong-tiananmen-vigil-organizers-call-on-xi-to-speed-reforms (accessed December 26, 2013).

CHAPTER 6

page 133. *A similar roar was echoing across*: McCurry, Justin, and Tania Branigan, "China-Japan Row Over Disputed Islands Threatens to Escalate," *The Guardian*, September 18, 2012, at http://www.theguardian.com/world/2012/sep/18/china-japan-row-dispute-islands (accessed on December 27, 2013).

page 137. *Socialism and Communism were no longer an ideology*: In interview with author.

page 137. *In the immediate aftermath of June 4th, Deng Xiaoping himself*: Deng Xiaoping, "Address to Officers at the Rank of General and Above in Command of the Troops Enforcing Martial Law in Beijing," June 9, 1989 at http://english.peopledaily.com.cn/dengxp/vol3/text/c1990.html (accessed December 8, 2013.)

page 138. *The "instigators of the riots" were accused*: Chen, 16.

page 138. *In this context, Western economic sanctions*: Wang, *Never Forget National Humiliation*, 183.

page 138. *"the tide of liberalization" had reached dangerous levels*: Li Peng, quoted in Willy Wo-lap Lam, "China's Tiananmen Verdict Unchanged," *CNN*, March 4, 2001 at http://edition.cnn.com/2001/WORLD/asiapcf/east/03/04/china.willy.tiananmen/ (accessed December 27, 2013).

page 138. *one American political scientist, William Callahan*: Wang, *National Humiliation, History Education and the Politics of Historical Memory*, 789.

page 139. *Gao Yong's hometown of Huludao*: Wang, *Never Forget National Humiliation*, 204.

page 141. *The most valuable object on display is a remnant of the original flag*: "National Museum Unveils Grand Exhibition 'Road to Revival,'" CCTV September 26, 2009 at http://english.cctv.com/program/newshour/20090926/102104.shtml (accessed on December 27, 2013).

page 141. *The seven men posed soberly for pictures*: "Xi Pledges Great Renewal of the Chinese Nation," Xinhua, November 29, 2012 at http://news.xinhuanet.com/english/china/2012-11/29/c_132008231.htm (accessed on December 27, 2013).

page 143. *Better still, his book had garnered a mention*: Kissinger, 504–507, 521.

page 144. *In 2008, after astronaut Zhai Zhigang completed*: Blanchard, Ben, "Chinese Astronaut Takes Historic Walk in Space," *Reuters*, September 27, 2008 at http://www.reuters.com/article/2008/09/27/us-china-space-idUSTRE48Q0RY20080927 (accessed December 27, 2013).

page 144. *This slogan picked from 210,000 possible entries*: Wang, *Never Forget National Humiliation*, 145.

page 145. *For foreign journalists, 2008 was an unsettling period*.: McLaughlin, Kathleen, "A Bad Omen," *American Journalism Review*, June/July 2008 at http://ajrarchive.org/article.asp?id=4534 (accessed December 27, 2013).

page 146. *Of the nearly 14 thousand performers*: Chang-tai Hung, "The Politics of National Celebrations in China" in Kirby, 367.

page 146. *In 2004, 15 television shows*: "Bashing Japan: Staged Warfare" *The Economist*, June 1, 2013 at http://www.economist.com/news/china/21578699-government-reins-overly-dramatic-anti-japanese-television-shows-staged-warfare (accessed December 8, 2013).

page 147. *During interviews, Shi hunches his back*: Qiangjiang Evening News, February 4, 2013 at http://chinadigitaltimes.net/2013/02/dying-for-a-living-anti-japan-war-actors/ (accessed December 11, 2013.)

page 147. *On his most productive day, Shi was slaughtered*: Lague, David and Jane Lanhee Lee, "Why China's Filmmakers Love to Hate Japan," *Reuters*, May 27, 2013 at http://www.abs-cbnnews.com/business/05/27/13/why-chinas-filmmakers-love-hate-japan (accessed December 27, 2013).

page 147. *The Founding of a Republic smashed box office records*: Yang Xiyun, "People, You Will See This Movie—Right Now," *New York Times*, June 24, 2011 at http://www.nytimes.com/2011/06/25/movies/chinese-get-viewers-to-propaganda-film-beyond-the-great-revival.html (accessed December 27, 2013.)

page 148. *In 2011, more than half a billion visitors*: Jinzhun "What Makes Red Tourism So Popular," *People's Daily Online*, November 7, 2012 at http://english.peopledaily.com.cn/90782/8009039.html (accessed December 10, 2013).

page 148. *A cavernous Revolutionary Memorial Hall*: "Ten Great Achievements for Tourism of Yan'an City in 2009" at http://www.westaport.com/english/guideinfo.asp?leaf_id=110 (accessed December 9, 2013).

page 148. *Tour buses clog every road as they shuttle some of the 20 million*: Lim, Louisa, "China's New Leaders Inherit Country at a Crossroads," *NPR*, October 29, 2012 at http://www.npr.org/2012/10/29/163622534/chinas-new-leaders-inherit-country-at-a-crossroads (accessed on December 27, 2013).

page 151. *In 2014, nearly 275 thousand Chinese students:* Lorin, Janet, "Chinese Students at U.S. Universities Jump 75% in Three Years," *Bloomberg*, November 17, 2014 at http://www.bloomberg.com/news/articles/2014-11-17/chinese-students-at-u-s-universities-jump-75-in-three-years (accessed March 21, 2015).

page 151. *In 2012, nearly 200 thousand Chinese students:* Zhao, Emmeline, "Chinese Students Struggle for Returns on U.S. Education," *China Real Time*, March 27, 2013 at http://blogs.wsj.com/chinarealtime/2013/03/27/chinese-students-struggle-for-returns-on-education-in-u-s/ (accessed December 11, 2013).

page 151. *the Massachusetts Institute of Technology became embroiled in controversy:* Carroll, Alison, "The Day the Internet Blew Up in My Face," *Asia Media Archives*, October 26, 2006 at http://www.asiamedia.ucla.edu/article.asp?parentid=56219 (accessed December 11, 2013).

page 151. *the Chinese Student and Scholar Association condemned:* MIT Chinese Student and Scholar Association, "On the 'Visualizing Cultures' Controversy and Its Implications," May/June 2006, at http://ocw.mit.edu/ans7870/21f/21f.027/throwing_off_asia_01/pdf/toa2_essay.pdf (accessed December 21, 2013).

page 151. *He called the print an "unusually frightful scene":* Dower, John W., "Throwing Off Asia II: Woodblock Prints of the Sino-Japanese War (1894-1895)" at http://ocw.mit.edu/ans7870/21f/21f.027/throwing_off_asia_01/pdf/toa2_essay.pdf (accessed December 27, 2013).

page 152. *the Chinese students called for an official apology:* Perdue, Peter C., "Reflections on the 'Visualizing Cultures' Incident," *MIT Faculty Newsletter*, Vol. 18, No 5 (May-June 2006) at http://web.mit.edu/fnl/volume/185/perdue.html (accessed December 11, 2013).

page 152. *that they had violated fundamental academic norms:* Perdue, Peter C., "Open Letter to Chinese Students at MIT," April 28, 2006 at http://www.xys.org/forum/db/1/74/148.html (accessed December 11, 2013).

page 152–153. *Cong paid the price for puncturing his students' illusions.:* "Battle of People in the Ryukyu Islands Against the U.S. Occupation," *People's Daily*, January 8, 1953.

page 154. *Japanese car exports to China plummeted by 80 percent:* Arnold, Michael S., "China Car Sales Rebound From Ire at Japan," *Wall Street Journal*, July 19, 2013 at http://online.wsj.com/article/SB10001424127887324244304578473192244080244.html (accessed December 11, 2013).

page 155. *In the central city of Xi'an, a Chinese driver was dragged from his car:* Qin, Amy and Edward Wong, "Smashed Skull Serves as Grim Symbol of Seething Patriotism," *New York Times*, October 10, 2013 at http://www.nytimes.com/2012/10/11/world/asia/xian-beating-becomes-symbol-of-nationalism-gone-awry.html (accessed December 10, 2013).

page 155. *Many Chinese have demonstrated their patriotism by responding appropriately:* Bi Yantao, "Nothing Wrong With Patriotic Education," *China Daily*,

September 21, 2012 at http://usa.chinadaily.com.cn/opinion/2012-09/21/content_15772327.htm (accessed December 10, 2013).

page 156. *The Chinese memory of national humiliation*: In Interview with Author.

page 156. *That was explicit in the police handling of the protests*: Wang Heyan, "Closer Look: How a Protest in Beijing Stuck to the Script," *Caixin Online*, September 17, 2012 at http://english.caixin.com/2012-09-17/100438867.html (accessed December 12, 2013).

CHAPTER 7

page 160. *Overlooking the Military Museum*: Vogel, 626-627.

page 162. *It was a task that Bao's then-secretary*: In telephone interview with author.

page 162. *This period of political liberalization was mandated*: Deng Xiaoping, "Help the People Understand the Importance of the Rule of Law," June 28, 1986, in *Selected Works of Deng Xiaoping: Volume III (1982-1992)*, Beijing: Foreign Languages Press, 1994, 167.

page 162. *Deng's idea of reform*: Vogel, 574.

page 162. *Four Principles of Socialism*: More commonly known as the Four Cardinal Principles, these are as follows:

We must keep to the Socialist road.
We must uphold the dictatorship of the proletariat.
We must uphold the leadership of the Communist party.
We must uphold Marxism-Leninism and Mao Zedong thought.

page 162–163. *He was both a sincere supporter of the reforms*: Cormier, 107.

page 163. *When it came to the question of how to handle the students*: Zhao, 27.

page 163. *In Bao Tong's original draft*: Chen, 21-22.

page 163–164. *I told myself that no matter what*: Zhao, 29.

page 165. *After June 4th, Beijing Mayor Chen Xitong*: Chen, 32.

page 165. *When he went on trial in 1992*: "The Trial of Bao Tong," Human Rights Watch, August 3, 1992, at http://www.hrw.org/reports/1992/08/03/trial-bao-tong (accessed December 9, 2013).

page 169. *one of the friends passed a message*: "'Prisoner of the State' Roundtable, Human Rights in China," July 2009 at http://www.hrichina.org/content/3823 (accessed December 11, 2013).

page 169. *The book included Zhao's own feisty letter*: Zhao, 84.

page 169. *Chen tried to abnegate responsibility*: Yao, 31.

page 169. *In his attempts to sidle away from responsibility, Chen cast himself*: Ibid., 35.

page 169–170. *For example, he insisted that he had played no role*: Yao, 61.

page 170. *Li Peng tries to shift the onus of the decision firmly onto Deng Xiaoping*: Li Peng diary, May 19th entry.

page 171. *Li Xiannian accused Bao Tong*: Zhang Liang, 313.

page 172. *that he did not yet have the idea of moving Zhao Ziyang*: Li Peng diary, May 28th entry.

page 172. *The second passage repeats a similar conversation*: Ibid., April 30th entry.

page 172. *On April 23rd, Li Peng wrote about his fears*: Ibid., April 24th entry.

page 173. *According to one eyewitness report, he had been lying*: Le Monde, November 7, 2012.

page 174. *"Mass incidents," as large protests are euphemistically known*: LaFraniere, Sharon, and Michael Wines, "Protest Over Chemical Plant Shows Growing Pressure On China From Citizens," New York Times, August 15, 2011 at http://www.bloomberg.com/news/2011-03-06/china-s-spending-on-internal-police-force-in-2010-outstrips-defense-budget.html (accessed December 11, 2013).

page 174. *In fact, disposable incomes have increased by a multiple of 17*: "China Disposable Income Per Capital" at http://www.tradingeconomics.com/china/disposable-personal-income (accessed December 11, 2013).

page 174. *Between 1978 and 1988, rural incomes grew*: Huang, 165.

page 175. *The political crackdown after Tiananmen was followed*: Hill, 195.

page 175. *A Bloomberg News investigation found that relatives of the current President Xi Jinping*: "Xi Jinping Millionaire Relations Reveal Fortunes of Elite," June 29, 2012 at http://www.bloomberg.com/news/2012-06-29/xi-jinping-millionaire-relations-reveal-fortunes-of-elite.html (accessed December 11, 2013).

page 175. *It discovered that in 2011 just three individuals*: "Heirs of Mao's Comrades Rise as New Capitalist Nobility," December 26, 2012 at http://www.bloomberg.com/news/2012-12-26/immortals-beget-china-capitalism-from-citic-to-godfather-of-golf.html (accessed December 11, 2013).

page 175. *As far back as 1990, one of the Immortals, General Wang Zhen*: Ibid.

page 175–176. *Even more explosive was the Pulitzer Prize-winning New York Times investigation*: Barboza, David, "Billions in Hidden Riches for Family of Chinese Leader," New York Times, October 25, 2012 at http://www.nytimes.com/2012/10/26/business/global/family-of-wen-jiabao-holds-a-hidden-fortune-in-china.html?pagewanted=all (accessed December 11, 2013).

CHAPTER 8

page 183. *The first memorial gathering in Tianfu*: Chengdu Yearbook Editorial Committee, 18.

page 184. *the movement's turning point came in the early hours of May 16th*: Detail from two unpublished papers written by American eyewitnesses, including Judy Wyman Kelly.

page 185. *Even the official account in a section on the unrest*: Chengdu Yearbook Editorial Committee, 19.

page 185. *Protesting became so commonplace that in certain circles*: Bernstein, Richard, "Turmoil in China; Far from Beijing's Spotlight, a City Bears Scars of Clashes," *New York Times*, June 15, 1989 at http://www.nytimes.com/1989/06/15/world/turmoil-in-china-far-from-beijing-s-spotlight-a-city-bears-scars-of-clashes.html?pagewanted=all&src=pm (accessed December 27, 2013).

page 185. *He wrote an article praising Zhao's agricultural reforms*: Yang Rudai, "Zhongguo Gaige Chuqi De Sichuan Tansuo" (An Exploration of the Early Reforms in Sichuan), *Yanhuang Chunqiu*, No. 7 (2010), 23-28; Reuters, "Chinese Magazine Breaks Zhao Taboos," *Sydney Morning Herald*, July 8, 2010 at http://www.smh.com.au/business/world-business/chinese-magazine-breaks-zhao-taboo-20100708-1022g.html (accessed December 11, 2013).

page 185. *the Sichuan government even took the symbolic step*: Sichuan Daily, May 19, 1989.

page 185. *Officials held talks with the students*: Ibid.

page 186. *According to official accounts, the remaining 51 students*: Chengdu Yearbook Editorial Committee, 20; Sichuan Daily Editorial Board, ed., *Chengdu Saoluan Shijian Shimo* (The Whole Story of the Chengdu Riots), hereafter *The Whole Story*, 21.

page 186. *Thousands marched down the main thoroughfare in Chengdu*: Chengdu Yearbook Editorial Commitee, 20; personal photos.

page 186. *Jostling turned into shoving*: Details from Anonymous (Author Withheld), *Chengdu Liusi Can'an Diaocha* (An Investigation into the Chengdu June 4th Massacre), hereafter, *Investigation*; see also Kelly.

page 186–187. *Thousands of onlookers were clogging the roads*: Rea, 39–44.

page 187. *Dennis Rea describes seeing a mob discover a barely disguised policeman*: Ibid., 40.

page 188. *The report mentions at least one student*: Investigation.

page 189. *The government did not attempt to cover up*: Li, 7 and 8.

page 189. *The book reports that 1,800 people sought medical treatment*: The Whole Story, 29.

page 189. *This cites medical personnel confirming seven deaths*: "Chengdu Stalemate," June 1989 at http://cablegatesearch.net/cable.php?id=89BEIJIN G15491&q=chengdu (accessed January 2, 2014).

page 189. *American consular officials told the New York Times*: Bernstein, Richard, "Turmoil in China; Far from Beijing's Spotlight, A City Bears Scars of Clashes" *New York Times*, June 15, 1989, at http://www.nytimes.com/1989/06/15/world/turmoil-in-china-far-from-beijing-s-spotlight-a-city-bears-scars-of-clashes.html?pagewanted=all&src=pm (accessed December 27, 2013).

page 189. *a mobile fire command post and three fire engines were deployed*: Sichuan Daily Editorial Board, ed., *Xuechao Dongluan Baoluan* (Student Movement, Turmoil, Chaos), hereafter *Student Movement, Turmoil, Chaos*, 209.

page 190. *one photograph showing a line of policemen helping shop owners*: The Whole Story, photo.

page 190. *The Sichuan Daily Editorial Board estimated the damage*: Ibid., photo caption.

page 191. *Using language that demonized the demonstrators as "hooligans" or "ruffians"*: Ibid., 38.

page 191. *Security forces were completely outnumbered*: "Chengdu Stalemate," June 1989 at http://cablegatesearch.net/cable.php?id=89BEIJING15491&q=ch engdu (accessed January 2, 2014).

page 192. *That phone call, in which de Wilde said, "There is no sign of police anywhere"*: "Events in China's Democracy Movement," June 5, 1989, in State Dept FOIA virtual reading room at http://foia.state.gov/Search/results.aspx?sear chText=chengdu+&beginDate=19881001&endDate=19911001&publishedBe ginDate=&publishedEndDate=&caseNumber= (pg 7) (accessed December 11, 2013).

page 193. *In a cable the next day, de Wilde reported rumors*: Cable sent to NSC Situation Room titled "Additional Attacks on Jinjiang Hotel Rumored for Later 6/6."

page 194. *She described what happened in testimony given to Amnesty International*: "Testimony on Events in Chengdu During 5 and 6 June," in Amnesty International, September 19, 1990 at http://www.amnesty.org/en/library/info/ASA17/009/1990/en (accessed December 11, 2013).

page 195. *One of their cables recounts the situation in terms similar to those of the eyewitnesses*: Cable sent to NSC Situation Room titled "Chengdu Protests Become Mob Riots on 6/5."

page 196. *Inside The Whole Story of the Chengdu Riots, there is a mention of the detentions.*: Li, 7.

page 196. *The book reports that by the time the armed police arrived*: The Whole Story, 37.

page 196. *This document describes how more than 300 Pap troops*: Chinese Peoples Armed Police Command (ed) Chuzhi Tupo Shijian Zhanli Xuanbian (Selected Battles Handling Sudden Incidents), Beijing: Chinese People's Armed Police, 1990, 65.

page 196. *Therefore, the rioters threatened they would "attack the Minshan [Hotel]*: Ibid., 61.

page 196. *He was attacked and wounded by our paramilitary police*: Student Movement, Turmoil, Chaos, 224.

page 196. *the foreigners staying at the hotel were so pleased to see the restoration of order*: The Whole Story, 81.

page 196. *One was Austrian anthropology professor Karl Hutterer*: "Letter to the Editor," New York Times, June 23, 1989, at http://www.nytimes.com/1989/06/23/opinion/l-chengdu-had-its-own-tiananmen-massacre-223689.html (accessed December 12, 2013).

page 197. *China rejected all the accusations*: Sanger, David E., "China Rejects Charges," *New York Times*, September 1, 1989 at http://www.nytimes.com/1989/09/01/world/china-rejects-charges.html (accessed December 27, 2013).

page 197. *The People's Armed Police Report describes a lack of ideological preparation*: Chinese People's Armed Police Command (ed) *Chuzhi Tupo Shijian Zhanli Xuanbian (Selected Battles Handling Sudden Incidents)*, Beijing: Chinese People's Armed Police, 1990, 51.

page 197. *Often they had only just lain down to rest*: Ibid., 50.

page 197. *The assessment disclosed that 25 canisters of tear gas were used*: Ibid., 33.

page 197. *It was the first time the division had used tear gas*: Ibid., 47.

page 197. *A total of 4,000 members of the People's Armed Police*: Ibid., 35.

page 197. *including reinforcements brought in from nearby cities*: Ibid., 37.

page 197. *'active cooperation with the army,' mentioning that an army detachment 'changed clothes,*: Ibid., 37.

page 197. *By June 16th, 106 people had been arrested.*: U.S. Congress, 409.

page 201. *Tan Zuoren was sentenced to five years*: "Chengdu Environmentalist Indicted for Blood Drive Commemorating June 4/Tiananmen: Trial of Second Dissident Begins in Chengdu," August 4, 2009, at http://cablegatesearch.net/cable.php?id=09CHENGDU141&q=tan%20zuoren (accessed December 12, 2013).

page 202. *The pitched battles and temporary loss of control*: Zhang Liang, 392.

page 203. *One factor ensuring their silence*: Chengdu Yearbook Editorial Committee, 17.

AFTERWORD

page 206. Lu Xun, *All blood debts must be repaid in kind*: "More Roses Without Blooms," *Selected Works*, Beijing: Foreign Languages Press, 1980, 2: 268

page 206. *The same sentiment was voiced another way*: Lim, Louisa, "Student Leaders Reflect, 20 Years After Tiananmen," *National Public Radio*, June 3, 2009 at http://www.npr.org/templates/story/story.php?storyId=104821771 (accessed December 28, 2013).

page 209. *Today, environmental issues are becoming the biggest cause*: "Chinese Anger Over Pollution Becomes Main Cause of Social Unrest," *Bloomberg News*, March 6, 2013 at http://www.bloomberg.com/news/2013-03-06/pollution-passes-land-grievances-as-main-spark-of-china-protests.html (accessed December 11, 2013).

page 209. *water that is largely undrinkable*: "China's Drinking Water in Crisis," Radio Free Asia, May 10, 2012 at http://www.rfa.org/english/news/china/water-05102012090334.html (accessed December 12, 2013).

page 211. *four Tibetans were shot dead and 50 injured*: "Four Tibetans Shot Dead as Protests Spread in Driru County," RFA, October 11, 2013 at http://www.rfa.org/english/news/tibet/shoot-10112013200735.html (accessed January 5, 2014).

page 211. *foreign press reports said that national leaders had been nearby*: Demick, Barbara, "China leaders were nearby during apparent Tiananmen Square attack," *LA Times*, Oct 29, 2013 http://www.latimes.com/world/world-now/la-fg-wn-tiananmen-square-china-leaders-20131029,0,359829.story#axzz2pZ7VnYEB (accessed January 5, 2014).

page 211. *the authorities have installed some 20 to 30 million closed-circuit video cameras*: Macleod, Calum, "China Surveillance Targets Crime—and Dissent," *USA Today*, January 3, 2013 at http://www.usatoday.com/story/news/world/2013/01/03/china-security/1802177/ (accessed January 5, 2014)

EPILOGUE

page 214. *whose picture appeared on the cover of Time magazine as 'The Face of Protest'*:Beech, Hannah and Emily Rauhala, "The Face of Protest," *Time*, October 8, 2014 at http://time.com/3482556/hong-kong-protest-teenagers/ (accessed December 30, 2014).

page 214. *Now the red light is on for Hong Kong's democratic future*: Lam, Jeffie, Chris Lau and Shirley Zhao, "Up to 3,000 Secondary School students join pro-democracy Movement on Final Day of Class Boycott", South China Morning Post, September 26 2014 at http://www.scmp.com/news/hong-kong/article/1600735/hong-kong-secondary-school-pupils-join-student-protesters-class?page=all (accessed December 29, 2014).

page 215. *He doesn't really talk about the Tiananmen Square protests*: Chan, Yannie and Joshua Wong, *HK Magazine*, May 15, 2014 at http://hk-magazine.com/city-living/article/joshua-wong (accessed December 29, 2014).

page 217. *The Beijing-backed Wen Wei Po newspaper*: "Huang Zhifeng 'Meiguobeijing' Daqidi" (Joshua Wong's 'American background'), *Wen Wei Po*, September 25, 2014 at http://paper.wenweipo.com/2014/09/25/HK1409250001.htm (accessed December 30, 2014).

page 217. *In response Wong replied*: Presse, Agence France, "Scholarism's Joshua Wong Answers 'Foreign Meddling' Claims," *South China Morning Post*, October 21, 2014 at http://yp.scmp.com/news/hong-kong/article/91617/scholarisms-joshua-wong-answers-foreign-meddling-claims.

page 218. *The students argued with lawyerly precision*: "Occupy Central - The Debate: Full Coverage of Student-Government Talks, South China Morning Post*, October 21, 2014 at http://www.scmp.com/news/hong-kong/article/1621141/live-hong-kong-students-prepare-meet-government-officials-democracy?page=all (accessed December 30, 2014).

page 221. *A gleeful China Daily editorial:* "'Umbrella Revolution' Defeated," *China Daily,* December 12, 2014 at http://usa.chinadaily.com.cn/epaper/2014-12/12/content_19075175.htm (accessed December 30, 2014).

page 221. *Zhang Rongshun, vice-chairman of the legislative affairs commission:* "Hong Kong Needs to be 'Re-Enlightened' on Law Following Occupy Protests, says Top Beijing Official," *South China Morning Post,* December 14, 2014 at http://www.scmp.com/news/hong-kong/article/1661865/hong-kong-macau-need-enlightenment-law-and-identity-says-npc-official?page=all (accessed December 30, 2014).

page 222. *More than a hundred mainland supporters:* "China: Political Repression at a High Mark," Human Rights Watch, January 29, 2015 at http://www.hrw.org/news/2015/01/29/china-political-repression-high-mark (accessed January 29, 2015).

page 222. *The reasons listed by one overseas human rights group:* "Detentions on mainland China related to Occupy Central Movement," Human Rights in China at http://www.hrichina.org/en/detentions-mainland-related-occupy-central-movement-2014 (accessed December 30, 2014).

page 222. *In an editorial, the state-run Global Times newspaper:* Tang, Didi, "China Bans Books by Pro-Hong Kong Protest Author," *AP,* October 14, 2014 at http://bigstory.ap.org/article/e44dd8b6939d4f3293f04fe21a02e6e3/china-bans-books-pro-hong-kong-protest-author (accessed December 30, 2014).

page 222. *Online censorship spiked to a record level:* Weiboscope, Journalism and Media Studies Centre, at http://weiboscope.jmsc.hku.hk/

page 222. *That day, censors deleted 1.5 percent of all posts on* weibo: Boehler, Patrick, "Record Censorship of China's Social Media as References to Hong Kong's Protests are Blocked," *South China Morning Post,* September 29, 2014 at http://www.scmp.com/news/china-insider/article/1603869/record-censorship-chinas-social-media-references-hong-kong (accessed December 30, 2014).

page 223. *It was a deletion rate twice as high as on June Fourth:* Luo, Chris, "Weibo more Heavily Censored During July First march than on Tiananmen Anniversary," *South China Morning Post,* July 3, 2014 at http://www.scmp.com/news/china-insider/article/1545652/chinas-government-pursues-more-censorship-july-1-it-did-june-4 (accessed December 30, 2014).

page 223. *"The history is like a blank":* Morillo, Isolda and Louise Watt, "25 Years On, No Fading of Wounds, Ideals," *AP,* May 30, 2014 at http://bigstory.ap.org/article/25-years-no-fading-tiananmen-wounds-ideals (accessed December 30, 2014).

page 223. *For that act, he was detained:* Jacobs, Andrew, "Chinese Artist Detained Before Tiananmen Anniversary," *New York Times,* May 9, 2014 at http://sinosphere.blogs.nytimes.com/2014/05/09/chinese-artist-detained-before-tiananmen-anniversary/?_r=0 (accessed December 30,2014).

Associated Press in Beijing, "Artist Chen Guang Detained for Tiananmen Anniversary Freed," *South China Morning Post*, June 14, 2014 at http://www.scmp.com/news/china/article/1532458/artist-chen-guang-detained-tiananmen-square-anniversary-freed (accessed December 30, 2014).

page 225. *The words read:* "The Art is Red," *The Economist*, December 20, 2014 at http://www.economist.com/news/china/21636783-propaganda-art-enjoying-new-lease-life-art-red (accessed December 30, 2014).

page 225. *In his hunger strike declaration:* Tang, Rose, "Declaration of a Hunger Strike, with English Translation," December 2, 2014 at http://rosetangy.blogspot.hk/2014/12/declaration-of-hunger-strike.html (accessed December 29, 2014).

BIBLIOGRAPHY

Amnesty International. *"China: The Massacre of June 1989 and Its Aftermath,"* London, March 31, 1990, http://www.amnesty.org/en/library/info/ ASA17/009/1990/en (accessed December 11, 2013).

Anon. (author name withheld). *Chengdu Liusi Can'an Diaocha ("An Investigation into the Chengdu June 4th massacre")*, Unpublished paper, 1989.

Asia Watch *China: Political Prisoners Abused in Liaoning Province as Official Whitewash of Labor Reform System Continues*. Vol. 4, No. 23 (September 1, 1992), New York: Asia Watch, 1992, at http://www.hrw.org/reports/pdfs/c/ china/china929.pdf (accessed December 27, 2013).

Bao Tong. *Bao Tong Wenji:Ershiyi Shiji Bian (A Collection of Essays by Bao Tong: Edited in the Twenty-First Century)* Hong Kong: New Century Press, 2012.

Barme, Geremie R. *"Confession, Redemption and Death: Liu Xiaobo and the Protest Movement of 1989,"* China Heritage Quarterly, March 2009, at http://www. chinaheritagequarterly.org/017/features/ConfessionRedemptionDeath.pdf (accessed December 27, 2013).

———*In the Red: On Contemporary Chinese Culture*. New York: Columbia University Press, 1999.

Beijing Municipal Bureau of Justice Educational Materials Editorial Board (ed.). *Zhizhi Dongluan Pingxi Fangeming Baoluan Falu Wenti Jieda (Q&A on Legal Issues About Curbing the Turmoil and Quelling the Counter-revolutionary Riots)*. Beijing: Beijing Publishing House, 1989.

Beijing Turmoil Editorial Committee (ed.). *Beijing Fengbo Jishi: The Truth about the Beijing Turmoil*. Beijing: Beijing Publishing House, 1989.

Beja, Jean-Philippe (ed.). *The Impact of China's 1989 Tiananmen Massacre*. New York: Routledge, 2011.

Berry, Michael. *A History of Pain: Trauma in Modern Chinese Literature and Film*. New York: Columbia University Press, 2008.

Brook, Timothy. *Quelling the People: The Military Suppression of the Beijing Democracy Movement*. Stanford, CA: Stanford University Press, 1998.

Buoye, Thomas, Kirk Denton, Bruce Dickson, Barry Naughton, and Martin K. Whyte (eds.). *China: Adapting the Past, Confronting the Future*. Ann Arbor, MI: University of Michigan Press, 2002.

Calhoun, Craig. *Neither Gods Nor Emperors: Students and the Struggle for Democracy in China*. Berkeley, CA: University of California Press, 1997.

Chai Ling. *A Heart for Freedom: The Remarkable Journey of a Young Dissident, Her Daring Escape, and Her Quest to Free China's Daughters*. Carol Stream, IL: Tyndale House Publishers, 2011.

Chan Koon-chung. *The Fat Years: A Novel* (tr. Michael S.Duke). New York: Doubleday, 2011.

Che Muqi. *Beijing Turmoil More than Meets the Eye*. Beijing: Foreign Languages Press, 1990.

Chen Xitong. *Report on Checking the Turmoil and Quelling the Counter-Revolutionary Rebellion*. Beijing: New Star Publishers, 1989.

Cheng Eddie. *Standoff at Tiananmen: How Chinese Students Shocked the World with a Magnificent Movement for Democracy and Liberty That Ended in the Tragic Tiananmen Massacre*. Highland Ranch, CO. Sensys Corp, 2009.

Chengdu Yearbook Editorial Board (ed.). *Chengdu Nianjian 1990 (Chengdu Yearbook 1990)*. Chengdu, CH: Chengdu Publishing House, 1990.

Cormier, Michel. *The Legacy of Tiananmen Square* (tr. Jonathan Kaplansky). Fredericton, New Brunswick, CA: Goose Lane Editions, 2013.

Cunningham, Philip. *Tiananmen Moon: Inside the Chinese Student Uprising of 1989*. Lanham, MD: Rowman & Littlefield, 2009.

Denton, Kirk A. "Heroic Resistance and Victims of Atrocity: Negotiating the Memory of Japanese Imperialism in Chinese Museums," *The Asia-Pacific Journal: Japan Focus*, Nov. 17, 2007 at http://japanfocus.org/-kirk_a_denton/2547 (accessed December 28, 2013).

Du Bin. *Tiananmen Tusha (Tiananmen Massacre)*. New York: Mirror Books, 2013.

Fenby, Jonathan. *Tiger Head Snake Tails: China Today, How It Got There, and Where It Is Heading*. New York: Overlook Press, 2012.

Feng Chongyi. "The Dilemma of Stability Preservation in China," *Journal of Current Chinese Affairs*, Vol. 42, No. 2 (July 2013), 3–19.

Gates Hill. *Looking for Chengdu: A Woman's Adventures in China*. Ithaca, NY: Cornell University Press, 1999.

General Political Department, Office of Cultural Essays (ed.). *Jieyan Yiri (Jingxuan Ben) (One Day of Martial Law [Selections])*, Beijing: PLA Publishing House, 1990.

Goldman, Merle. *From Comrade to Citizen: The Struggle for Political Rights in China*. Cambridge, MA: Harvard University Press, 2005.

Han Minzhu (ed). *Cries for Democracy: Writings and Speeches from the 1989 Chinese Democracy Movement*, Princeton, NJ: Princeton University Press, 1990.

He Qin, *Zhonghua Renmin Gongheguo Shi (The History of the People's Republic of China)*, 2nd ed. Beijing: Higher Education Press, 1999.

He Rowena Xiaoqing. "Curriculum in Exile: Teaching Tiananmen at Harvard," *Curriculum and Teaching Dialogue*, Vol. *14*, No. 1–2 (2012), 53–66.

Hong Lijian. "Provincial Leadership and Its Strategy Toward the Acquisition of Foreign Investment in Sichuan," in *Provincial Strategies of Reform in Post-Mao China: Leadership, Politics and Implementation* (eds. Cheung Peter T. Y., Chung Jae-ho, and Zhimin Li). Armonk, New York: M. E. Sharpe, 1998, 372–411

Huang Xiaorui and Ge He. "Study on the Problems and Countermeasures of 'Limited Property Rights Houses,'" *Asian Social Science*, Vol. *7*, No. 9, Sept. 2011 (168–174).

Huang Yasheng. "How Did China Take Off?" *Journal of Economic Perspectives*, Vol. *26*, No. 4, Fall 2012 (147–170).

Hutterer, Karl L. "*The Massacre in China: A Report from the Provinces—Chengdu, Sichuan Province.*" (unpublished paper).

Kelly, Judy Wyman. "*'The Chengdu Spring' and Some Chinese Intellectuals.*" (unpublished paper).

Kirby, William C.(ed.). *The People's Republic of China at 60, An International Assessment*. Cambridge, MA: Harvard University Asia Center, 2011.

Kissinger, Henry. *On China*. New York: Penguin, 2011.

Lee Ching Kwan and Yonghong Zhang. "The Power of Instability: Unraveling the Microfoundations of Bargained Authoritarianism in China," *American Journal of Sociology*, Vol. *118*, No. 6 (May 2013), 1475–1508.

Lee Haiyan. "The Charisma of Power and the Military Sublime in Tiananmen Square," *Journal of Asian Studies*, Vol. *70*, No. 2 (May) 2011, 397–424.

Li Linsen. "*From Tiananmen Square to Tianfu Square—the 1989 Student Protests in Chengdu*" (M.A. thesis, University of Michigan), 2012.

Li Peng. "*The Critical Moment: Li Peng's June 4th Diary*" (Unpublished Manuscript).

———. *Li Peng Liusi Riji Zhenxiang: Fu lu Li Peng Liusi Riji Yuanwen (The Truth About Li Peng's June 4 Diary: With an Appendix Containing the Original June 4 Diary)*. Hong Kong: Aoya Chuban Youxian Gongsi, 2010.

Liao Yiwu. *The Corpse Walker: Real Life Stories, China From the Bottom Up*. tr. Wen Huang. New York: Pantheon, 2008.

———. *For a Song and a Hundred Songs: A Poet's Journey Through a Chinese Prison* (tr. Wenguang Huang). New York: Houghton Mifflin Harcourt, 2013.

Liu Xiaobo. *No Enemies, No Hatred: Selected Essays and Poems* (eds. Perry Link, Tienchi Martin-Liao, and Liu Xia). Cambridge, MA: Belknap Press of Harvard University Press, 2012.

Ma Jian. *Beijing Coma* (tr. Flora Drew). New York: Farrar, Straus and Giroux, 2008.

McGregor, Richard. *The Party: The Secret World of China's Communist Rulers.* New York: Harper, 2010.

Miles, James A.R.. *The Legacy of Tiananmen: China in Disarray.* Ann Arbor, MI: University of Michigan Press, 1996.

Minzner, Carl. "*Social Instability in China: Causes, Consequences and Implications,*" Center for Strategic and International Studies, 2006, at http://csis.org/files/media/csis/events/061205_mizner_abstract.pdf   (accessed December 28, 2013).

Munro, Robin. "Who Died in Beijing, and Why," *The Nation,* Vol. 250, No. 23 (June 11, 1990), 811–821.

Munro, Robin, and Mickey Spiegel (eds.). *Detained in China and Tibet: A Directory of Political and Religious Prisoners.* New York: Human Rights Watch, February 1994.

Ogden, Suzanne et al. (eds.). *China's Search for Democracy: The Student and Mass Movement of 1989,* Armonk, NY: M.E. Sharpe, 1992.

Oksenberg, Michel, Lawrence R. Sullivan, and Marc Lambert (eds.). *Beijing Spring, 1989 Confrontation and Conflict, The Basic Documents.* Armonk, NY: M. E. Sharpe, 1990.

Pal, Nyiri. "From Starbucks to Carrefour: Consumer Boycotts, Nationalism and Taste in Contemporary China," *PORTAL Journal of Multidisciplinary International Studies,* Vol. 6, No. 2, July 2009 at http://epress.lib.uts.edu.au/journals/index.php/portal/article/view/936/1505 (accessed December 28, 2013).

Pan, Philip P. *Out of Mao's Shadow: The Struggle for the Soul of a New China.* New York: Simon & Schuster, 2008.

Pomfret, John. *Chinese Lessons: Five Classmates and the Story of the New China.* New York: Henry Holt, 2006.

Rea, Dennis. *Live at the Forbidden City: Musical Encounters in China and Taiwan.* Bloomington, IN: iUniverse, 2006.

Rhodes, Greg. *Expat in China: The Chengdu Blues.* CreateSpace Independent Publishing Platform, 2013.

Schak, David. "*Learning Nation and Nationalism: A Longitudinal Examination of Primary School Moral Education Texts in China,*" unpublished paper, 2013.

Schell, Orville. *Mandate of Heaven: the Legacy of Tiananmen Square and the Next Generation of China's Leaders.* New York: Touchstone Edition, Simon & Schuster, 1995.

Schell, Orville, and John Delury. *Wealth and Power, China's Long March to the Twenty-first Century.* New York: Random House, 2013.

Schell, Orville, and David Shambaugh (eds.). *The China Reader: The Reform Era.* New York: Vintage Books, 1999.

Shen Tong. *Almost a Revolution: The Story of a Chinese Student's Journey from Boyhood to Leadership in Tiananmen Square*. Ann Arbor, MI: University of Michigan Press, 1998.

Sichuan Daily Editorial Board (ed.). *Chengdu Saoluan ShijianShimo (The Whole Story of the Chengdu Riots)*. Chengdu: Sichuan People's Press, 1989.

——. *Xuechao Dongluan Baoluan (Student Movement, Turmoil, Chaos)*. Chengdu: Sichuan People's Press, 1989.

Spence, Jonathan. *The Gate of Heavenly Peace: The Chinese and Their Revolution 1895–1980*. New York: Viking, 1981.

State Education Comission Political Thought Work Group (ed)., *Jingxin Dongpo De 56 Tian: 1989 Nian 4 Yue 15 Ri -9 Yue Meiri Jishi (A Frightening 56 Days: Daily Documentary from April 15 to September 1989)*, Beijng: Dadi Publishing House, 1989.

Szeto Wah. *Dajiang Dongqu: Situ Hua Huiyilu (The Big River Flows East: Szeto Wah's Memoir)*. Hong Kong: Oxford University Press, 2011.

Unger, Jonathan (ed.). *The Pro-Democracy Protests in China, Reports from the Provinces*. Armonk, NY: M. E. Sharpe, 1991.

U.S. Congress. Senate Committee on Foreign Relations. Subcommittee on East Asian and Pacific Affairs. *Sino-American Relations: One Year After the Massacre at Tiananmen Square*. 101st Congress, 2nd Session, 1991.

Vogel, Ezra F. *Deng Xiaoping and the Transformation of China*. Cambridge, MA: Belknap Press of Harvard University Press, 2011.

Wang Chaohua (ed.). *One China, Many Paths*. New York: Verso, 2003.

Wang Dan. *Wang Dan Huiyi Lu: Cong Liu Si dao Liu Wang. (Wang Dan's Memoirs: From June 4 to Exile)*, Taipei: Shibao Wenhua Qiye Gufen Youxian Gongsi, 2012.

Wang Shunsheng, Huang Yanmin, and Wang Jiugao. *Xinbian Zhongguo Gongchandang Lishi Jiaocheng (New Edition of Lectures on Chinese Communist Party History)*. Beijing: Higher Education Press, 2011.

Wang Zheng. "National Humiliation, History Education and the Politics of Historical Memory: Patriotic Education Campaign in China," *International Studies Quarterly*, Vol. 52, No 4 (December 2008), 783–806.

——. *Never Forget National Humiliation; Historical Memory in Chinese Politics and Foreign Relations*. New York: Columbia University Press, 2012.

Wasserstrom, Jeffrey N. *China in the 21st Century: What Everyone Needs to Know* (2nd ed). New York: Oxford University Press, 2013.

Wong Jan. *Red China Blues: My Long March from Mao to Now*. New York: Anchor Books, 1996.

Wu Mouren. *Bajiu Zhongguo min yun jishi (Daily Reports on the Movement for Democracy in China)*, Not published, 1989.

Wu Renhua. *Liusi Shijian Zhong de Yanjin Budui (The Martial Law Troops During the June 4th Incident)*. Alhambra, CA: Zhenxiang Publishers, 2009.

Wu'er Kaixi. *Wei ziyou Er Zishou: Wu'er Kaixi De Liuwang Biji (Giving Myself Up for Freedom: Wu'er Kaixi's Notes from Exile)*. Xinbeishi: Baqi Wenhua Publishing, 2013.

Wu'er Kaixi and Chris Taylor. *Road to Exile* (unpublished manuscript), 2004, at http://www.christaylorwriter.com/road-to-exile/ (accessed January 1, 2014).

Yang Jisheng. *Zhongguo Gaige Niandai de Zhengzhi Douzheng (China's Reform and Political Struggle)*. Rev. ed. Hong Kong: Cosmos Books, 2010.

Yao Jianfu comp.. *Chen Xitong Qinshu: Zhongkou Shuo Nan Shuozhen (Conversations with Chen Xitong: It is Difficult to Tell the Truth in Shining Testimonials)*. Hong Kong: New Century Media, 2012.

Yu Hua. *China in Ten Words* (tr. Allan H. Barr). New York: Pantheon Books, 2011.

Zhang Liang (compiler), *The Tiananmen Papers*, ed. Andrew J.Nathan and Perry Link. New York: Public Affairs, 2001.

Zhang Qizhi (ed.). *Zhongguo Lishi Xin Bian (A New Chinese History)*. Beijing: Higher Education Press 2011.

Zhao Ziyang, *Prisoner of the State: The Secret Journal of Premier Zhao Ziyang* (ed. and tr. Bao Pu, Renee Chiang, and Adi Ignatius). New York: Simon & Schuster, 2009.

INDEX